# *Maimonides's "Guide" on Obstacles to Knowledge, Being, and Action*

Much of the scholarship on Maimonides is notoriously riven by vigorous debate sifting out the esoteric from the exoteric to arrive at either positive assertions or an overall skepticism related to creation, providence, and prophecy. Joshua Parens offers a brilliantly insightful and novel reading of Maimonides which argues that existential political philosophy is the key to unravelling theoretical Maimonidean metaphysics. His study profoundly demonstrates how the doubt, contradictions, and vagueness that pervade the *Guide of the Perplexed* are precisely what illuminate rather than obscure its core meaning.

—James A. Diamond, Joseph and Wolf Lebovic
Chair in Jewish Studies, University of Waterloo

In his compelling new book, Joshua Parens sails into the center of current debates about the great thinker Maimonides. He masters those debates by persuasively working through them, employing careful reading and sophisticated argumentation. He shows how Maimonides sticks closely to his high-minded principles in order to pursue the truth, aided by philosophy while still supporting theology. As such, Parens makes a truly original contribution to the growing field of Maimonides studies.

—Kenneth Hart Green, professor, department of
the Study of Religion, University of Toronto

Moses Maimonides delved deeply into some of the most delicate and difficult problems of philosophical theology; and he chose a deliberately elusive writing style with which to share his deliberations and conclusions. It should come as no surprise, then, that interpretations of his thought have been many and highly variegated. Joshua Parens, an established scholar of medieval philosophy, adds another learned voice to the ongoing, and never-ending, discussions of Maimonides's "true stance" on controversial issues.

—Y. Tzvi Langermann, emeritus professor
of Arabic, Bar-Ilan University

MERCER UNIVERSITY

MERCER UNIVERSITY PRESS

*Endowed by*

TOM WATSON BROWN

*and*

THE WATSON-BROWN FOUNDATION, INC.

# *Maimonides's "Guide" on Obstacles to Knowledge, Being, and Action*

JOSHUA PARENS

MERCER UNIVERSITY PRESS
*Macon, Georgia*

MUP/ P715


Published by Mercer University Press
1501 Mercer University Drive
Macon, Georgia 31207


29 28 27 26 25     5 4 3 2 1

Books published by Mercer University Press are printed on acid-free paper that meets the requirements of the American National Standard for Information Sciences—Permanence of Paper for Printed Library Materials.

Printed and bound in the United States.

This book is set in Adobe Caslon.

Cover/jacket design by Burt&Burt.

Library of Congress Cataloging-in-Publication Data

Names: Parens, Joshua, 1961- author
Title: Maimonides's "guide" on obstacles to knowledge, being, and action / Joshua Parens.
Description: Macon, Georgia : Mercer University Press, [2024] | Includes bibliographical references and index. |
Identifiers: LCCN 2024056612 (print) | LCCN 2024056613 (ebook) | ISBN 9780881469639 paperback | ISBN 9780881469646 ebook
Subjects: LCSH: Judaism—Works to 1900 | Jewish philosophy—Early works to 1800 | Philosophy, Medieval | Maimonides, Moses, 1135-1204
Classification: LCC BM545.D3413 P38 2024 (print) | LCC BM545.D3413 (ebook) | DDC 181/.06--dc23/eng
LC record available at https://lccn.loc.gov/2024056612
LC ebook record available at https://lccn.loc.gov/2024056613

# CONTENTS

Preface vii
Acknowledgments ix
Introduction 1

*Part I: Obstacles to Knowledge* 15

Chapter 1: The Half-and-Half Teaching and the Two Accounts of God 17
Part 1—The Half-and-Half Teaching 20
The First Statement of the Half-and-Half Teaching: 1.67 20
The Second Statement of the Half-and-Half Teaching: 2.29 26
The Half-and-Half Teaching in *Eight Chapters* 36
Part 2—The Two Accounts of God 40
The Wedge Built into the Half-and-Half Teaching 40
There are Two Accounts of God, Not One Synthesis 56

Chapter 2: The Vagueness of the Limits of Knowledge 65
Survey of the Scholarship on the Limits of Knowledge since 1979 68
From Prohibitions to Limits: 1.31 through 34 83
The Sphere of the Moon as Limit and Disorder or Lack of a Causal Explanation: 2.22 and 24 87
Counterindications to the Limits of Knowledge in Maimonides's Treatment of Prophecy and Providence: 2.32, 3.17 through 18, and 3.51 92

Chapter 3: The Space of Doubts and the Problem of Authority 101
Doubts, Authority, and Disgrace: The New Post-Alexandrian World 103
Disgrace before Authority in Greater Detail 112
Doubts regarding Creation and Eternity 131

*Part II: Obstacles to Being and Action* 137

Chapter 4: Privation, Particularized and Absolute 139

The Differences between Particularized and Absolute Privation 142
Matter, Touch, and Shame 152
Re-thinking the Relation between Matter and Privation: 3.8 through 10 162
Toward Impediment as the Leading Example of Privation 166

Chapter 5: Prophecy, God's Will, and Impediments 169
The Creation-Prophetology Puzzle Expanded 171
Who or What Might God Impede? 181
Prevention or Impediment in the Prophetology 182
*Guide* 2.32 and the *Letter on Astrology* 190

Chapter 6: Providence, General and Particular? 201
Impediments and Particular Providence: 3.9–10 and 3.25 203
The Problem of Evil as Privation: 3.10 through 18 210
The Primacy of Intellectual Virtue in Maimonides's Job: 3.22, 23, and 51 226
Providence, General and Particular? 235

Chapter 7: Creation, Impediment or Will? 239
The Privation of General Providence and Will 242
Impediments, the Necessary Existence Argument, and Eternal Creation 255
Impediments to God or Active Intellect? 264
The Itinerary of Will in *Guide* 2.18 through 21 267

Conclusion 281
Appendix: Strauss's Outline of the *Guide* 293
Bibliography 297
Index 305

# PREFACE

What then does the title mean? When you look at the table of contents, you will see that there are at least six words in the chapter titles with negative connotations: vague, limit, doubt, problem, privation, and impediment. The stand-in for them in the title of the whole work is "obstacle." This is one of the translations Pines has used for two or three Arabic words in the *Guide*: *ʿāʾiq* and *mānīʿ*. He renders these by the following English words: hindrance, obstacle, impediment, and in its passive verbal form as "being prevented." I say, "two or three" because one probably should add to this list of two words one more familiar to our Western ears, *ḥijāb* or "veil."

I did not set out to write a book about negativity. This fell into my lap after many years of thinking, teaching, and writing about Maimonides's *Guide*. It began with my Master's thesis in which I tried to make sense of the connection between Maimonides's critique of the dialectical theologians and his own argument for creation, both of which employ the key concept of "particularization." It is not by chance that you will find that word in the title of perhaps the key chapter of this book, chapter 4, "Privation, Particularized and Absolute." The title's reference to "obstacles to knowledge, being, and action" is meant to refer first to the obstacles or limits to knowledge, which we discuss in part one when we weigh in on the limits of knowledge debate surrounding the *Guide*. Ultimately, this book argues that especially by reference to "doubts" as identified in 2.23, the limits prove not to be nearly as clear or definitive as they've been taken to be. Contrary to other authors, however, I argue that that lack of clarity is intentional—and serves the purpose of defending philosophy. "Obstacles to being and action" is meant to refer to the recurring prevalence of privation or obstacle or impediment in the highest themes of the *Guide*, creation, prophecy, and providence, which are taken up in part two, here not as obstacles to knowledge but to being and action. Although most readers notice the oddity of Maimonides's third opinion on prophecy—that it is the result of the right nature and the right education, except that God may will that it be prevented—I am not aware of anything written on how impediments also play a prominent role in relation to creation and providence. The specter of privation grew in importance in my mind also once I came to see that in recent scholarship so much emphasis has been placed on matter and the limitations it imposes on knowledge. Ultimately, I will try to show that matter is actually something of a red herring. Blame is initially placed on matter that ultimately falls at the feet of privation. Of course, not much satisfaction can be gotten out of reifying privation—unless one really believes in devils or the "reality" of evil. Ultimately, Maimonides does not share any such view. Although he is no relativist, he does view privation as relative rather than absolute.

Despite all the talk of negativity or privation, I should be very clear that Maimonides's view of the whole is quite positive. As he puts it in one of the most important chapters for this book (namely, *Guide* 3.10) in one of his most memorable sentences, "The true reality of the act of God in its entirety is the good, for the good is being" (440). Strangely, this sentence and its relation to his arguments about privation have gone underappreciated. Of course, variations on this sentence have been stated by many other great authors. Yet what Maimonides does with this claim and its relation to privation has not been sufficiently attended to.

# ACKNOWLEDGEMENTS

I dedicate this book to my wife, Lenny. Although her tastes run more along the lines of Jane Austen and George Elliot than Maimonides, her broad and deep experience with editing has helped me to sound out ideas especially when they risk becoming too obscure. Above all, she helped me arrive at an acceptable title, which was harder than usual.

I thank Doug Kries of Gonzaga University for working with me to hold panels on medieval political philosophy at the Southern Political Science Association meetings, where I was able to test out some of the ideas in chapter 2. I am especially grateful to Joe Macfarland of St. John's College for a question he asked me several years ago that helped me come to see how important it is to distinguish the defense of the Law from the defense of philosophy. This insight has been key not only to this book but also to a forthcoming project on Leo Strauss.

I thank the University of Dallas and especially its president, Jonathan J. Sanford, for granting me an extraordinary full-year's sabbatical after my nearly ten-year service as the Braniff Graduate Dean.

I'm grateful to Marc Jolley the editor-in-chief of Mercer University Press for his generosity and great flexibility in bringing this book into being.

I thank the University of Chicago Press for its permission to quote at great length the Pines translation of Maimonides's *Guide of the Perplexed*, as well as for permitting me to use Strauss's outline in the Pines edition as my appendix. Most end-of-line page citations in this book are to the Pines translation.

# INTRODUCTION

Without aiming at it, this book finds itself roughly in the middle of contemporary Maimonidean scholarship, with respect to what Josef Stern has characterized as the opposition between the "'dogmatic'" and "'skeptical'" responses to Shlomo Pines's 1979 "Limitations of Knowledge" piece.[1] Pines argues that the limits of knowledge are so clearly placed that Maimonides means to limit us to knowledge of the earthly or what appears in natural science or physics or what is beneath the sphere of the moon. Of course, this is the strong skeptical view. Josef Stern published in 2013 by far the most sophisticated elaboration of this view. As a result, we will find ourselves in dialogue with Stern throughout. His primary modifications of Pines's skepticism are that he does not accept that our only resort is to "political happiness," and he does not follow Pines in accepting the presence of esotericism in the *Guide.* As we will see in chapter 2, many Maimonides scholars responded to Pines by arguing that there are some things above the limit of the sphere of the moon that human beings can know. They are, of course, the so-called "dogmatists." This book finds itself somewhere in the middle of this debate: it will argue that the limits of knowledge, though a very real theme in the *Guide*, are not nearly as clear or definite as Pines insinuates

---

[1] Josef Stern, *The Matter and Form of Maimonides' "Guide"* (Cambridge, MA: Harvard University Press, 2013), 5n4. Shlomo Pines, "Limitations of Human Knowledge According to al-Fārābī, Ibn Bājja, and Maimonides," in *Studies in Medieval Jewish History and Literature,* ed. I. Twersky (Cambridge: Harvard University Press, 1979), 82–109; reprinted in *Collected Works of Shlomo Pines,* vol. 5, ed. W. Z. Harvey and Moshe Idel (Jerusalem: Magnes Press, 1997), 404–431; "Les Limites de la métaphysique selon al-Fārābi (sic), Ibn Bājja et Maïmonide; sources et antithèses de ces doctrines chez Alexandre d'Aphrodise et chez Themistius," in *Miscellanea Mediaevalia, Akten des VI Internationalen Kongresses für Mittelalterliche Philosophie,* August-September 1977 (Berlin: De Gruyter, 1981), 211–225.

when he draws analogies between Maimonides and Kant.[2] Indeed, if not for this vagueness in the *Guide*, we will argue, the theme of limits could not serve one of its primary functions, namely, to defend philosophy. A vaguely specified limit can act as a deterrent to inquiry to those who are faint of heart while being an enticement to those who are braver.[3]

Having said all that, the limits of knowledge, though important, do not stand out first and foremost in one's initial impression of the *Guide*. That first impression warrants the tendency among scholars to label Maimonides as someone who synthesizes or harmonizes the Jewish and philosophic positions. The most superficial surface of the *Guide*, and indeed of Maimonides's *oeuvre* is what we will call his "Half-and-Half Teaching." Most notably, in *Guide* 1.67, 2.29, and *Eight Chapters*, chap. 8, Maimonides appears to teach that the world is created and subject to a lack of fixity over the six days of creation; thereafter, the world is subject to the natural order described by Aristotle. Thus, Maimonides declares repeatedly, especially in *Guide* part 2, that Aristotle is correct about everything up to the sphere of

---

[2] It is worth underlining here that even those whose arguments I will at moments build out most from in both temporal order and extent of building out, namely, Strauss, Pines, and Stern, all agreed at one point or another that the limits are very clear. Of course, those whom Stern refers to as "dogmatists" in contrast to his "skeptical" position have raised their own doubts about these limits identified especially in *Guide* 2.22 and 24. However, I am not aware of any other author who focuses on what I will call the "vagueness" of the limits. See Leo Strauss, *Philosophy and Law*, trans. Eve Adler (Albany: SUNY Press, 1995); *Philosophie und Gesetz*, (Berlin: Schocken Verlag, 1935). See Josef Stern, *Matter and Form*, 133n2 on Pines's "Limitations" piece.

[3] This may be my greatest departure from Stern. He interprets key moments of the *Guide* as resulting in skeptical dilemmas as part and parcel of spiritual exercises that relish the limits of our knowledge and assent to the truths taught by the Torah. For Stern, the *Guide* is "Torah/philosophy": a teaching that is a revised version of the older, more dogmatic conception of "Jewish philosophy."

the moon.[4] This Half-and-Half Teaching[5] is what comes closest to being compatible with the label "Jewish philosophy."

In his "Literary Character of the *Guide for the Perplexed*," Leo Strauss rightly highlighted what is typically lost in the rush to label Maimonides a Jewish philosopher, namely, the primacy of the defense of Judaism in the *Guide*—what Strauss labels "enlightened *kalām*."[6] Maimonides defends Judaism most directly and succinctly in 2.25, when he notes that neither creation nor eternity can be proven, but in the absence of any such proof we must side with creation. We must side with creation because without it the teaching of Aristotle "destroys the Law in its principle" (2.25, 328). Aristotelian necessity is at odds with biblical creation. Insofar as the intensity of the dialectic between philosophy and Law reinforces our sense that these two sides are irreconcilable, this aspect of the surface of the *Guide*, the Half-and-Half Teaching, is the most superficial.

In his "Restatement on Xenophon's *Hiero*," Strauss adds to his earlier suggestion—that the *Guide* is first and foremost a defense of Judaism[7]—the claim that Maimonides engages (presumably not only in the *Mishneh Torah* but also in the *Guide*, though Strauss does not specify) in "philosophic politics" or "the defense of philosophy."

---

[4] *Guide* 2.19, 306–7, 311; 2.22, 319–20; 2.24, 326.

[5] The phrase "Half-and-Half" is here being used imprecisely. I refer to a combination of elements of creation with those of eternity—or of the fixity of nature based on eternity. Obviously, creation makes possible all the miracles. Given that nearly all the miracles are thought to take place after the six days of creation, it is far from readily apparent that the two "halves" of this whole can go together.

[6] Leo Strauss, *Persecution and the Art of Writing* (Chicago: University of Chicago Press, 1952, 1988), 40–41. Strauss applies this label after observing that in *Guide* 1.71 Maimonides indicates that he shares the intention of the traditional *Mutakallimūn* to "defend the law."

[7] Note that Strauss already emphasized in PL (1935), p. 89, that the *Guide* is not primarily the legal defense of philosophy—rather it is primarily the philosophic foundation of the Law.

In "Restatement," Strauss includes Maimonides at the end of the following who's who of philosophic politics: just as Plato engaged in such a defense of philosophy "in the Greek city and for it," Cicero "in and for Rome," Fārābī "in and for the Islamic world," so did Maimonides "in and for Judaism."[8] Because Maimonides is so continuously defending this from that, it is easy to muddle these two defenses, of philosophy and of Judaism, with one another. We doubt their equivalence[9] not only because of what we've already seen of the opposition between creation and eternity, but also because in an even earlier writing than "Literary Character," namely, *Philosophy and Law* (PL), Strauss identifies in Maimonides and his predecessors (such as Alfarabi) what he calls the legal foundation of philosophy and the philosophic foundation of the Law. As I have argued elsewhere, the term "foundation" is a vestige of the Neo-Kantian influence on Strauss of his teachers.[10] It will have to suffice here to say that he came ultimately to understand that these should be termed "defenses" rather than "foundations"—or the defense of Judaism before philosophy and the defense of philosophy before the Law.[11] The Neo-Kantian language of "foundation" bespeaks an all-too-modern philosophic grounding of the sciences, while the language of defense bespeaks a long and complicated rhetorical task. The presence of Neo-Kantian overtones in Strauss's early terminology was definitely out of sync with the pitched dialectical battle between philosophy and Law that becomes apparent in *Guide* 1.71: the

---

[8] Leo Strauss, *What Is Political Philosophy?* (Chicago: University of Chicago Press, 1959, 1988), 95–133, esp. 126–27.

[9] Cf. Michael Millerman, "On 'The Literary Character of the *Guide for the Perplexed*': Aporia and Euporia" *Interpretation* 42 (2015) 1: 51–67.

[10] In "Political Happiness or Political Philosophy in Maimonides: Pines vs. Strauss," unpublished paper, presented online for the APSA 2021 meeting.

[11] Note that even in PL, Strauss already also refers to the "legal foundation of philosophy," at least in the case of the *falāsifa,* in this case, especially Averroes in the *Decisive Treatise,* as the "defense of philosophizing before the bar of revelation" (p. 81).

defense of Judaism grew out of centuries of battle between various revealed religions (first Christianity, then Islam, and finally the first of these religions, Judaism) and philosophy (1.71, 177)! Of course, that battle represents the status quo before the interventions of Alfarabi and Maimonides. Both authors brought about a revised relationship between philosophy and *kalām*;[12] however, that conflict continues, if only in the background. Despite the apparent paradox of defending *both* philosophy and Law, as Strauss indicates across PL, "Literary Character," and "Restatement," Maimonides can and does engage in both these defenses especially in the *Guide*.

As was mentioned above, the most obvious manifestation of the **defense of Judaism** is in *Guide* 2.25. There Maimonides argues that since neither eternity nor creation can be demonstrated, we must side with the Law. To maintain eternity as Aristotle does would undermine the Law in its principle, that is, at least initially the claim of creation. In effect, we side with creation because we side with the Law. In Strauss's *Philosophy and Law*, he inferred that Maimonides arrives at this conclusion because he holds that the Law manifests supernatural knowledge that exceeds that of the philosopher. This argument appears in Strauss's treatment of the legal defense of philosophy as a limit of that defense that coincides with what he portrays as the very clear limit of knowledge to physics or the earthly.[13] As this introduction has already indicated, we are not as confident as was Strauss in PL that Maimonides viewed those limits as so clear.

Leaving aside for now the clarity or vagueness of the limits of knowledge, the defense of Judaism is most obviously carried out in the section on creation vs. eternity (2.13–31). Although Maimonides acknowledges some of the arguments for eternity, he packs his

[12] On this change from the vulgar *kalām* to the enlightened *kalām* views, see Joshua Parens, *Leo Strauss and the Recovery of Medieval Political Philosophy* (Rochester: University of Rochester Press, 2016).

[13] PL, 91–2.

strongest arguments for creation in a relatively brief span: 2.18–21. Of course, the debate between eternity and creation is the Account of the Beginning. Given that Joseph ben Judah's greatest deficiency is in physics or natural science or the Account of the Beginning,[14] we're not surprised that the peak of the Maimonidean defense of Judaism comes in these chapters. It is true that from one point of view the discussion of God, including divine names, in 1.50 through 70 is a higher subject, since it concerns metaphysics or divine science or the Account of the Chariot. However, given that that discussion took place before Maimonides had even set forth the arguments for God's existence, unity, and incorporeality (2.intro and 2.1), it had to take place at a somewhat lower level than the defense of creation. The sections on prophetology (2.32–45) and particular providence (3.8–24), as Strauss so convincingly argues in "The Place of Providence" are part or perhaps the center of Maimonides's political science or political philosophy.[15] Also, he explains there that Maimonides appears to rest his political science on the metaphysics, as one would expect based on prior Jewish dialectical theology; however that appearance is deceiving. In effect, the political science or political philosophy of the *Guide* may be more determinative for the

[14] Strauss, "How to Begin to Study *The Guide of the Perplexed*," Pines ed., xx.

[15] Strauss, "The Place of the Doctrine of Providence according to Maimonides," Gabriel Bartlett and Svetozar Minkov, trans., *Review of Metaphysics* 57 (2004): 537–49. Here, it is worth noting that at least in PL, Strauss seemed to place the prophetology section at the center of Maimonides's "philosophic foundation of the Law"—at least apparently in contradiction of what I'm arguing here. That is, Strauss opens chapter 3, "The Philosophic Foundation of the Law" with the observation that the prophetology is "a central part of the doctrine of the *Guide of the Perplexed*," and in the pages that follow he focuses on both how Maimonides uses the philosopher-king teaching of Plato's *Republic* as the lens through which he interprets biblical prophecy and then goes on to treat the psychology of prophecy with an eye to clarifying that teaching. That prophetology is central no one would gainsay. However, it is debatable whether it is central to the defense of Law or the defense of philosophy.

direction of the *Guide* as a whole than the Account of the Beginning. Although metaphysics is obviously higher than political science, it may be that Maimonides here is guided by something like the essential insight of Plato alluded to by Socrates in his miniature autobiography in the *Phaedo*: one cannot approach the Good directly lest one be blinded by it. Consequently, one must necessarily begin with the speeches about the human things if one ever hopes to work one's way around to the divine things. Despite his greater liking for Aristotle, Maimonides is like Plato in another respect, he does not separate out his inquiries into these things neatly from one another into works on political philosophy, natural science, and divine science any more than he establishes rigid lines between the defense of Judaism and the defense of philosophy. Here, all we intended was to give a sense for where these two defenses are most centrally located in the *Guide*.

There is a strange consequence, however, of the placement of the three highest themes of the *Guide*, creation (2.13-31), prophecy (2.32-45), and providence (3.8-24) in this order: although creation seems to have primacy not only temporally but also in theoretical gravity (due to its proximity to the grandest problems of philosophy—ones that partake as much of metaphysics as they do of physics), there is another point of view from which creation and prophecy can be viewed as particular cases of providence. Assuming that God did create the world, creation is surely the greatest manifestation of divine providence. It is even more obvious that prophecy would be a manifestation of God's care for humankind. It is surely passingly strange then that discussions of matters such as the extent of God's power and God's foreknowledge (3.8 through 24) appear so late in a section that Strauss argues is part of Maimonides's political science or philosophy. It seems to me again that this bears witness to the Platonic character of Maimonides's teaching. Although creation precedes both prophecy and providence in the order of the *Guide*, we will try to show that we will be better served philosophically if our understanding of creation in some sense takes the lead from our understanding of providence as a part of political philosophy.

Maimonides **defends philosophy** by transforming the Talmudic prohibitions on inquiry into the Account of the Beginning and the Account of the Chariot into the declaration that there are limits to what we can know about the highest things. The similarity between the Talmudic prohibitions on inquiry and the attacks of Athens on Socrates are not difficult to see. Both prohibit inquiry into what is above and below for fear of what knowledge about these might do to subvert the law.[16] Maimonides transforms the Talmudic prohibition into something less punitive, namely, indications of limits to our knowledge. By leaving those limits vague, he also enables the philosopher to proceed with inquiry, even about those limits themselves.

On the one hand, the defense of Judaism reaches its peak in *Guide* 2.25. Indeed, one could argue that the highest theoretical moments of the *Guide* (the negative theology in 1.52 through 62 or thereabouts and the account of creation vs. eternity in 2.13 through 31) serve as part of Maimonides's "intelligent *kalām*." And, as it happens, that peak is more or less at the center of the dispute over the limits of knowledge. On the other hand, we believe and will try to show in chapter 2 that the peak of the defense of philosophy consists primarily of both the transformation of the Talmudic prohibitions surrounding inquiry into the Account of the Beginning and the Account of the Chariot into limits of knowledge and the very vagueness of those limits so crucial to the defense of the Law at its peak. Although the political science or political philosophy of the *Guide* includes at its core the prophetology and particular providence sections, it must also necessarily include the defense of philosophy. It is little wonder then that it has been argued that Strauss means by

[16] See Plato, *Apology* 23d and *Guide* 1.32.

"intelligent…or enlightened *kalām*" precisely the political philosophy of the *Guide*.[17]

Given that the defense of Judaism reaches its peak in 2.18 through 21, at or near the theoretical peak of the *Guide*, and that defense of Judaism is summed up most clearly in 2.25; we are somewhat surprised to see that the *Guide* achieves a moment of extraordinary clarity about how to adjudicate the dispute between philosophy and Law in 2.22 through 24. We will make the case that the putatively clear limits of knowledge referenced in these chapters (2.22 and 2.24) are, in accordance with the guidance of 2.23 in their center, anything but clear. Rather these limits are clouded by doubts on each side of the dispute between eternity and creation, philosophy and Law. Once again, the very vagueness of these limits but also the cloudiness of these doubts serve greatly to defend philosophy. Here, then, the effort to separate out sections of the *Guide* devoted to the defense of Judaism from those devoted to the defense of philosophy breaks down. Maimonides can and does engage in both activities at once; however, I do not believe that we can simply reduce "enlightened *kalām*" (or the defense of the Law) to the "defense of philosophy." Ultimately the former is more superficial, and the latter runs deeper.

Let us turn now from the defense of Judaism and defense of philosophy to the weighing of doubts regarding the highest themes of the *Guide*: creation, prophecy, and providence. Given what we already know about creation vs. eternity, we will not expect to be able to settle such disputes between Law and philosophy by means of demonstrative arguments. One of the things that has most fueled the debates over the limits of knowledge is confusion about what can and what cannot be settled by demonstrative argument. This book shares the view espoused by two formidable scholars, Arthur Hyman and Joel L. Kraemer, that particularly in Pines's Limitations article

[17] See note 9 above.

too little attention and openness have been granted to the role of dialectic in Maimonides's armory of arguments.[18] We will try to show that the weighing of doubts that Maimonides outlines in 2.23 promises to yield more than would the approach that says all that we can depend on are demonstrative arguments. If we were limited to demonstrative arguments, Maimonides could not say, as he does so often, that Aristotle is right about everything up to the sphere of the moon. Too little of Aristotle's *Physics* and the commentaries on it by Hellenistic commentators whom Maimonides trusted such as Alexander of Aphrodisias and Themistius consist in demonstrative or apodictic arguments to suppose that trustworthy science consists only in certain demonstrations.

Be that as it may, we will try to show that the key insights in settling the weighing of doubts about these highest theoretical themes—creation, prophecy, and providence—come not from the side of pure metaphysics but from the side of political philosophy. Let us preview an example: in the dispute between eternity and creation, what seems to speak in favor of eternity is what Maimonides refers to in *Guide* 1.71 as the "nature of existence." What seems to speak in favor of creation is that it serves to uphold the relevant sort of miracles—namely, the possibility that God could give the Law to a particular people at a particular time and place. The leading doubt on the side of eternity is that it does not uphold those sorts of miracles. The leading doubt on the side of creation concerns being at

[18] See Arthur Hyman, "Demonstrative, Dialectical and Sophistic Arguments in the Philosophy of Moses Maimonides" and Joel L. Kraemer, "Maimonides on Aristotle and Scientific Method," both in *Moses Maimonides and His Time*, Eric L. Ormsby, ed. (Washington DC: The Catholic University of America Press, 1989), respectively, pp. 35–51 (esp. p. 50) and pp. 53–88 (esp. 86–87). For their references to Pines's article, see Hyman, "Demonstrative, Dialectical and Sophistic Arguments in the Philosophy of Moses Maimonides," 43n18 and Kraemer, "Maimonides on Aristotle and Scientific Method," 57n7. Also cf. Stern's relatively minimal discussions of dialectic as noted in the index to *Matter and Form* on pp. 56, 137, 302.

odds with the nature of existence. As we will see in chapter 1, Maimonides offers a synthesis of creation and eternity, which we refer to as the Half-and-Half Teaching, to try to undercut the doubts attaching to creation.[19] It is not difficult to see that political philosophy is immediately in play here because that God gives the Law to a particular people is essential to its authority. Of course, Aristotle is no enemy of law. His account merely cannot support such miracles as the giving of the Law at Sinai. We will show that, as theoretical as the "nature of existence" appears to be, it serves to protect human freedom. In contrast, the sort of omnipotence required to guarantee the giving of the Law to a particular people at a particular time and place may put human freedom at risk. Even if the dispute between creation and eternity cannot be settled at a theoretical level, we believe that political philosophy will provide essential guidance in weighing these doubts.

While the weighing of doubts will be our primary task from chapter 3 forward, a theme or *motif* will assist us greatly in this inquiry. At first it appears unrelated to doubt. We refer to the theme of obstacle. As we have already noted in the preface, we use obstacle in two ways referring to the two parts of this book: on the one hand, obstacles to knowledge, including the limits of knowledge and doubts surrounding the highest themes of the *Guide*; on the other hand, obstacles to being and action or in Maimonides's commonplace language, he refers to a number of obstacles or impediments or veils. To use the more technical physical and metaphysical language that he uses far less often, we refer to "privation." One of the oddest features of the *Guide* is that in his highest themes many of the doubts weighing on each side stem from "privation." To use the most salient example, in Maimonides's account of prophecy the opinion he claims to prefer is the one that coincides with the philosophic opinion, except that God can will to "prevent" prophecy in

[19] Also cf. *Guide* 2.17.

one with a suitable nature and adequate preparation. The term he uses for "prevent" is the same as the term Pines renders as "obstacle" and "impediment" elsewhere.[20] Strangely, there are parallels in the case of creation and providence too. The more one looks, the more "privation" pops up at peak moments of the *Guide*. As it happens, the most formidable elaboration of the skeptical view of the *Guide* relies heavily on the opposition between matter and form in the *Guide*. We will try to show that too little attention has been paid to "privation," which of course forms a threesome with matter and form.

This book consists of two parts: part one concerns the obstacles to knowledge and part two concerns the obstacles to being and action. Part one includes chapters 1 through 3.

Chapter 1 is about the Half-and-Half Teaching, the teaching that during the six days of creation the natures of things are in flux, but after those six days they fit Aristotle's account of what is beneath the sphere of the moon. This teaching would be more sustainable if we could understand how one might combine the account of God in the Bible with the account in Aristotle's philosophy; however, these are two quite different accounts of God. Chapter 2 concerns the limits of knowledge. It is obvious by now that one of our main contributions to the debates surrounding the limits of knowledge is that though they might appear at first to be clear, which serves the defense of Judaism, ultimately, they are not, which serves the defense of philosophy. We will see evidence in favor of the view that Maimonides is not as clear as he first seems to be about the limits of knowledge not only in chapter 2 but also in subsequent chapters, perhaps especially chapter 7 on creation. Chapter 3 concerns what

[20] As we will see later, there are two Arabic words, which appear to be interchangeable.

we refer to as the "space of doubts." The vagueness of the limits of knowledge open up this space of doubts. It is about various matters beyond the supposedly clear limits of knowledge that we are encouraged by Maimonides in *Guide* 2.23 to weigh doubts, according to a method Maimonides develops beyond the approach of Alexander of Aphrodisias. At the same time, while weighing doubts Maimonides discourages the reader from submitting to "authority." Yet Maimonides is not beneath appealing to the reader's fear of "disgrace" before various authorities on each of the opposing sides regarding creation, prophecy, and providence. Subtle as these threads of authority and disgrace are, they give clear indications that Maimonides sees this dialectic as part of a dispute between philosophy and Law with a great deal at stake that is not purely theoretical.

Part two includes chapters 4 through 7. Chapter 4 brings out the important but neglected role of privation in the *Guide*. Privation first shows up in the puzzling phrase "particularized privation" in *Guide* 1.17. This curious phrase with its loud echoes in both the vulgar *kalām* argument in 1.74, Fifth Method and Maimonides's own enlightened *kalām* argument in *Guide* 2.19 sets the reader thinking about what sets Maimonides's approach to privation apart from that of the Mutakallimun. The key difference concerns how the Mutakallimun treat privation as absolute, while Maimonides emphasizes the relativity of privation. The very absoluteness of privation blinds the Mutakallimun to the rich role (not to say "presence") of privation in what Maimonides refers to, as of 1.71, as the "nature of existence." Far from meaning that Maimonides is a relativist, the relativity of privation ultimately proves to be the necessary buffer between God's goodness and privation. This exploration of privation will enable us to put *Guide* 3.8, too often treated as revealing Maimonides's asceticism, in proper perspective. With the frame provided by chapter 4 on privation, chapters 5, 6, and 7 will treat the doubts on each side of the debate in prophecy, providence, and creation—each in turn. We begin with prophecy in chapter 5, because the role of privation is so much in evidence there. God's will to prevent prophecy has given rise to what W. Z. Harvey identified as the "Cosmogony-Prophetology Puzzle"—which we will refer to as the "Creation-Prophetology Puzzle." With the help of the debate among Laurence Kaplan, Herbert Davidson, and Harvey, we will explore the contours of the puzzle as it relates especially to prophecy, though we will also foreshadow the direction of our final chapter on creation. Of course, Maimonides draws the reader's attention to the link between creation and prophecy in the opening of *Guide* 2.32. We will make the initially improbable argument in chapter 6 that, despite the appearance of a great profusion of opinions about providence, there are ultimately only two relevant views: the view of the Law and of philosophy. If this were not the case, then we would have to weigh innumerable doubts on innumerable sides of the question of providence. In addition, we will need to show that despite the late appearance of providence in the *Guide*, Maimonides's inquiry into it is meant to reflect back not only on prophecy—since particular providence and prophecy are both said to result from overflow from God (presumably by way of the Active Intellect)—but also on creation. Once again, creation is only the most extraordinary manifestation of God's providence, according to the Bible.

# PART I

# OBSTACLES TO KNOWLEDGE

# CHAPTER 1

# THE HALF-AND-HALF TEACHING AND THE TWO ACCOUNTS OF GOD

What we have dubbed the "Half-and-Half Teaching" is a recurring argument at key rhetorical moments of the *Guide*, as well as the end of Maimonides's *Eight Chapters*. The most notable appearances of this teaching are in *Guide* 1.67 and 2.29[1] and in Chapter 8 of the *Eight Chapters*. It will be crucial to consider these striking harmonizing or synthesizing moments in their wider Maimonidean rhetorical contexts. The appearance of harmony between eternity and creation in the Half-and-Half Teaching is mirrored by the directly correlated accounts of God. Some interpreters of the *Guide* argue as if there were only one account of God in the *Guide*.[2] As we will see, the key to uncovering the contradictory accounts is Maimonides's evasive use of the concept of "relation," starting in 1.52. As we

[1] For summary restatements of what I'm calling the Half-and-Half Teaching, also see 2.17, 296 and 2.30, 355.

[2] For example, Kenneth Seeskin, *Searching for a Distant God* (New York: Oxford University Press, 2000). When interpreters take for granted that the negative theology most prominent in 1.52 through 66 is Maimonides's final view on God, the underlying assumption is that there is only one serious account of God in the *Guide*. Cf. Josef Stern, *The Matter and Form of Maimonides' "Guide"* (Cambridge, MA: Harvard University Press, 2013), where the author frequently distinguishes what he calls the "Aristotelian first mover" from the "Abrahamic particularizer." I will refer to these as the Prime Unmoved Mover and YHVH. Whether the latter should be so linked to Abraham is complicated by what I believe is the fact that Maimonides develops not one but two accounts of Abraham (the Abraham of the binding of Isaac, e.g., 3.24, and Abraham as proto-philosopher, e.g., 2.39 and 3.29). Stern treats these as one account.

uncover the contradictions between the two accounts of God, we will be enabled to see more clearly the contours of the opposition between eternity and creation.[3]

This chapter is divided into two main parts: the first part surveys Maimonides's presentations of the Half-and-Half Teaching. The second part will cover the two accounts of God in the *Guide*. The purpose in this second part will be to indicate where one would expect the Half-and-Half Teaching to run into difficulties. After all, though Maimonides insinuates that the God of the Bible is capable of accounting for both halves of this teaching,[4] he relies on opposing accounts of God in philosophy and Law to build out the Half-and-Half Teaching.

Let us anticipate here the three main moments when the Half-and-Half Teaching appears, in the first part of this chapter. *Guide* 1.67 marks a pivot in Maimonides's account of God from his negative theological account of God as YHVH (in Guide 1.52–66) to an account of God as the Prime Unmoved Mover of Aristotle's *Metaphysics* 12 (in *Guide* 1.68–69). In other words, this first appearance of the Half-and-Half Teaching occurs at the meeting of the account of YHVH with the Prime Unmoved Mover. It is a moment in which Maimonides attempts to elide the distinction between these two accounts. He is so successful in this that many readers don't notice that

---

[3] For two different views of these two accounts, see Barry Kogan, "What Can We Know and When Can We Know It?" in *Moses Maimonides and His Time,* Eric Ormsby, ed. (Washington, DC: Catholic University of America Press, 1989), 121–137, esp. 130–132 and Alfred Ivry, "The Logical and Scientific Premises of Maimonides' Thought," in *Perspectives on Jewish Thought and Mysticism*, Alfred Ivry, Elliot R. Wolfson, and Allan Arkush, eds. (Amsterdam: Harwood Academic Publishers, 1998), 63–97, esp., 71. Ivry does not consider the two accounts to be reconcilable; Kogan believes they are but views the notion that they are irreconcilable as a widely received view.

[4] See, for example, Maimonides's assurance that with respect to miracles God is capable of changing any species He might want but chooses to limit Himself to changing particulars only (2.29, 346).

there are two incompatible accounts of God in the *Guide*. That there should be such accounts should not surprise anyone, given the highly dialectical character of the work.

In *Guide* 2.29, Maimonides is bringing to a close his arguments in defense of creation. Much like 1.67, 2.29 precedes a chapter in which Maimonides provides a figurative interpretation of the Account of the Beginning, but a figurative interpretation that interprets it through the lens of the four elements: air (*ruaḥ*), earth, water, and fire. Back in 2.25, Maimonides acknowledged that if the eternity of the world had been proven, then we would be compelled to interpret the Account of the Beginning figuratively—that is, to interpret creation as in fact eternity. However, he claimed there that eternity has not been proven. Strangely, in 2.30, Maimonides provides a figurative interpretation of the Account of the Beginning that is compatible with eternity. The most obvious similarity with 1.67 then is that the chapter that follows (in this case, 2.30—and in the earlier case, 1.68) appears to affirm or presuppose the eternity of the world.

Chapter 8 of *Eight Chapters* (EC) is the end of Maimonides's introduction to his commentary on *Pirqei Avot* or the *Ethics of the Fathers*. Lest we lose sight of our proper focus, that is, the *Guide*, we won't linger long over EC. We will acknowledge that there are respects in which EC makes the perfect setting for the Half-and-Half Teaching. Most obviously, the EC can appear at first to be a sort of synthesis of Torah and philosophy. However, the cracks in that synthesis appear early, as we will show. Chapter 8 as a whole emphasizes the shared ground between the Law and philosophy against the astrologers. As we will see in the *Guide*, astrology serves as a foil for Maimonides's favored position, but a foil that conceals beneath it its more pressing kindred spirit, fideism. The greatest danger posed by the revealed position is its tendency to drift into fideism. Given this context, when Maimonides presents the Half-and-Half Teaching in EC, he is taking advantage of the harmony between the Law and philosophy regarding human freedom. That freedom represents the polar opposite of the specter of fideism hidden within the Law through its dependence on creation.

In the second part of this chapter, we will consider the necessary existence argument as it first emerges in Maimonides's account of God and the negative theology in *Guide* 1.50 through 70. Our exploration of the necessary existence argument will lead us to see what Avicenna was up against in Maimonides's account of the views of the Mutakallimun in *Guide* 1.71, 73, and 74 The arguments of the Mutakallimun reveal that Avicenna's talk of existence as an accident served to gloss over the differences between his views and those of his dialectical theological opponents. Above all, the Mutakallimun treat being and non-being (for example, life and death) or existence and non-existence as if they had equal status. This evidently harmless claim will haunt us till the end of the book, where we will confront Maimonides's appeal to Alghazali's claim that it is the reality of (God's) will to will and not to will (2.18, 301). Too much else that Maimonides says flies in the face of such a view. If Maimonides cannot ultimately abide these equivalencies regarding being and non-being, he may not be able to maintain the Half-and-Half Teaching as a coherent teaching.

## Part 1: The Half-and-Half Teaching

### *The First Statement of the Half-and-Half Teaching: 1.67*

1.67 comes toward the end of the negative theological account of God, specifically following several chapters on what Strauss has called God's "utterances." "Saying" has been linked over several chapters to the "nature" of YHVH as "I will be what I will be." Indeed, "saying" has come to be identified specifically with God as characterized by "will" (*al-mashī'a*, will or desire; 1.67, 161). In contrast, in 1.68–69, God will come to be identified clearly with "intellect" (*al-ʿaql*; 1.68, esp. pp. 164–65). As we will see eventually, the presumption that God like human being is characterized by both intellect and will, though fitting perhaps in the Christian tradition due to the Incarnation, is at least less plausible in the Hebrew Bible and Jewish tradition.

Returning to our context in the *Guide*, in 1.63, Maimonides turns from a highly general discussion of the names of God of varying lengths and complexity (in 1.61 and 62), all of which point to the primacy of the simplest name, YHVH. The end of this discussion is marked by the following brief paragraph, "We have gone beyond our noble subject and our subtle speculation [about negative attributes], turning to speculation designed to invalidate vain imaginings the lack of validity of which is manifest to every beginner in speculation. However the necessity that made us mention the *names* and their meaning and the opinion concerning them that is generally accepted by the vulgar has led us to do so. I shall now return to my subject." The return to their subject is marked by the turn to discuss God's self-identification as "I will be what I will be" (Exod. 3.14). But this subject in turn requires an introduction, which emphasizes that this is a distinct moment in the argument. 1.63 dramatizes when Moses implored God for a name that would be his calling card to allay the doubts of the Hebrews. His situation is novel in comparison not only to the Sabians but also to the *Patriarchs* who were addressed by God regarding only their private matters. Moses must publicly persuade the Jewish people. To do so, he believes that he will need to give them "knowledge" that God exists. "I will be what I will be" is intended to convey this. Maimonides draws very close to the suggestion that this name is meant to indicate that God is the "necessarily existent." For now it will have to suffice to say that "necessary existence" has a highly mixed provenance, both kalamic and philosophic.

In 1.64, Maimonides turns to an ambiguity in the usage of YHVH: that at times it refers to God and other times to His commandment. As his commandment, it is "an instrument of [His] will and volition." But to honor God is not to speak a name of His, but rather to apprehend God to the extent to which each is capable. Ironically, "saying" is often attributed to things devoid of apprehension, namely, that they praise God, despite their inability to think or speak. 1.65 pursues the equivocality of "*speaking* and *saying*" further. It can refer to (1) "utterance by the tongue," (2) "notions represented by the intellect," and (3) "wishing (*al-irāda*)" or "will and volition (*al-mashī'a wa-l-irāda*)." Only the latter two are used of God since God is incorporeal. But even intellect and will are used equivocally.

Maimonides begins 1.66 with the following somewhat startling interpretation of Exodus 32:16: "*And the tables [of the commandments] were the work of God.* He intends to signify by this that this existence was natural and not artificial...." This claim is startling, of course, because of how remote it is from a voluntaristic approach to the commandments, which all the talk of "will" might have led us to expect, as part of what would today be called a divine-command view of the Law. Maimonides seems to express a turn away from the preceding pages, where God's will has acquired increasing importance. After all, artifice or convention is the result of a will rather than of nature. Interestingly, Maimonides goes on in 1.66 to take Onqelos to task for reifying God's will.[5] Since the Torah refers to the tables of the Law as the "*work of God*" and as the "*writing of God*," Onqelos, rather than decorporealizing (and naturalizing), reinforces the corporeal language of the Torah. Rather than treating the passage "*with the finger of God*" (Exod. 31:18) as meaning something like "*by the word of God*," which could be readily interpreted as "*by the will of God*," he translates the Hebrew into Aramaic as "*written with a finger belonging to God.*" It is as if Onqelos temporarily forgets

[5] As we will see later, this critique of Onqelos will be echoed subsequently in a small disagreement with that other Hellenistic interpreter of the Bible, Jonathan ben Uziel, amid the obscure discussion of the Account of the Chariot in *Guide* 3.1–7 (especially in 3.2 and 4). Although Hellenistic interpreters were capable of decorporealizing, they still insisted on a more voluntarist view of God than does Maimonides.

his ambition to decorporealize the Torah out of a desire to underscore that the table of the commandments is the will of God.

When we turn finally to 1.67, Maimonides opens with the following: "As the term *to say* [*'amirah*] is figuratively used for the will in regard to everything that has been created in the *six days of the beginning*…." Here we see the revealed first part of the Half-and-Half Teaching which resonates so loudly with Onqelos's interpretation of the finger of God. It is strange how tentative is Maimonides's announcement of the Half-and-Half Teaching. It appears as one option among several, all of which are concerned to explain the relation between God's "saying" and His "repos[ing]" (*niḥah*). Maimonides begins with God's repose after six days of creation in Genesis 2:2, turns to Job for the cessation of (or rest or repose from) "saying" or "speaking" by Eliphaz, Bildad, and Zophar (Job 32:1), and then gives a somewhat lengthy discussion of the cessation of speaking of the ten young men David sends to *Nabal* (I Samuel 25:9). Maimonides's purpose seems to be to show that when *niḥah* is used, it generally does not mean "rest" after being tired, as God is often interpreted as being when God is said to "rest" on the seventh day. Rather, much as it meant merely that his ten young men ceased speaking, so God ceased speaking as willing on the seventh day. Maimonides speaks out of both sides of his mouth when describing the view of the *Sages* and the commentators: apparently, they leave it unclear whether God is "resting" or merely ceasing to act.

Maimonides then proposes a third alternative, and this is where he sets forth the Half-and-Half Teaching.

> It is also possible that [the verb *va-yanaḥ*, meaning He reposed] is one of those verbs the first or third radicals of which are weak. Thus Scripture would say that on every day of the preceding six, events occurred that did not correspond to the established nature that exists at present in the whole of existence, whereas on the seventh day the state of things became lasting and established just as it is at present. This assertion made by us is not refuted by observation that the conjugation of the verb in question is not

> like that of the verbs the first or third radical of which are weak. For sometimes conjugations are irregular and may be found not to correspond to other analogous examples. This occurs more particularly in the case of these weak verbs. The doing-away with the notion in question, which gives rise to vain imagining, should not be negated because of the rules of conjugation obtaining in the [Hebrew] language, for we know that today we have no complete [or do not have a complete] understanding of the science of our language and that in all languages rules merely conform to the majority of cases.

Maimonides proceeds in a similar vein, leaving the reader wondering just how strongly he intended this first appearance of the Half-and-Half Teaching. Furthermore, though we cannot be certain, we suppose that, when he writes, "The doing-away with the notion in question, which gives rise to vain imagining. . ." the notion in question is the *Sages'* mistaken notion that God would need to rest after the exertions of the six days. *Niḥah* refers only to the cessation of God's will in creating, not to any need on His part for rest after the six days. The last word of this chapter is "His will" (*mashī'atihu*). And with this he concludes the first half of the Half-and-Half Teaching.

We will conclude this section with a few observations about 1.68–69, that is, the second half of the Half-and-Half Teaching, concerning God as intellect. Although these two chapters are clearly indebted to Aristotle's *Metaphysics* 12, there are a few moments of apparent deviation from the exploration of God as intellect. At the end of 1.68, the human intellect comes to be likened to God, the Creator's. In each case, when it thinks its object as a pure immaterial actuality, it becomes one with its object.[6] But the human intellect is not capable of this at all times. Similarly, the active intellect, which

---

[6] Cf. *Guide* 1.1. Maimonides's choice of the Arabic for "Creator" (*al-bārī*) (165 [88a]) seems intended to cause cognitive dissonance in the well-versed philosophic reader, who recognizes in this passage very loud echoes of Aristotle's *De anima* 3.4–5, esp. 430a3 and *Metaphysics* 12.9, 1074b34.

as we will see plays a pivotal role in prophecy, can suffer an impediment—or at least so it appears at this moment in Maimonides's inquiry. (This theme of "impediment" will take on greater and greater significance over the course of our inquiry into obstacles.) That God can suffer no impediment is affirmed not only near the end of 1.68 but also near the beginning of 1.69, where he contends with the Mutakallimun's habit of calling God the maker rather than the first cause. Speaking of God as a maker leaves one with the mistaken impression that he might be subject to impediment.

Later in 1.69, Maimonides acknowledges that there is disagreement whether God should be thought of in terms of will or wisdom but insists that whichever is the case they or it must be synonymous with God's essence. The genesis of the question whether God should be thought of as will or wisdom arises in the wake of the claim that God is not only the efficient and formal cause of the whole but also its final cause. Much like "first cause," all these characterizations of God befit more a Prime Unmoved Mover than they do YHVH. Declaring God the final cause cannot but lead to the search for a series in which God proves to be the ultimate final cause. Maimonides will wait until 3.13 to uncover all the twists and turns associated with this claim. For now, he begins the search with the portrayal of God as sitting on a throne, eventually determining that He might be "feared and regarded with awe" and "obeyed" in order to "prevent harm" and so on, until

> This should be done with regard to every end occurring in time until one finally arrives at His mere will, may He be exalted—according to a certain opinion, as shall be made clear so that ultimately the answer will be: God willed it so; or—according to the opinion of others, as I shall make clear—one finally arrives at the decision of His wisdom so that ultimately the answer will be: His wisdom decided it so. Thus according to these two opinions the order of all ends is ultimately due to His will and wisdom, that they are identical with His essence: His will and His volition or His wisdom not being extraneous to His essence. I

> mean to say that they are not something other than His essence. Consequently, He, may He be exalted, is the ultimate end of everything; and the end of the all is similarly a seeking to be like unto His perfection as far as is in its capacity. This, as shall be made clear, is the meaning of His will, which is His essence.

In 3.13, Maimonides will make it apparent that asking for the end of the all or whole beyond the ultimate final cause, that is, God, indicates a misunderstanding of the character of the ultimate end. Such an end is not wholly unlike a will, insofar as at some point the questioning cannot lead any further—much as a child who asks why to every command of his parents cannot continue ceaselessly without finally reaching a point at which the parent must say because the parent said so. Despite the similarity that at a certain point one must stop: a will, an end, and the wisdom of such an end are not all synonymous.

### *The Second Statement of the Half-and-Half Teaching: 2.29*

Much like 1.67, 2.29 comes toward the end of a series of exegetical chapters somewhat reminiscent of 1.63 through 66. Here, Maimonides is arguing against the suspicion that there are moments in the Bible that affirm the eternity *a parte ante* of the world—*a parte post* perhaps, but not *a parte ante*. The denial of eternity *a parte ante* is meant to prepare the way for the first or revealed half of the Half-and-Half Teaching. Given that in 2.25 Maimonides adopts perhaps the closest rapprochement of the Bible and philosophy in the whole of the *Guide*, when Plato's view of eternity is shown to be closer to the Bible than Aristotle's[7] we might be forgiven for interpreting these exegetical chapters on the Torah and even the Midrashim (2.26, Rabbi Eliezer; 2.27, the Bible and the Talmudic sages; 2.28, Solomon and David) as confirming some similarity between the Law and philosophy. Just as in 1.63–66 the will came to the fore, so here in 2.26–28, despite any apparent similarity between the views of Rabbi Eliezer

---

[7] That is, 2.25, pp. 328–9; cf. Strauss, Introduction, pp. liv–lv.

and Solomon, on the one hand, and the philosophers, on the other, the will, that is, God's will, again comes into its own.

Of all these quasi-eternalist moments in and connected with the Bible, Rabbi Eliezer comes closest to whispering of the possibility of the eternity *a parte ante* of the world. Borrowing passages from Psalm 104 and Job 37, Rabbi Eliezer pieces together an account of the whole as being created by God in much the way that a tailor makes a garment out of cloth, except that he uses the image of God drawing the light from His own garment as the material out of which He makes, what the Psalmist envisions as, the heavens stretched out as a curtain. And echoing Job, Rabbi Eliezer invokes a theophanic image of the throne of Glory as like snow that God throws and out of which He makes earth. If Rabbi Eliezer "wished to signify by *the light of His garment* an uncreated thing and similarly by the *throne of glory* something uncreated, this would be a great incongruity. For he would have admitted thereby the eternity of the world, if only as it is conceived according to Plato's opinion" (2.26, 330–31). Maimonides demurs on whether Rabbi Eliezer understands the Torah properly. He gives some hints that the rabbi might not, but, ultimately, he cannot abide the notion that the Law conceives of God as a sort of Platonic *demiourgos*[8] who fashions creation out of eternally pre-existing matter.

In 2.27, without citing any biblical or rabbinic text, though he alludes to the Midrash when discussing immortality in passing, Maimonides states very clearly the animus of the Bible. "Creation" (*ḥ.d.th.*) or what Pines here translates as "production" of the world (where elsewhere he translates "production in time") is, as he underscored in 2.25, the "foundation of the entire Law." What is required for creation, in contrast to Platonic making out of eternally pre-existent matter, is that "things exist and perish according to His will ...and not in virtue of necessity." In the span of a few sentences,

[8] Cf. the Maker of 1.69.

Maimonides invokes the opposition between will and necessity that was so prominent in his most concerted argument in favor of creation in 2.19. Much like 2.19, he oscillates from that clear opposition to the opposition he is less willing to maintain openly—namely, the opposition between will and intellect. Here, using the key equivalent to intellect, namely, wisdom. Maimonides affirms the primacy of the will only to question its primacy in 2.27 in a manner highly reminiscent of 1.69, the closing pages of which wander back and forth between will or volition and wisdom. Given that 1.69 is devoted to God as efficient or motive, formal, and final cause of the whole, echoing loudly the account of Aristotle as elaborated on by the Hellenistic commentators, one can hardly read that end of 1.69 without foreseeing the pitched battle that is to come between philosophy and the Mutakallimun (in 1.73–76).

2.28 turns away from the more crucial matter of God's nature to the less heated one of eternity *a parte post* as it occurs in David and Solomon. Although this moment is less heated, it encapsulates nicely the upshot of the Half-and-Half Teaching, creation is followed by *eternity a parte post*. As we know from other works, though Maimonides defends both the World to Come for each individual and some account of Bodily Resurrection, his account of the End of Days is by no means a typical one—primarily because he does not envision an end to the world in keeping with the Millenarian visions of some Jewish and most other monotheistic sects. The way he puts it here is "*David*, peace be on him, likewise makes clear and manifest the eternity *a parte post* of the heavens and the permanence in an immutable state of their statutes and of all that is in them.... He means by this that the statutes, which He has laid down, will never be changed.... However, he makes it clear that they are created. . ." (2.28, 335).

Despite the emphasis on the eternity *a parte post* of the world, Maimonides must give some ground, as he will in 2.29, on the problem of miracles. How can miracles take place if God's statutes after the 6 days of creation are inviolable? According to Maimonides, if they could be changed, then God's perfection would seem to be detracted from. In other words, if His statutes can change, then it can only be due to some "deficiency." (Much as it is impossible that God should be impeded [1.69], God cannot be subject to "deficiency.") Solomon then "stated an end for what has come to exist or given an excuse for what changes, saying in the final part of the verse: *And God hath so made it, that they should fear before Him*[9]—he refers to the production in time of miracles." Now the context of this (italicized to indicate Hebrew) quotation from Ecclesiastes is far from unambiguous in its reference to miracles. On the one hand, Eccles. 3:11 could be thought to highlight the human desire to anticipate all future events, as if human beings were guided either by prudence or prophecy; on the other hand, the more immediate context in the rather long verse that is 3:14 itself, Solomon writes, appearing to emphasize eternity: "I realized, too, that whatever God has brought to pass will recur evermore: Nothing can be added to it/And nothing taken from it...." This is then followed immediately by the passage quoted above about moving us to fear before Him. The allusion to miracles is at best rather faint. It would seem that Maimonides may be more intent than Solomon to allude to the problematic status of miracles in the Half-and-Half Teaching. The chapter concludes on a note emphasizing divine sapience more reminiscent of a pre-Socratic philosopher like Anaximander than the voluntarism of the first half of the said teaching: "Similarly all that is being accomplished for and by created things is absolute justice and follows from the requirement of wisdom, as shall be made clear in some of the chapters of this Treatise."

Part 2, chapter 29 is somewhat ungainly. We cannot explore it in any detail here. It will have to suffice to say that the majority of it is devoted to Isaiah and what Maimonides interprets as his highly

[9] Eccles. 3:14.

figurative use of miracles. In other words, the bulk of 2.29 is devoted to dismissing miracles, as one should perhaps expect based on two things: 2.27 emphasized the unchangeable character of God's statutes regarding heavens and earth, and as we will see shortly 2.30, goes to the extreme of interpreting Genesis in keeping with the teaching of eternity. Maimonides's argument is perhaps most plausible when it comes to Isaiah's interest in motivating the Jews to rise up against *Sennacherib* by portraying God's assistance as miraculous (340). All the miraculous talk is not only figurative but parabolic, in the same sense as Maimonides argued all talk of God as corporeal in the Torah is parabolic in *Guide* part 1. What underlies all this talk of miracles, however, appears to be a good dose of confidence on Isaiah's part in God's particular providence for Israel.

Having established the figurative character of Isaiah's references to miracles, Maimonides pivots (on p. 343) to other prophets, about whom he states, "Inasmuch as these figurative expressions occur often in *Isaiah*, I have examined all of them. However, they also occur sometimes in the speech of others." Maimonides does not go so far yet as to claim that all prophets mean all talk of miracles merely parabolically. However, he engages the reader in a forced march through select passages about large scale miracles involving the heavenly bodies, mass locust infestations, and the like, from Jeremiah, Ezekiel, Joel, Amos, Micah, Haggai, Psalms, the Deuteronomic account of the salvation of the Hebrews from God's destruction of the Egyptians in the flight from Egypt (Deut. 33:29)—and back to echoes of the Deuteronomic account in Psalms, followed by passages from Habakkuk, Judges, Joel, and the Talmudic sages. In the wake of the passages from Joel, he sums up: "The notion toward which we are driving has already been made clear; namely, that the passing-away of the world, a change of the state in which it is, or a thing changing its nature and with that the permanence of that change, are not affirmed in any prophetic text or in *any* statement of the *Sages* either."[10] In what follows, Maimonides follows up with an analysis of the Talmudic view of the Messianic Age in light of Solomon's statement in Ecclesiastes that "there is nothing new under the sun." Of course, he rejects any suggestion by the rabbis that eternity *a parte post* is contrary to a proper understanding of the Messianic Age. After acknowledging Mosaic miracles as merely temporary events (evidently of a sort that even Plato might admit),[11] despite the earlier treatment of the miraculous drowning of the Egyptians and miraculous salvation of the Hebrews as merely parabolic,[12] Maimonides pivots to an account of the rabbinic sages that reminds one of the most widely espoused view among all monotheists reconciling natural order with obvious claims about miracles in various scriptures: "The *Sages, may their memory be blessed,* have made a very strange statement about miracles.... This notion consists in their holding the view that miracles too are something that is, in a certain respect, in nature. They say that when God created that which exists and stamped upon it the existing natures, He put into these natures that all the miracles that occurred would be produced in them at the time when they occurred." He goes on to explain that the reason this is strange is that "it indicates the superiority of the man who made it." That man found it difficult to accept that any nature should change "or that another volition may supervene" after the six days of creation. What I have referred to as "the most widely espoused view among all monotheists" is, then, a version of the Half-and-Half Teaching. The prevalence of this view says little, since what really counts is what undergirds this superficial teaching.

After marshalling rabbinic interpretations of Isaiah to confirm his approach, Maimonides sets forth his fullest expression of the Half-and-Half Teaching in the *Guide*:

---

[10] I add italics for emphasis here.

[11] Review 2.25, 328–9.

[12] Cf. p. 345 top with bottom of p. 343.

> The matter has now become clear to you and the doctrine epitomized. Namely, we agree with Aristotle with regard to one half of his opinion and we believe that what exists is eternal a parte post and will last forever with that nature which He, may He be exalted, has willed; that nothing in it will be changed in any respect unless it be in some particular (*juz'iyya*) of it miraculously—although He, may He be exalted, has the power to change the whole of it, or to annihilate it, or to annihilate any nature in it that He wills. However, that which exists has had a beginning, and at first nothing at all existed except God. His wisdom required that He should bring creation into existence at the time when He did do it, and that what He has brought into existence should not be annihilated nor any of its natures changed except in certain particulars (*juz'iyyāt*) that He willed to change; about some of these we know, whereas about others that will be changed in the future we do not know (346).

Immediately thereafter, he characterizes Aristotle's view as adding the other half, namely, eternity *a parte ante* and having "recourse to the law of necessity." Maimonides then prepares the way for the figurative interpretation of the Account of the Beginning. Lest we get ahead of ourselves, let us pause to reflect on this striking statement of the Half-and-Half Teaching.

Although one must parse this passage with care, the initial impression is that the prevalence of talk of will and of the possibility of God's annihilating all that is runs counter to the tone of the rest of the *Guide*—not least of all the tone of the context in and surrounding 2.29. Above all, it flies in the face of the stinging critique of the Mutakallimun that Maimonides provides in 1.73 through 76, following the very strong underlining of what characterizes his approach to the defense of the Law in 1.71, namely, that what is argued must comport with the "nature of existence" or "nature of being (*ṭabīʿat al-wujūd*)." The main upshot of 1.73 through 76 is that the Mutakallimun facilitated their arguments for creation by setting existence and non-existence on par with one another. Maimonides, however, clearly sides with Aristotle in privileging being over nonbeing. Much like his shocking echo of the Avicennian claim that existence is an accident in 1.57, which cannot mean that whether something exists or does not is merely a matter of chance, Maimonides here comes rhetorically very close to the Mutakallimun. Of course, why he should do so here is quite obvious. The context shows just how far Maimonides goes in resisting a robust voluntaristic interpretation of miracles. Only here in such an anti-miraculous setting, where he sets forth the Half-and-Half Teaching, is it safe for him to indulge in pseudo-fideistic rhetoric. When eventually we look at 2.19 will we see just how fast and loose Maimonides is willing to play with the supposed opposition between will and necessity. Over the course of that one chapter, "purpose" (that is, God's purposiveness or character as the final cause) goes from being identified with "will" to being identified with "necessity."

The counterpoint to the shocking prevalence of the talk of God's will and the apparent possibility of annihilation is God's wisdom. His wisdom not only dictates the time of the creation of the world but also that the natures of things should have the durability they have. As we will see, the matter of a time of creation will prove to be one of the most enduring and troubling doubt associated with creation primarily because it seems to insinuate that God was either impeded from starting earlier or simply willed arbitrarily to 'start' the world, giving it its limited time existing. At least since 1.68, the reader has known that the notion that God should suffer some impediment is impossible. If it is not due to an impediment but is somehow an expression of God's wisdom, can we get any sense as to how or why it would express wisdom rather than an arbitrary will?

As we did with the first appearance of the Half-and-Half Teaching in 1.68, we will conclude this section with a few observations about 2.30. Much like 1.69, 2.30 moves into a register that emphasizes the eternal or natural side of the Half-and-Half Teaching. 2.30 is prepared by two "preambles" appearing at the end of 2.29. The first preamble is that, though the *Guide* is dedicated in part to "explaining what can be explained of the *Account of the Beginning*...not everything mentioned in the *Torah* concerning the *Account of the Beginning* is to be taken in its external sense as the vulgar imagine." Maimonides goes on to describe what might happen if one took the Torah literally, namely, "a grave corruption of the imagination" or "denial of the action of the deity" and "disbelief in the foundations of the Law." The second preamble, which like the first seems all too familiar from part 1, notes that the prophets use equivocal words and "words that are not intended to mean what they indicate according to their first signification." Although there are moments when Maimonides does not stick to the first signification of a term, the strangest feature of 2.30 is the way he relies on such first significations in very unexpected ways, especially in settings in which historically interpreters had not adopted a literal approach! In other words, Maimonides's interpretation of the *Account of the Beginning* in 2.30 is, to the reader's great surprise, extremely literal at key moments. Conversely, the moment when Maimonides does rely heavily on non-literal interpretations is in his critique of some of the more fanciful rabbinic interpretations of Genesis—especially as they relate to Adam, Eve, and the serpent.[13]

Maimonides opens 2.30 with an exploration of what is perhaps the most contentious moment in any interpretation of the Torah. Does the opening indicate a temporal beginning or not? This cannot but recall all the doubts surrounding creation, especially as they relate to the Aristotelian way of conceiving of the relation between time and motion that has dogged the reader at least since 2.13. It may not be an exaggeration to say that until Maimonides no one in the tradition had felt the full weight of the opposition between eternity and creation. Maimonides's presentation of the interpretations

[13] See pp. 355 through 357. See especially the statement: "Among the amazing dicta whose external meaning is exceedingly incongruous, but in which...you will admire the wisdom of the parables and their correspondence to what exists...."

of the rabbinic *Sages* suggests that they did not feel that weight. Rather they, like most contemporary interpreters, perceived the account of creation as temporal. In opposition to this, Maimonides argues that the word one would use if one were thinking of a temporal first is *teḥillah*. *Bereshit* with its focus on *rosh* refers rather to the "principle" or as the Greeks would have it the *archē*. For now, that is, until we discuss the doubts surrounding creation, we will have to set aside Maimonides's critique of the rabbinic confusions about creation and time. Once we get past these opening mysteries, Maimonides turns to what he transforms into a discussion of the four elements. In this passage running in the Pines edition from 350 through 353, Maimonides treats earth, fire, air, and water in the order of their appearance in Genesis, having noted near the middle that their "natural positions" are those identified by Aristotle (earth, water, air, and fire).[14] Along the way, he attempts to make sense especially of the talk of the water above the firmament by translating biblical references into their natural correlates. He concludes the whole discussion with reference to the four who entered Pardes—appearing to allude to the fact established in the *Book of Knowledge*, "Laws concerning the Study of the Torah," that the better part of

[14] Cf. Sara Klein-Braslavy, *Maimonides' Interpretation of the Story of Creation* (Hebrew), (Jerusalem: Reuben Mass, 1978, 1988). Maimonides set the stage for this shocking literalism back in part 1. He did so in the midst of a series of chapters that could be described as presenting the Bible's anthropology. In 1.39, he discusses the all-important Hebrew word *lev*; in 1.40 *ruaḥ*; in 1.41 *nefesh*; and in 1.42 *ḥay*. It is not surprising that he addresses the literal meaning of *ruaḥ* as one of the elements, that is, "air," first. However, he uses as proof text, the opening of Genesis, as Pines renders it, fittingly shockingly, "And the air of God hovered" (Gen. 1:2). This shock hardly wears off, when, by the end of 1.40, he suggests that the term when used in reference to God refers either solely to God's intellectual overflow or in some cases also to His will. The dissonance between the literal reference to the element air and these figurative meanings in 1.40 is considerable, and it resonates again in the background here in 2.30. Note the numerical affinity (both add up to 5) between these chapters (1.40 and 2.30).

Talmud is the inquiry into the Account of the Beginning and the Account of the Chariot—and by exhorting the reader to study Aristotle's *Meteorology*. Within a couple of pages, Maimonides reminds the reader of the Half-and-Half Teaching as the unanimous view of the rabbinic *Sages*. Yet 2.30 has devoted precious little attention to the miraculous character of the *six days of the Beginning*. From this point forward, Maimonides deals with the strange musings of the *Sages* regarding Adam and Eve, the serpent, Cain and Abel, Seth—and concludes with a discussion of God's relation to the heaven.[15] God here appears to be a creator or maker, though His primary role is that of governor over the heavenly bodies.

This second statement of the Half-and-Half Teaching adds to the suspicion that the God responsible for six days of creation seems ill suited to being fitted together with the God who rules the earthly realm like the God of Aristotle. Whether the Half-and-Half Teaching is coherent rests in no small part on what we will consider later about the two accounts of God in the *Guide*. One thing is amply evident: Maimonides gives little evidence of conceding ground to miracles, which if he were serious about creation we might expect him to concede. The specter of Plato in these chapters is considerable. As we will see, a surprising number of interpreters hold that Maimonides sides with Plato as a way of siding with creation and miracles. We will question that view later.

### *The Half-and-Half Teaching in "Eight Chapters"*

The initial impression left by *Eight Chapters* (EC) is that it is importing Aristotelian ethical ideas and terminology into the moral teaching of the Fathers, and this by itself gives the EC the appearance of being a synthesis of Torah with philosophy. In this sense,

---

[15] See Josef Stern, *The Matter and Form of Maimonides' "Guide,"* 177–78nn58–9, for his interpretation and his citation of the interpretation of others of this passage. I do not find the parallels Stern draws to God as rider in 1.70 convincing.

EC is the ideal setting for introducing the Half-and-Half Teaching. The first indications that Maimonides is not simply engaged in a synthesis appear early in chapter 2. There it appears that the Law attributes sin to both appetite and flesh or as Maimonides translates it into Aristotelian terms, the sentient or sensible or sensitive part, as well as the appetitive part.[16] The translation into Aristotelian terms is made all the more striking by the conflict between this view and Aristotle's own view as stated at the end of chapter 2 that appetite alone is the cause of sin or vice. The EC is far more than a mere synthesis. Unfortunately, now is neither the time nor the place for further exploration of the details of various tensions between the Torah and philosophy regarding ethics in EC.[17] For now, it must suffice to observe that though the EC appears at first glance to be a synthesis, it is not that. Seen in that broader context, the Half-and-Half Teaching finds a natural place in EC as a whole. In a position so close to the end of Maimonides's introduction to his commentary on *Pirqei Avot*, the Half-and-Half Teaching serves to reinforce the initial impression of a synthesis of philosophy and Law, which we might reasonably assume Maimonides would hope the average reader of this portion of his *Commentary on the Mishnah* to carry into the commentary on *Pirqei Avot*.

Very usefully for our purposes, in chapter 8 of EC Maimonides joins the argument against "the senseless ravings fabricated by the astrologers" (84).[18] This argument against the astrologers enables Maimonides to make common cause between the Law and philosophy—or at least between philosophy and one trend in the Law. As I have implied previously, astrology serves as a foil for the Torah's

---

[16] See Aristotle, *De anima* 2.2, esp. 413b ff.

[17] We will touch on this in greater depth in chapter 4.

[18] All references, unless otherwise noted, are to the excellent translation of EC by Weiss and Butterworth: *The Ethical Writings of Maimonides* (New York: New York University Press, 1975; New York: Dover, 1983).

own tendency toward fideism.[19] Astrology and fideism have the same effect on human action, namely, to undermine any sense of freedom human beings might believe they possess. Ultimately, the metaphysical details regarding such freedom are less pressing than the question whether human beings exert themselves rather than awaiting the action of mysterious forces beyond our ken. Maimonides has little difficulty in showing that if we are to obey the Law, we must possess sufficient room to act (84–85).

Maimonides alludes to the connection between astral determinism and fideism in their effects on human action, after inveighing against fideistic interpretations of the rabbinic adage: "*Everything is in the hands of Heaven except the fear of Heaven.*"[20] He draws this connection by following a path through denigrating proponents of astral determinism to inveighing against fideistic tendencies in rabbinic thought and thence to an attack on the fideism of the Mutakallimun. This is how he sets the stage for the Half-and-Half Teaching:

> The account generally accepted among the people, examples of which may be found in the discourse of the *sages* and in the texts of books, is in a way correct: man's standing up, sitting down, and all his movements derive from the volition (*mashī'a*) of God, may He be exalted, and from His will (*irāda*). Let us suppose, for example, that someone throws a rock into the air, and it then falls down. If we say that it fell down by the volition of God, this is a correct account because God wanted the whole earth to be in the center. Therefore, whenever a piece of [the earth] is thrown up, it moves toward the center; similarly, every single particle of fire moves upward through the volition that occurred in the past making fire move upward. It is not the case that now, when this pieces of earth is in motion, God wishes it to move down.

[19] I implied this both earlier in this chapter and in *Maimonides and Spinoza* (Chicago: University of Chicago Press, 2012), chapter 4.

[20] EC, chap. 8, 85n13, referencing *BT,* Berakhot, 33b; Megillah 25a; Niddah 16b.

> The dialectical theologians disagree with this. I have heard them say that volition with respect to each thing takes place one moment after another, continuously. We do not believe that; rather, volition occurred during *the six days of Creation*, and [since then] all things act continuously in accordance with their natures. As [Solomon] said: *What was is what will be; what has been done is what will be done; there is nothing new under the sun.* Therefore the *sages* insisted that there was a prior volition, during *the six days of Creation*, for all the miracles which deviate from custom and which have come about or will come about as promised. At that time the natures of those things were determined in such a way that what has taken place in them would take place. When it takes place at the time it is supposed to, something new is presumed to occur, but that is not so.

Here, we see the Half-and-Half Teaching in a different light. Perhaps one can say that the world has the nature it has due to God's will in the *six days of Creation*, but what Maimonides means by "volition" in this case is far from the obvious meaning we attach to the word. Here, God's volition appears to have little or nothing directly to do with individuals. Indeed, if God creates during the six days of Creation, He must somehow create the species rather than the individuals—or so this account seems to imply. In other words, such talk of God's volition in the days of creation appears to be equivalent to general providence in a purely intellectual account of God's causal role. The talk of "volition" appears to be figurative or parabolic. He concludes this striking version of the Half-and-Half Teaching by treating miracles much as he will go on to treat them in *Guide* 2.29, which anachronistically we have already seen. That is, Maimonides's treatment of miracles in EC is highly similar to views he attributes to the sages in the *Guide*. There, a "very strange statement" about miracles by the rabbis "indicates the superiority of the man who made it" because he recognized that no nature should change, at least not after the days of creation (2.29, 345).

## Part 2: The Two Accounts of God

### *The Wedge Built into the Half-and-Half Teaching*

To see the problems with the Half-and-Half Teaching, it is essential to see that it implies the compatibility of two different accounts of God. Here we oversimplify for purposes of clarity: those two accounts are the God of the philosophers and the God of the Bible or the Prime Unmoved Mover and YHVH. One of the primary means of obscuring the difference between the two is by way of the necessary existence argument. It is well known that Avicenna attempted a harmonization of philosophy and Law in the Muslim tradition by obscuring the differences between these two accounts. It is less well known that the necessary existence argument was one of the primary means of obscuring this difference. In this part of chapter 1, we will inquire not only into Maimonides's use of the necessary existence argument as a means of concealing the differences between these two accounts, but we will also inquire into how that argument was used in the pitched battle between the Mutakallimun and Avicenna, which will become necessary if we are to see how different the *kalām* account is from the philosophic one. Despite the intensity of Maimonides's critique of the *kalām*, he is not beyond obscuring the differences between philosophy and *kalām*, even if he does it in a way that is more responsible than the way Avicenna did so.

Although Maimonides does echo Avicenna on the distinction between essence and existence (1.57) and in using elements of the so-called necessary existence argument (2.intro and 2.1), there is little evidence that Maimonides follows Avicenna in seeking to obscure so thoroughly the divide between eternity and creation. The dialectic of the *Guide* runs quite contrary to the more thoroughly harmonizing tendency of Avicenna—much as Maimonides's contemporary, Averroes, resisted that tendency in Avicenna. True, Maimonides does use the Half-and-Half Teaching to produce a thin veil of harmony, and he also takes advantage of the fact that the necessary existence argument can be made to fit both eternity and creation.[21] That does not mean, however, that Maimonides is willing to follow Avicenna, as Averroes puts it, in confusing the lines between *kalām* and philosophy.[22] *Guide* 1.71 through 76 is too blistering in its critique of the Mutakallimun to say he follows Avicenna so fully in harmonizing *kalām* and philosophy. Above all, I do not see evidence that Maimonides maintains some version of "eternal creation," akin to the position, say, of Avicenna and eventually Thomas Aquinas and Hasdai Crescas, as a serious way of sidestepping the opposition between eternity and creation.[23]

---

[21] See, for example, Maimonides's use of the language of the necessary existence argument both in describing the *kalām* positions (1.74, the Sixth Method, the method of preponderance, 219) and in describing what he characterizes as Aristotle's, despite the clear connection also to Avicenna (see both 219 and 2.1, Third Philosophical Speculation, pp. 247–8, esp. the opening on p. 247). I cannot agree, though, with J. Stern's suggestion that the necessary existence argument ultimately references what he calls the "Abrahamic particularizer" of *Guide* 2.19, 310–11 (*Matter and Form*, 154–7).

[22] See, for example, Cristina Cerami, "A Map of Averroes' Criticism of Avicenna: *Physics, De Caelo, De generatione et corruptione* and *Meteorology*," in *The Arabic, Hebrew and Latin Reception of Avicenna's Natural Philosophy*, 163–240, A. Bertolacci and D.N. Hasse, eds., (Boston, Berlin: W. de Gruyter, 2018), esp. p. 171, citing the Long Commentary on the *Physics* 2, c. 22, 56m–57b.

[23] Cf. Warren Zev Harvey, "A Third Approach to Maimonides' Cosmogony-Prophetology Puzzle," originally in HTR 74 (1981): 287–301; reprinted in *Maimonides: A Collection of Critical Essays*, Joseph Buijs, ed. (Notre Dame, IN: University of Notre Dame Press, 1990), 71–88, esp. p. 79n54 and Howard Kreisel, "Maimonides on the Eternity of the World," in *Judaism as Philosophy: Studies in Maimonides and the Medieval Jewish Philosophers of Provence* (New York: Academic Studies Press, 2015), 40–69, esp. p. 63. Kreisel, like Harvey, leaps to the inference that Maimonides must have embraced some notion of eternal creation, apparently because it is "conceptually possible" and because Hasdai Crescas followed this path. Also see Lopez-Farjeat, "Avicenna's Influence on Aquinas' Early Doctrine of Creation in 'In II Sent.,'

"Eternal creation" as a teaching seems to have two primary possible meanings: either it is merely a repackaging of Neoplatonic teachings on emanation, in which divine causality is purely necessary, or it is meant as a serious harmonization of eternity and creation. The former meaning appears to me to be characteristic of Avicenna; the latter of Thomas Aquinas. Although Avicenna's understanding of the necessary existence argument emphasizes the gulf between God as necessary existent and all other beings as possible existents, it is generally accepted that Avicenna has a strongly necessitarian view of God's causal role. In this respect, Avicenna's conception of God as necessary existent does not differ appreciably from what Maimonides characterizes as Aristotle's view of divine necessity.[24] In contrast, Thomas Aquinas takes the Avicennian conception of the distinction between essence and existence in a direction opposed to a necessitarian view of God's causality. Through his novel teaching about *esse* as both the actuality of the individual being and God's own essence, Thomas draws a connection between God and individuals that is nowhere to be found in Avicenna or—as I will try to show—Maimonides.

With these arguments in mind, we may turn now to the challenges inherent in the Half-and-Half Teaching. The main challenge is posed by what Maimonides identifies as the "nature of existence" or of "being."[25] One wonders whether the "nature of existence" does not require a God who possesses less latitude than YHVH.[26] Of

---

D.1, Q.1. A.2." *Recherches de théologie et philosophie médiévales* 79 (2012)2: 307–37, esp. 320–22.

[24] Cf. W. Z. Harvey, "Maimonides's Avicennianism," *Maimonidean Studies* 5, Arthur Hyman and Alfred Ivry, eds. (New York: Yeshiva University Press, 2008), 107–119.

[25] Pines sometimes translates the relevant Arabic term, *wujūd*, as "existence" and sometime as "being."

[26] See, for example, Maimonides's characterization of Aristotle's view regarding God's latitude in 2.13, p. 283. In short, Aristotle's Prime Unmoved Mover is constrained by the limits of what is possible.

course, YHVH's latitude is most obvious in the case of miracles (Heb., *nais, nisim*). They seem to require a God possessed of will, who would resist the suggestion that the order He causes possesses the kind of fixity associated with "the nature of existence."

That there is at least a potential problem implicit in the Half-and-Half Teaching is evident from the way Maimonides portrays the opposition between the views of the Mutakallimun and the "nature of existence" in *Guide* 1.71. There he argues that the Mutakallimun "did not conform in their premises to the appearance of that which exists (*al-ẓāhir min amr al-wujūd*), but considered how being ought to be in order that it should furnish a proof for the correctness of a particular opinion" (178).[27] In 1.73, Maimonides sets forth those very premises. And the particular opinion they sought to furnish was the proof that the world is created—or to disprove eternity.[28] Maimonides goes on to argue that "men of later periods" read

[27] For the stronger phrase, "*ṭabīʿat al-wujūd*" see pp. 182–3. Pines also omitted to translate this key phrase when it first appears in the context of the quotation from Themistius on p. 179. That quote should read: "To sum up: I shall say to you that the matter is as Themistius puts it: that which exists does not conform to the various opinions, but rather the correct opinions conform to **the nature of** that which exists."

[28] Their proofs of creation, which is the way they are characterized by Maimonides (see 1.74, introduction, p. 215), are essentially at the same time proofs of a creator's existence. Indeed, the leading aim of the Mutakallimun was not to prove that God exists but to disprove eternity. See the structure of Harry Austryn Wolfson's, *The Philosophy of the Kalam* (Cambridge: Harvard University Press, 1976), for evidence that these two arguments are for the Mutakallimun wrapped up in one another, see 1.71, 181. Cf. Stern, *Matter and Form*, pp. 151–2. I do not agree that the argument (in 1.71) on the bottom of p. 181 is a "simple constructive dilemma" because what that presentation, there in particular, appears to be intended to show is that if one invokes creation as an assumption, one has already presupposed the existence of a creator. In effect, one is assuming what one needs to prove. Such is not the case with the assumption of eternity. This then is why whenever he seeks to prove God's existence (not only in his legal works), he assumes eternity.

the writings of the Mutakallimun without a sufficient appreciation of why they argue as they do. They think that they wrote these things merely to "confuse the opinions of the philosophers." On the contrary, the dialectical theologians did this "because of the harm that would come if this were not done—even if it were after a hundred propositions—to an opinion whose recognition as correct was desired by them. These ancient Mutakallimun did away with the disease starting with its root." This passage and all that it implies seems to fly in the face of attempts especially in the last twenty years of scholarship to show that rather than writing esoterically, Maimonides is merely presenting the skeptical challenges inherent to the highest reaches of physics and metaphysics. It seems to be too rosy a picture to suppose that all that is at stake in the arguments between eternity and creation is the realization that one cannot know where the truth lies regarding them—or to so harmonize them that the result is "eternal creation." Maimonides's words in 1.71 portend more than that; they suggest that he would not settle merely for sweeping the conflict under the rug. Put differently, the 7th Cause of Contradiction, which seems to be strongly referenced by the talk above of "the harm that would come... after a hundred propositions" seems to be more than a purely pedagogical matter of skepticism or an effort to harmonize.[29]

---

[29] Cf. Stern, *Matter and Form*, 33n19, 44n30—and especially Yair Lorberbaum's article on the 7th Cause, which Stern cites in Hebrew, as "The Seventh Contradiction: On the Contradictions in the *Guide*—A Reevaluation" *Tarbiz* 69 (2000): 213-37; which was subsequently published in English as "On Contradictions, Rationality, Dialectics, and Esotericism in Maimonides's *Guide of the Perplexed*" *Review of Metaphysics* 55 (2002) 4: 711–50, especially 722 ff. Lorberbaum attempts to show that the whole animus of the 7th Cause of Contradiction is pedagogical. He does so through an ingenious drawing of distinctions between Arabic terms that can be translated by some cognate of "necessary" (*ḍarūra* and *yanbaghī*), the former of which is in a nominal form and the latter of which is a deontic verb form. He also calls on research by Aviezer Ravitzky into the thirteenth- and fourteenth-century

Given that throughout 1.73 through 76 and beyond, Aristotle is referred to frequently as "our adversary who maintains the eternity of the world" (for example, 1.74, Fourth Method, p. 217; Sixth Method, p. 220; Seventh Method, p. 221; and 2.1, First Speculation, p. 245), it seems likely that by "doing away with the root" in 1.71, Maimonides is referring to the eternity of the world—and as for what flows from it after hundreds of propositions that might well be the "nature of existence." After all, in making being conform to the belief they wish to uphold, namely, creation, the Mutakallimun adopt premises that conflict with the "nature of existence." Moreover, all or most of these premises are embraced by those who opposed Aristotle among the Greeks. Of course, it is well known that they borrow premises from the atomists, apparently because the enemy of my "adversary" is my friend. However, it should be emphasized that what the Mutakallimun do with these premises is much more extreme than what the atomists did. What makes that possible is their fideistic vision of God. As we will see later in this book, even atomists like Democritus and Leucippus share far more in common with Aristotle than do the Mutakallimun.

In 1.73, the premise that is the culmination of most of the preceding premises[30] is the so-called "admissibility" premise, the Tenth Premise. This premise makes possible both the Fifth and Sixth Methods of attempting to prove the world is created in 1.74. The

---

commentary tradition on the *Guide* ("The Secrets of the *Guide of the Perplexed*: Between the Thirteenth and Twentieth Centuries," in *Studies in Maimonides*, Isadore Twersky, ed., 7 [Cambridge: Harvard University Press, 1971], 159–207). The basic upshot of Ravitzky, Lorberbaum, and Stern is that Strauss and then Pines politicized the 7th Contradiction (or Cause of Contradiction)—while the medieval commentators who emphasized esotericism seemed to view it as purely theoretical (Ravitzky, p. 180–82). I hope to show here that as ingenious as these arguments are they don't get to the bottom of Strauss's interpretation.

[30] See 1.73, 207 for Maimonides's explanation of how the Tenth Premise is the culmination of the preceding 9 premises.

Fifth Method is the method of particularization and the Sixth is the method of preponderance, which, according to Maimonides, ultimately amount to the same thing.

The following is how Maimonides presents the Fifth Method:

> This is the method of particularization. And it is a method to which [the Mutakallimun] accord very great preference. Its principle refers back to what I have made clear to you in regard to the tenth of their premises. For [the Mutakallim] directs his thought to the world as a whole or to any part of it he likes and says: it is admissible that...it should be in the time and place in which it exists; and it is also admissible that it should...exist prior to or after the time in which it exists or in another place than that in which it is found. Accordingly it is particularization in respect of...a particular time and therewithal the admissibility of all this being different, is a proof of the existence of someone who particularizes, who has freedom of choice, and who has willed one of two admissible things (*mukhtar irād aḥad hadhayin al-jā'zayin*)[31]. Now the fact that the world as a whole or any part of it requires someone who particularizes is a proof of it being created in time (*muḥdathan*). For there is no difference between your saying someone who particularizes or who makes or who creates (*khāliq*) or who brings into existence or who creates in time (*muḥdath*) or who purposes (*qāṣad*) the universe—all these terms being intended to signify one single notion.[32]

---

[31] Here, Pines translates "two admissible possibilities." Given the opposition between the admissible and the possible that Maimonides intends, adding "possibilities" muddies the whole matter.

[32] Here, Pines distinguishes two very similar words in Arabic, both of which could be translated as "creates" (based on the roots ḥ.d.th. and kh.l.q.) by adding "in time" to the former. By the time we get to 2.13 ff., Maimonides will most frequently use the Arabic term based on ḥ.d.th., and Pines will continue to translate it as "create *in time.*" It should be noted that in 2.13 the very idea of "in time" will be made problematic. To complicate matters even further, Maimonides will eventually bring into play the Hebrew word *bara*, which has a cognate form in Arabic, *bara'a*.

Despite Maimonides's implied harsh indictment of the argumentative means used by the Mutakallimun in 1.71, he concludes his whole account of the Fifth Method in 1.74 with the following assessment: "To sum up: this is to my mind a most excellent method. I have, with regard to it, an opinion which you shall hear." Of course, Maimonides will go on to offer his own modified "particularization" proof for creation in 2.19—though he acknowledges there that it does not rise to the level of being demonstrative. Above all, we take for granted, based on 1.71, that Maimonides will employ a version of the particularization argument that conforms to the "nature of existence." This seems to be what Leo Strauss meant by "intelligent *kalām*."[33] However, here in 1.74, we see a version of "particularization" that flies in the face of the "nature of existence." It is worthwhile to consider these *kalām* arguments here because doing so will prepare us for Maimonides's departures from them in 2.19 and because it will help to reveal the gap between those who defend the "nature of existence" and those who make experience conform to their preferred premise, creation.

Several things draw our attention in the Fifth Method: connections between admissibility, the time of God's action, and the centrality of "freedom of choice" or "will" in *kalām* conceptions of God as creator. When he set forth the admissibility premise in 1.73, Maimonides highlighted some key points of departure of the Mutakallimun. Their most important departure is their abandonment of the Aristotelian distinction of modes of being into necessary, possible, and impossible. For the "possible," they substituted the "admissible" (1.73, 211).[34] As early as Maimonides's *Eight Chapters*, chap.

[33] See Leo Strauss, *Persecution*, 40–41.

[34] It is worth noting that Pines does not always distinguish in his English translation the Arabic words "admissible (*al-jā'iz*)" from "possible (*mumkin*)." Cf. especially pp. 207 and 210. On both pages Maimonides engages a philosopher and a Mutakallim in a dialogue, which may account for some of this fluidity. On p. 207, Pines renders *mumkin* as "possible" and turns then to the

1, he acknowledged this "innovation" on the part of the Mutakallimun, and there, as in 1.73, Tenth Premise, Maimonides underscored the connection between their talk of "admissibility" and their reliance on the "imagination" (EC, chap. 1, 63 and *Guide* 1.73, "A Call upon the Reader's Attention," pp. 209–212). He puts the matter succinctly in EC, "They thought, or made people fancy, that everything that can be imagined is possible." Relying excessively on the imagination and failing to cultivate the intellect properly is the psychological basis of their abandonment of the "nature of existence." Although they recognize logical impossibilities, they do not recognize that there is any limit to what is naturally possible—that is, they do not recognize the "nature of existence."[35]

That the Mutakallimun abandon the "nature of existence" may not be difficult to see; however, we need to inquire further into 1.73 to see what it can tell us by contrast about what is required for the

key set of three modes, the "necessary, admissible, and impossible." Here he accurately renders *jā'iz* as "admissible." However, on p. 210, perhaps because the philosopher seems to be speaking, Pines renders the series, "necessary, possible, and impossible," when the Arabic has *jā'iz* for the second term. Cf. also the Weiss-Butterworth translation of *Eight Chapters*, chap. 1, of the series with *jā'iz* as "admissible." Less significantly, Maimonides does not always use the same term for "impossible": most frequently it is *mumtaniʿ* (210), but sometimes it is *mustaḥīl* (207).

[35] For evidence that they recognize the logically impossible, see 3.15, 459–60, where this is implied because, according to Maimonides, "all men of speculation" recognize its impossibility. One might say rather than dividing things into the "necessary, the admissible, and the impossible," as Maimonides puts it in EC, they or at least the most extreme among them, the Ashʿariyya, ultimately distinguish only between the admissible and the impossible. As omnipotent, God can do whatever is admissible; that which is logically impossible is impossible for God. It is unclear what would be necessary for their God. I find it strange that some who read 3.15 are persuaded by its latter half in which Maimonides questions everything required for the maintenance of the "nature of existence," including the distinction between the imagination and the intellect (see Stern, *Matter and Form,* 241–2).

"nature of existence" and whether the "nature of existence" is compatible with creation. Although Maimonides initially presents the Tenth Premise as if it were the culmination of the preceding nine premises (1.73, 207), on the next page he refines this claim by setting forth a Mutakallim's response to the philosopher's claim that there is a real difference between accidents linked to matter and accidents linked to form. Ultimately, the Mutakallim repudiates the philosopher's view because he rejects the very notion that things have a form (see Eighth Premise). From his point of view, there are merely atoms and accidents. Form it would appear is central to the "nature of existence." To mount his argument against the "nature of existence," in this elaboration of the Tenth Premise, the Mutakallim appeals to all 11 of the other premises except for the Fourth, Seventh, and Eleventh (1.73, 208). We may leave aside for now these omitted premises and focus on the remaining ones, though we cannot consider all the remaining premises. Our interest here is in seeing whether Maimonides gives us any indications, albeit indirectly, that defenders of creation will tend to ignore or discount some feature(s) of the "nature of existence." To lead us off, it is worth considering the Twelfth Premise, which is unique in being the only premise the Mutakallim appeals to that hasn't yet been covered. This premise denies the trustworthiness of the senses. As early as his *Treatise on the Art of Logic*, Maimonides has acknowledged first and foremost the basic trustworthiness of the senses.[36] Like Aristotle and every other philosopher, he is aware of illusions of the senses such as the appearance that a straight stick is bent in water. Nevertheless, he knows that so long as a person's body is healthy, his senses may be trusted.[37] It almost goes without saying that many miracles give the lie to the senses. This Twelfth Premise sits in the middle of the premises used to bolster what appears as the point the Mutakallim

[36] Weiss and Butterworth, *Ethical Writings*, chapter 8, p. 156.
[37] See *Eight Chapters*, chap. 3 (*Ethical Writings*, p. 66).

is attempting to make, namely, the Eighth Premise's denial of a real distinction between matter and form or form and accident. The other six premises to which the Mutakallim appeals to make his point are the following: 1, 2, 3 (12) 9, 6, and 5, in that order. They are Premise 1, the world is composed of atoms; Premise 2, all other than the atoms is vacuum or void; Premise 3, time is composed of instants; Premise 9, accidents don't serve as substrata for other accidents, only atoms are the substrata for accidents; Premise 6, accidents do not last during two units of time; and Premise 5, accidents do not exist apart from atoms. Premise 6 comes close to where the rubber meets the road: That what is must be created anew at every moment is shocking and surely runs counter to the apparent continuity that we experience through sensation, as well as the texture of continuity that Maimonides seems to have in mind by the phrase "nature of existence." In the course of explaining this premise, Maimonides acknowledges that "what led them to this opinion is that it is not to be said that there is a nature in any respect whatever and that the nature of one particular body may require that this and that accident be attached to that body" (201). In other words, they deny the existence of the kinds of accidents associated with the form of a being. But what is most absurd is the vehemence with which all but one Muʿtazilite mutakallim treat privations as if they existed. Things such as death in a dead thing must be constantly created by God (204). In effect, they establish a kind of parity between existence and non-existence that cannot but undermine the continuity of the natural that is expressed by the phrase "nature of existence."[38] In accordance with the "nature of existence," it is form or actuality that

[38] As we will see later, that is, in chapter 4, when we analyze *Guide* 3.10, matters are slightly more complicated than this. In fact, the Mutakallimun treat both accidents and privations of accidents as existent—in opposition to the void as the only thing that truly does not exist.

has preponderance over privation.[39] Or as Aristotle argues throughout the *Metaphysics*, an individual being's achievement of form or a state of health is what is "for the most part." Disease and even death are what is "otherwise than for the most part."[40] The other name that Aristotle uses to capture what is "for the most part" is the "possible," which is of course at odds with the *kalām* term "admissible."

The importance of privation in the *Guide* can hardly be overstated. It is alluded to as early as 1.17, in Maimonides's distinction among matter, form, and particularized privation. But, as we will see later, privation's importance does not really become apparent until 3.10, in the wake of the initially apparently ascetic 3.8. Initially, Maimonides inflames the reader's animus against matter or flesh, until he tempers it in 3.10 with the realization that it is privation rather than matter that is the problem.[41]

There is a key moment that we ought to tie to Maimonides's discussion of the Mutakallimun on existence and non-existence, namely, his prior discussion of God's nature in 1.50 through 70. Near the peak of his account of the negative theology, Maimonides affirms things about existence that are highly reminiscent of Avicenna's teaching. In 1.57, he claims that God's essence is his existence, his existence is necessary, and he adds that for other beings in whom their essence is not equivalent to their existence, their existence is accidental. In fact, that last point is nearly the first thought of this chapter: "It is known that existence is an accident attaching to what exists." That Avicenna claims something like this is well

[39] Even though the atomists, Democritus and Leucippus, reject Aristotelian form, according to Aristotle himself, they accept that actuality has priority over potentiality (*Met.* 12.6).

[40] See *Met.* 6.2 and 9.9.

[41] Also see Strauss, "Literary Character," in *Persecution and the Art of Writing*, 75–76 on Maimonides's repeated misquotation of Aristotle's refrain in EN regarding the sense of touch, which makes Aristotle into a fellow ascetic admonisher to all potential philosophers. Above all, consider the undercutting of this attack on touch in 1.46–47, esp. 101 and 104.

known. However, at least since Averroes first criticized Avicenna for this claim, it seems to have been misconstrued. One thing is certain: He does not mean by accident the sort of accident associated with matter.[42] More importantly, he is enough of an Aristotelian and especially of a Neoplatonist to *not* be arguing, as do the Mutakallimun, that whether a being exists or not are equally possible. Aristotle, Avicenna, and Maimonides agree—as we will see later, indeed, as all philosophers seem to agree—on the superiority and priority of existence over non-existence. None of them hold the view of the Mutakallimun who treat non-being as on a par with being. Maimonides states the primacy of being over non-being in 3.10 (439–40)—and implies as much throughout his critique of the Mutakallimun. Yet, as we will see, Avicenna's development of the necessary existence argument for God's existence, I believe intentionally, provides cover for the Mutakallimun. Indeed, it is not by chance that Maimonides uses the language of necessary existence to characterize the Sixth Method of proving creation (and thereby the existence of the creator), the so-called method of preponderance (1.74, 219). This is how Maimonides puts it:

> One of the later [Mutakallimun] thought that he had come upon a most excellent method superior to all the methods known before. This method is concerned with the preponderance (*tarjīḥ*) given to existence over nonexistence. He said: According to everyone, the world is possible in respect of existence; for if its existence were necessary, it would be the deity. Now we engage in discussion only[43] with those who, on the one hand, affirm the existence of the deity and, on the other, maintain the eternity of the world. Now that which is possible is that of which it is possible that it should exist and it is equally possible that it should

[42] See Yegane Shayegan, "The Accidentality of Existence in Avicenna and Its Critique in Averroes," *Journal of Persianate Studies* 10 (2017): 218–39, esp. p. 223.

[43] I have moved the word "only" to its proper position in this English sentence. Pines placed it before "engage."

> not exist, existence not being more appropriate to it than nonexistence. Now the fact that this thing, which is possible in respect of existence, exists in spite of the equal validity of its status as an existent and its status as a nonexistent proves that there is someone who gives preponderance to its existence over its nonexistence.

The claim early in this explanation that in effect views the world as possible in contrast to God as necessary indicates to us the world in which this author posited the "preponderance" argument. On the one hand, according to Wolfson, Alghazali (1058–1111) initiated the "preponderance" argument as a reply to Avicenna (980–1037).[44] On the other hand, according to Davidson, even the "particularization" argument, which Maimonides presents as the Fifth Method, is traceable not only back to al-Juwayni[45] (1028–1085) but even further back to one of the earliest *kalām* arguments for creation, that of al-Baqillani's (950–1013) proof from accidents.[46] One definitely sees vestiges of the proof from accidents in Maimonides's articulation of the particularization proof. And, once again, Maimonides observes that the preponderance argument is really just a modification of the particularization argument. I descend to this level of detail to underscore that this was a two-way street. That Alghazali was responding to Avicenna is widely understood. What is less widely understood is that Avicenna's necessary existence argument, though it surely contains some extraordinarily novel theoretical innovations, is also couched in such a way as to appeal to Mutakallimun who preceded him, such as al-Baqillani, with a very simply structured proof for God's existence. Indeed, it was both ingenious and dangerous to

[44] Harry Austryn Wolfson, *The Philosophy of the Kalam* (Cambridge: Harvard University Press, 1976), 447.

[45] Wolfson, *Kalam*, 447.

[46] Herbert A. Davidson, "Arguments from the Concept of Particularization in Arabic Philosophy," *Philosophy East and West* 18 (1968) 4: 299–314, and cf. Wolfson, *Kalam,* 374 and 392–409.

provide so simple a proof which could be used by Mutakallimun to try to prove creation (against the philosophers' arguments for eternity) and philosophers to prove God's existence. As Wolfson explains when describing the content and history of the preponderance proof, he begins by recalling that before Alghazali formulated his response to Avicenna, Avicenna had fashioned one of his versions of the necessary existence argument as part of a proof for the eternity of the world. Wolfson writes, "The crux of Avicenna's argument, then, is that on the assumption of the world proceeding from God by necessity, it could not have proceeded from Him in time—and this on the ground that there is no adequate explanation why it proceeded at a certain given time and not sooner or later." Avicenna's necessary existence argument, which was originally aimed at eternity, employed the language of preponderance that Alghazali would then try to turn back round against Avicenna.[47] That Avicenna's necessary existence argument was used both to prove eternity and to prove creation helps to explain why some would now argue that when Maimonides uses the necessary existence argument, which he appears to borrow from Avicenna, that he has in mind an "Abrahamic particularizer."[48] Of course, Avicenna did not have such a particularizer in mind but at best an eternal creator in keeping with the Neoplatonic tradition he sought to elaborate. As we will see, Maimonides follows in Avicenna's footsteps in using the necessary existence argument in part because it is palatable to both philosophers and Mutakallimun, despite the fact that the character of the necessary existent they envision is completely different. Both the greatest value and greatest danger of this argument is its pliability for both sides in the argument between the *kalām* and philosophy.

Let us return to our discussion of 1.73, Tenth Premise, to conclude our analysis of Maimonides's inquiry into admissibility,

[47] Wolfson, *Kalam*, 444–47.

[48] Stern, *Matter and Form*, 156–7.

imagination, the nature of existence, and God's nature. In "A Call upon the Reader's Attention," Maimonides also connects the over-extension of the imagination and the embrace of the admissible (as well as the rejection of the nature of existence) to an emphasis on divine will rather than wisdom. Reverting to his earlier mini-dialogue between a philosopher and a Mutakallim (pp. 207–9), Maimonides writes, "Consider thou who art engaged in speculation, and perceive that a method of profound speculation has arisen. For with regard to particular mental representations, one individual claims that they are intellectual representations, whereas another affirms that they are imaginative representations. We wish consequently to find something that would enable us to distinguish the thing cognized intellectually from those imagined. For if the philosopher says, as he does: That which exists [or 'existence'] is my witness and by means of it we discern the necessary, the possible, and the impossible; the adherent of the Law says to him: The dispute between us is with regard to this point. For we claim that that which exists was made in virtue of will and was not a necessary consequence." The nature of existence depends on what is "cognized intellectually." For the philosopher, it is the intellect that grasps what is possible in nature. The God who causes what is necessary and what is possible—nature—is, as we know from 1.68–69, an intellect. For the Mutakallimun, what is partakes of three modes: the necessary, the admissible, and the impossible. Human imagination, not nature or intellect, is the guide to what is admissible. The only things that are impossible are the things logically impossible. God and God alone is necessary. I acknowledge that the above passage taken by itself could be made to square with the Half-and-Half Teaching. In context, though, I believe that Maimonides is pointing to the yawning gulf between divine wisdom and divine will. Of course, I am well aware of those passages running throughout 1.50 through 70 that seem to treat wisdom and will as merely equivocal in God's case.[49] Although this claim is true of YHVH, I will try to show that it is not true of the Aristotelian God of 1.68–69. Ultimately, the "nature of existence" can speak to us only through our intellects.

*There Are Two Accounts of God, Not One Synthesis*

The Half-and-Half Teaching, if successful, would require an account of a God who combines elements of the account of God in 1.52 through 66, namely, YHVH, with elements of the account of God in 1.68 through 69, namely, the Aristotelian God. Some seem to see these two accounts as of a piece. Those who adopt what Josef Stern has called a dogmatic approach to the *Guide* are more likely to embrace the view that Maimonides achieves such a synthesis.[50] Some have attempted to square this circle by arguing that Maimonides adopts a vision of eternal creation. Although such an approach may have suited Hasdai Crescas, there is little if any evidence that Maimonides adopted this approach, unless one means this in the way Plotinus or Avicenna might have had a notion of eternal creation in mind. Here, the creation dimension is little more than a way of trying to imagine what Neoplatonists had in mind when treating of emanation from the One. Of course, such emanation never had any temporal meaning. In some sense, emanation, even among pagan Neoplatonists, is by its very nature an accommodation to human imagination.[51] Although Maimonides acknowledges a place for the

---

[49] For example, 1.53, 1.56, and 1.64.

[50] Stern, *Matter and Form*, p. 5.

[51] However, once one blends together Plotinus with elements of Aristotle's teaching regarding the causal hierarchy of heavenly bodies and with an explanation of prophecy, emanation (*f.y.ḍ.*), or "overflow" as Pines renders the term in his translation, becomes highly figurative (see *Guide* 2.12, 279; also see Alfarabi, *Political Regime* and *Virtuous City*: Alfarabi: *The Political Writings*, Vol. 2, *"Political Regime" and "Summary of Plato's Laws,"* Charles E. Butteworth, trans. [Ithaca: Cornell University Press, 2015], §§ 34, 68, 80.); *Al-Farabi on the Perfect State,* Richard Walzer, trans. (Oxford: Clarendon,

imagination in the acquisition of knowledge even if based merely on the summary things said about the soul in *Eight Chapters*, he has some rather harsh things to say about the imagination in the *Guide*: such as that it is itself the evil inclination![52] Leaving the imagination aside, our main point is that, though the Half-and-Half Teaching may appear to establish harmony between six days of creation and subsequently unchanging nature, Maimonides while often glossing over the differences between YHVH and the God of necessity, ultimately intends the reader to see the disharmony between the two accounts and to consider its implications for claims such as the Half-and-Half Teaching.

In contrast to the interpretation we are offering, Kenneth Seeskin is one of the leading authors promoting a synthetic view of the account of God in the *Guide*. He appears to be convinced of two things: Maimonides's whole view of God is captured in the negative theology. And when Maimonides claims there is no relation between God and man, he means by this no relation in any sense.[53] Even on the basis of the negative theology of YHVH, it seems unreasonable to think that Maimonides is claiming there isn't even what we would call a "causal relation" between God and creation. Such a view might be conceivable in the case of an occasionalist, but Maimonides seems to strive with every fiber of his being against the kind of occasionalism rampant among the Mutakallimun. I suspect

1985; reprint: Kazi Publications, 1998), chap. 3, § 1; chap. 13, §§ 1–2; chap. 14, §§ 7–11; chap. 15, § 10. Also see Seymour Feldman, "The Theory of Eternal Creation in Hasdai Crescas and Some of His Predecessors," *Viator* 11 (1980): 289–320. Feldman speaks of even Alfarabi as purveying a version of "eternal creation"; however, as we will see over the course of this book, we would prefer to limit the use of this term to those who are not merely glossing over the differences between eternity and creation, as did Alfarabi, Avicenna, and Averroes.

[52] See 2.6, 264–5 and 2.12, 280.

[53] Kenneth Seeskin, *Maimonides on the Origin of the World* (Cambridge: Cambridge University Press, 2005), 8–9.

that Seeskin overstates this matter because he does not see that when Maimonides denies "relation" (in 1.52) he has a quite narrow meaning, namely, the Aristotelian category of "relation" in mind.[54] True, when he moves away from Aristotle's claim into the full territory of his negative theology he denies relation in an even broader sense; however, in both cases what he is denying is "relation" in a sense tied to predication. Maimonides's sense of lack of relation is meant to refer to and bear on the matter of what human beings can know of God. It does not bear either on the issues of God's causal relation to or knowledge of us.

That being said, the claim of lack of relation in human knowledge of God does create challenges regarding some of the most important and striking claims about God made in the Bible—and attended to and underlined by Maimonides. The most obvious problem is posed by the crucial passage on man being made in the image and likeness of God (Genesis 1:26), which is surely intended to convey something of how man is to think of God. This passage is a key focus of Maimonides from the first chapter of the *Guide*. In the Christian tradition, this biblical passage takes on special meaning in connection with the doctrine of the Incarnation. Almost from the beginning of the *Guide*, Maimonides is at great pains to argue that image and likeness refers to man's possession of an intellect like God's—and certainly no corporeal likeness. Wouldn't such a likeness indicate something essential about God, namely, that God is an intellect? It should not be surprising that at least in this moment of his argument, though he relies upon a proof text from Genesis, he is in fact offering an interpretation that reminds us more of the Aristotle's God than YHVH. And when we claim that God transcends human knowing, are we thinking of God as essentially intellect, essentially will, or both? I will argue that, when we claim

[54] See Aristotle, *Categories,* chap. 7.

likeness, we are on firmest ground to insist upon intellect;[55] however, when we insist upon the greatest degree of lack of relation we have in mind will (1.53). After all, we rarely speak of a God of inscrutable *intellect*—rather we speak only of a God of inscrutable *will.*

Returning more directly to the issue of our lack of relation to God, the limits of our knowledge of the God of Aristotle are not as great as those on our knowledge of YHVH. On the one hand, Jews refer to God by these letters, YHVH, of course, known as the Tetragrammaton, to avoid pronouncing the name of God, which was permitted only by the high priest in the Holy of Holies on the holiest day of the year, the Day of Atonement. And, of course, many orthodox Jews use simply the Hebrew phrase for the Name, ha-Shem, to avoid appearing to be impious through the pronunciation of the name. Indeed, for this reason some will even avoid the use of the word "God." All of these facts are meant to indicate the extent of intellectual distance of the believer from God. On the other hand, according to Aristotle, though immaterial beings are indefinable—and lack relation in the technical sense that they escape a sufficiently proximate species or genus for speech to be able to grasp the relation (*Guide* 1.52, 118)—the Prime Unmoved Mover has an essence that can be grasped intuitively.[56] Indeed for Aristotle, human thinking begins with the intuition of primary intelligibles (such as that the whole is greater than the part) and ascends through discursive argument, which appears to rise in the strict sense of demonstration no higher than material beings, to the intuitive grasp of immaterial

---

[55] When I say that we're on firmest ground regarding likeness, in relation to intellect, I do not mean that this is what the Bible has in mind when speaking of being made in the image and likeness of God.

[56] The claim on indefinability in *Met.* 7.15, 1040a25–27 puts the odd back and forth between *Guide* 1.51, 112–13 and 1.52, 114–15 "First Group" of attributes predicated of things in perspective. For the indications that discursive inquiry does not exhaust the possible ways of acquiring knowledge of the immaterial, see *Met.* 7.17, 1041b10–11 and book 12, chaps. 6 through 10.

separate beings in a manner that transcends demonstration.[57] In contrast, YHVH cannot be grasped even intuitively. It is this stronger sense of lack of relation that is the ultimate basis of the negative theology. It is precisely because YHVH is altogether transcendent that Maimonides has recourse to negation. Although one might use negation in connection with the God of Aristotle: for example, Aristotle's God does not have a body and does not have parts;[58] Aristotle developed a positive account at least of the divine essential attribute of intellect; he spoke of essence and form to capture that which transcends the material; and he spoke aptly of divine simplicity to convey the lack of parts. He did not have recourse to negative theology per se because, despite our limited ability to define or explain the divine essence in words, our ability to think enables us to grasp intuitively something of what it might mean to be pure thought thinking itself (*Met.* 12.10).[59]

---

[57] Although it is the case that it would take the commentators on Aristotle such as Alexander of Aphrodisias and Themistius to develop a robust notion of primary intelligibles, Aristotle alludes to them in the opening chapters and concluding chapter of the *Posterior Analytics*.

[58] Cf. Thomas Aquinas, *Summa contra gentiles* 1.17–18

[59] An anecdote may help explain the point I am trying to make here. As someone who teaches at a Catholic university, I have had a bit of a misunderstanding with my colleagues in my own department of Philosophy. We once discussed the course description for a graduate version of a course called Philosophy of God. My Catholic colleagues insisted that Thomas Aquinas's three ways of demonstrating God's existence (causality, remotion or negation, and eminence or analogy) were all part of *natural* theology. I was stumped because I knew that for Maimonides his way of negation was emphatically his account of YHVH—what would be, if he used the term, a part of *revealed* theology (cf. Leo Strauss, "Literary Character," in PAW, 46). What accounts for the difference is that Thomas Aquinas does not distinguish between Aristotelian negation and the kind of negation Maimonides demands. Similarly, Thomas's moment of "causality," which is sometimes also referred to as the "positive" moment, refers at least primarily to the arguments for God's existence from motion such as the ones Maimonides presents in *Guide* 2.1. Perhaps even

What Maimonides does with Aristotle's technical meaning of relation is intentionally to make an overly broad claim about human ignorance, which seems to cover both YHVH and Aristotle's Prime Unmoved Mover. On the one hand, although it is in a narrow technical sense true that for Aristotle there is no "relation" between us and God, that does not mean that for Aristotle and philosophers like him there is no knowledge of God—rather that knowledge is limited to a form of rational intuition (*noesis*). On the other hand, the extent of ignorance of YHVH and inability to predicate anything about Him is significantly greater. The Torah's vision of YHVH does not leave room even for rational intuition.[60] What Maimonides achieves through this intentionally overly broad claim about relation is to appear to harmonize the philosophic and Jewish understandings of God. Like the Half-and-Half Teaching, the apparent harmonization or blending of these two senses of God enables Maimonides to present an appearance of harmony that is useful for welcoming philosophic inquiry into the Jewish fold. The crux of this harmonization is the human being. Because we human beings possess both an intellect and will or desire, it is tempting to suppose that God does too. Although Aristotle speaks analogically of the Prime Unmoved Mover (PUM) as if it had a soul and might even possess desire—all of this is imagery, since Aristotle also denies discursive access to the immaterial intelligible beings—it is not by chance that, ultimately, he characterizes it as thought thinking

---

analogy in Thomas does not really point to the truly ineffable, at least as Maimonides portrays it.

[60] By "rational intuition" I do not even mean Plotinian intuition of a Good beyond Being. Rather, I refer to the sort of intuition implied by talk of God as First Cause in Alfarabi. However, all the Islamic and Jewish rationalists in this monotheistic period resist the idea of direct intuition of God, speaking instead of conjunction with the Active Intellect, lest they trample the remoteness of the pure monotheistic Creator.

itself.[61] The PUM cannot possess desire or will,[62] because desire implies lack, as Socrates explains in the *Symposium*. The PUM is decidedly an intellect. In contrast, YHVH cannot be captured by any humanlike power or faculty (*qūwa*). However, because YHVH is said to be the creator of all things out of nothing and because such creation would surely require omnipotence, it seems inevitable that the greatest danger is that YHVH should be thought of as an unlimited, unconstrained, and inscrutable will. This danger is the watchword of the *Guide*, whether it appears in the form of Ashʿarism or astral determinism. It is little wonder then that in the lexicographic chapters (1.1 through 49) Maimonides oscillates between characterizing God as wisdom or will or both. More on this in our final chapter.

Just how problematic characterizing God as will is emerges only in the section on creation vs. eternity (2.13–31). But the danger is already alluded to much earlier. Though it is hinted at perhaps as early as 1.11 with the earliest discussion of providence and becomes apparent throughout the chapters on the biblical human anthropology (1.39–42), the first serious hint of a problem appears at the end of 1.68, shortly after the pronouncement of the Half-and-Half Teaching. God is pure thought thinking itself in this chapter. Such a being cannot be impeded. Only lesser beings such as the Active Intellect can suffer an impediment—or so it seems here.[63] This small theme of "impediment" will blossom into a central problem of the *Guide*, not only in connection with prophecy and providence but also in relation to creation. For now it will have to suffice to say that Maimonides hints that, like Avicenna, he has difficulty finding his way to the claim that God could act in time.

---

[61] Cf. *Met.* 12.7 with 12.9.

[62] I refer to "desire" or "will" (cf. [Gr.] *boulēsis* with [Ar.] *irāda*) because like Maimonides he does not have a notion of will that is distinct from desire. And both speak of "choice" (and similarly cf. *proairesis* with *ikhtiyār*).

[63] This will be revised in *Guide* 2.18, as we will see later.

Although the Half-and-Half Teaching is supposed to combine six days of creation with an earthly order fitting Aristotle's account, this combination would seem to imply some sort of synthesis of the biblical account of God with the philosophic account. We have seen how difficult it is to achieve a synthesis of these two accounts. The God of the Bible, YHVH, seems to require above all omnipotence and a will; the philosophic God is, of course, an intellect. The Christian tradition finesses this problem by way of the teaching of the Incarnation. In other words, it finesses it by resting confident in the notion that God is akin to man in having both intellect and will. Yet that combination is due to the finitude of the human. Even when that tradition insists on essential differences between human will and divine will, it still relies on this kinship between the divine and the human. Of course, Judaism cannot do this. God is not only the Most High but in some sense infinitely high. Human beings have no means of knowing YHVH, not even by some form of intuition. There is reason to think, then, that it might be better not to finesse some things. As Strauss has suggested in other contexts, such syntheses don't really work. Either the philosophic God becomes absorbed into the biblical by assuming that the omnipotent God of the Bible would, after having created the world, stand by an earthly world following the order set forth by Aristotle, or the biblical God is retained only in name, as we see, for example, in 1.69.

# CHAPTER 2

# THE VAGUENESS OF THE LIMITS OF KNOWLEDGE

Already in chapter 1, we have seen hints of some of the difficulties surrounding the limits of knowledge. To put the matter bluntly, the limits on the knowledge of God as Aristotle conceives of God (as portrayed in 1.68 through 69) is a far cry from the limits of knowledge of YHVH (as portrayed especially in parts of 1.52 through 62). The former are not absolute limits; the latter are nearly absolute, permitting only the meager light from the negative theology.

Once again, we have Shlomo Pines's 1979 article on the limits of knowledge in Alfarabi, Ibn Bajja, and Maimonides to thank for our focus on the limits of knowledge.[1] As we argued in the introduction, the responses have been divided into "skeptical" responses from those who adhere more or less closely to Pines's argument and "dogmatic" responses from those who deny these limits.[2] We will try to argue that, in spite of Maimonides's thematization of limits of knowledge in part 1, chapters 31 through 34, and his apparent underscoring that the limit is at the sphere of the moon in part 2, chapters 22 and 24, Maimonides intended for the limits to be vague. We

[1] Shlomo Pines, "Limitations of Human Knowledge according to al-Fārābī, Ibn Bājja, and Maimonides," in *Studies in Medieval Jewish History and Literature,* ed. I. Twersky (Cambridge: Harvard University Press, 1979), 82–109; reprinted in *Collected Works of Shlomo Pines,* vol. 5, ed. W. Z. Harvey and Moshe Idel (Jerusalem: Magnes Press, 1997), 404–431; "Les Limites de la métaphysique selon al-Fārābi (sic), Ibn Bājja et Maïmonide; sources et antithèses de ces doctrines chez Alexandre d'Aphrodise et chez Themistius," in *Miscellanea Mediaevalia, Akten des VI Internationalen Kongresses für Mittelalterliche Philosophie*, August–September 1977, (Berlin: De Gruyter, 1981), 211–225.

[2] Josef Stern, *The Matter and the Form*, 5n4.

will show that while the limits of knowledge serve the defense of Judaism—that is, the Law—the very vagueness of those limits serves the defense of philosophy. In other words, as part of the defense of Judaism, Maimonides makes it appear that there are clear limits; as part of the defense of philosophy, however, he gives counterindications to these limits, which render the exact location of the limits unclear. Of course, we do not mean to argue that human knowledge has no limits. We do, however, intend to argue that the vagueness of the limits serves to defend philosophy. The simply pious reader may rest satisfied with the defense of Judaism; the more intellectually courageous reader is enabled to see by means of the vagueness of the limits that the limits are themselves subject to further investigation. The ongoing debates about the limits of knowledge even over forty years after Pines's landmark article testify at least to the possibility of our interpretation.

Because so much has been written in response to Pines's article, we would be remiss to ignore the prodigious set of responses plowing ahead to offer yet another response. A survey of the literature will enable us to gain some clarity about what is at stake in these debates. The first section in this chapter will be devoted to laying out the plot, as it were, of these debates. There are at least two "generations" of responses:[3] the initial responses primarily in the late 1980s and the 1990s, followed by a second generation of responses to Herbert Davidson's musings regarding *Guide* 2.24, which contains among the most skeptical remarks made by Maimonides. Davidson's piece led not only to a piece shortly thereafter by W. Z. Harvey in 1997, but also to a response to Harvey and Davidson by Joel L. Kraemer in 2006 and an issue of the journal *Aleph* (volume 8) in 2008 devoted to the passage. It is not much of an exaggeration to say that Josef Stern's book, *The Matter and Form of Maimonides'*

[3] As will become apparent when we outline the history of responses to Pines, we do not mean by "generation" to refer to an actual human generation of anywhere from 22 to 33 years.

*"Guide,"* is the most extended development of the skeptical view first voiced by Pines and to the second generation of responses to Pines. Indeed, Stern's own piece in *Aleph* anticipates among the most important arguments in his subsequent 2013 book.

The second section will outline the steps by which Maimonides transforms the Talmudic prohibitions or strictures (some mild and some extremely severe) on inquiry into mere indications of limits of human knowledge in part 1, chapters 31 through 34.

The third section will explore the moments in part 2 of the *Guide* that seem to delineate most clearly the limits of knowledge, namely, 2.22 and 24. Closer examination will reveal that far too much heat was generated by the offending passage in 2.24 as one author, T. Zvi Langermann, made apparent in his contribution to the *Aleph* 8, "My Truest Perplexities." In addition to Langermann's insights we will remind the reader of the necessity of paying attention to the rhetorical arc of the *Guide* here. Above all, it is not by chance that 2.24's skeptical conclusion precedes immediately the most important moment in the defense of Judaism in the *Guide*, 2.25.

In the fourth section, we will raise the question: how could Maimonides even posit his account of God's will preventing prophecy if the limits were what they seemed to be, that is, clearly at the sphere of the moon or limited to knowledge only of the earthly? Although we will return to look in some depth at prophecy and providence in chapters 5 and 6, here we will take a quick look at 2.32 and 3.17 through 18 as well as 3.51 solely with an eye to the conundrum: if the limit were simply at the sphere of the moon, then why would Maimonides even be willing to speculate about God's will preventing prophecy (2.32). Maimonides's subsequent claim that the sole cause of the worthy not receiving divine "overflow" is the worthy's failure to continuously contemplate God (3.51) leads one not only to doubt the clarity of the limits but also to revise the earlier interpretation of the third opinion about prophecy, since prophecy is simply a special case of providence.

## Survey of the Scholarship on the Limits of Knowledge since 1979

Pines's article, or at least some of its features, has only grown in influence. The main evidence for this is that the response of what we will refer to as the "first generation," even including his own students,[4] was largely to criticize Pines's thesis. Subsequently, however, the skeptical school has grown in stature and influence. The most well-known of these scholars of the "first generation"—Alexander Altmann, Herbert Davidson, and Alfred Ivry—all wrote articles begging to differ with Pines.[5] Although it is often the case that controversial new approaches are rejected by contemporaries and embraced by later generations, we don't believe that it is as much that dynamic in play here as the evidence abounding in the *Guide*—that is, the evidence that Maimonides does not recognize a clear limit at the sphere of the moon. Still, starting with W. Z. Harvey's "skeptical" response to Herbert Davidson's "dogmatic" translation recommendations regarding 2.24,[6] the subsequent issue of the journal

---

[4] Among this "first generation," we include scholars who in one or another place count themselves as students of Pines, such as W. Z. Harvey (though his views have changed over time) and Herbert Davidson. We also include a scholar who was a slightly younger contemporary of Pines (1908–1990), Alexander Altmann (1906–1987).

[5] An interesting exception is Marvin Fox. As I note in an appendix on Pines's Limitations article in my last book, although Fox resists the comparison with Kant, he himself speaks of antinomies and of his surprise that other scholars have failed to recognize the importance of "the limits of reason" in Maimonides. See *Leo Strauss and the Recovery of Medieval Political Philosophy* (Rochester: University of Rochester Press, 2016), 138n4.

[6] W. Z. Harvey, "Maimonides' First Commandment, Physics, and Doubt," in *Ḥazon Naḥum: Studies in Jewish Law, Thought, and History Presented to Dr. Norman Lamm on the Occasion of His Seventieth Birthday*, Yaakov

*Aleph* about 2.24, followed by the increasingly persistent inquiries of Josef Stern, as well as the periodic new publication by Kenneth Seeskin; the next generation seemed to find ever more to recommend itself in the skeptical approach.

Let us begin by giving a thumbnail sketch of some of the features of Pines's Limitations article. Since I have already published a critique of Pines's article based on careful scrutiny of it and others of his articles comparing Maimonides to Kant and Spinoza, especially his 1990 article "Truth and Falsehood Versus Good and Evil," where I found contradictions among Pines's own interpretations of Ibn Bajja and Alfarabi, I will avoid repetition of what I argued there to the extent possible.[7] Pines built his interpretation of the limitations of knowledge not only by overstating Maimonides's similarities to Kant but also on a careless comparison of Maimonides with Alfarabi by way of an unnamed manuscript by Ibn Bajja. That careless comparison depended on Alfarabi's now infamous lost Commentary on Aristotle's *Nicomachean Ethics*. Although Pines viewed the Ibn Bajja manuscript as a sort of smoking gun, the appeal to it presupposes that most of his readers accept the profound influence of Alfarabi on Maimonides. As it happens, I do accept this influence, but a decent number of others do not. Furthermore, this unnamed manuscript about a lost work is not the sort of thing one wants to build an interpretation of Maimonides on. Perhaps Pines viewed this link by way of Ibn Bajja and Alfarabi as adding merely one more crucial piece of evidence. Let it suffice to say that two

---

Elman and Jeffrey S. Gurock, eds. (New York: Yeshiva University Press, 1997), 149–162.

[7] "Truth and Falsehood Versus Good and Evil. A Study in Jewish and General Philosophy in Connection with the Guide of the Perplexed, I,2," in Studies in Maimonides, ed. Isadore Twersky (Cambridge: Harvard University Press, 1990), 95–157. See my *Leo Strauss and the Recovery of Medieval Political Philosophy* (Rochester: University of Rochester Press, 2016), appendix, pp. 137–47.

things have tended to fall by the wayside as the repercussions of Pines's article have been felt: the direct comparison with Kant has often been rejected and the heavy reliance at least on the "new" evidence from the Ibn Bajja ms has gradually receded into the background.[8] What remains is the relatively obvious fact that Maimonides does indeed discuss the limits of human knowledge or limits on human intellect's grasp of metaphysical knowledge—and there is the superficial similarity with Kant that both seem (in Maimonides's case, only at times) to put the limit well short of God. The main difference, however, is that Maimonides does not give reasons in-principle why the limits should be at the sphere of the moon. There are reasons pointing to the sphere of the moon as the limit: it is true that Maimonides states repeatedly that Aristotle is correct about everything up to the sphere of the moon, and it is true that Maimonides states clearly that Aristotle's causal explanation of the motions of the heavenly bodies is faulty. It is also true that Maimonides's argument for creation by way of particularization in 2.19 seems to insinuate that everything above the sphere of the moon is mysterious. However, as we will see when we consider the second generation of scholarship, according to at least T. Zvi Langermann, with whom we agree, Maimonides does not ever rule out the possibility that human beings might discover the lacking causal explanation for the at-times apparently disordered motions of the planets. Furthermore, we do not agree that Maimonides gives clear indications that

[8] For the rejection of the comparison with Kant, see Marvin Fox as cited in the previous note and W. Z. Harvey as cited in my appendix to *Leo Strauss and the Recovery of Medieval Political Philosophy*, 138n5. My remarks should not be taken to indicate that scholars have not been spurred on to inquire further into Ibn Bajja's ms or Alfarabi's lost commentary on EN. I thank Josef Stern for making me aware of Chaim Meir Neria, "Al-Fārābī's Lost Commentary on the Ethics: New Textual Evidence," *Arabic Sciences and Philosophy* 23 (2013): 69–99.

human beings are limited to earthly sense experience.[9] Still, it is undeniable that as Fox observed, Pines contributed mightily to taking the problem of the limits of reason in Maimonides more seriously.

When we turn to that first generation of scholars, including Altmann, Davidson, and Ivry, the main focus is on showing that Maimonides's views on the potential of the human intellect exceed the limits specified by Pines by focusing attention on what little Maimonides says about the nature of the human intellect, especially the role of the Active Intellect and other states of the human intellect in the process of cognition.

As Altmann explains, his "Maimonides on the Intellect and the Scope of Metaphysics" was written with the intention of avoiding a "polemical stance" toward Pines's "Limitations" piece.[10] As a result, he argues somewhat obliquely against Pines's thesis. On the one hand, Altmann's paper is very useful because it is so detailed an exploration of Maimonides's views on the intellect's process of cognition; on the other hand, because Maimonides says so little about his views and then only intermittently and in passing, it is difficult to avoid the sense that Altmann may be importing too much from Maimonides's forbears. Those Altmann focuses on are Alexander of Aphrodisias, both his *De anima* commentary and his *De intellectu*.[11] Of course, he also touches on Alfarabi's "Letter concerning the

---

[9] Cf. Josef Stern, *The Matter and Form of Maimonides' "Guide,"* chap. 4. We refer to "earthly" sense experience because obviously we have sense experience even of the heavenly bodies and their motions.

[10] Alexander Altmann, "Maimonides on the Intellect and the Scope of Metaphysics," in *Von der mittelalterlichen zur modernen Aufklärung* (Tubingen: J.C.B. Mohr, 1987), 60–129.

[11] For these works, the interested reader should see both the critical editions listed by Altmann, 66n50, *Alexandri Aphrodisiensis praeter commentaria scripta minora: de anima liber cum mantissa*, I. Bruns, ed. (Berlin, n.p., 1887) and in English translation, Alexander of Aphrodisias, *The De Anima of Alexander of Aphrodisias: A Translation and Commentary*, Athanasios Fotinis, trans. (Lanham, MD: University Press of America, 1979, 1980).

Intellect," which at least has the advantage of being a text that Maimonides references in relation to the intellect in the *Guide*. In relation to Alexander, Altmann works primarily from similarities between Alexandrian and Maimonidean statements about intellect. To my knowledge, Maimonides, despite frequent reference to Alexander, does not reference him on the intellect in the *Guide*. When Davidson takes up the baton, he adds to Altmann's inquiries into Maimonides on the intellect the suggestion that Maimonides's understanding of the intellect is also perhaps even more deeply influenced by Avicenna's.[12] In this, Davidson is extending an argument apparently first made by Barry Kogan.[13] More valuable than attempting to construct a detailed account of Maimonides's relatively thin claims regarding the intellect are Altmann's subsequent forays into what Maimonides understands by "metaphysics" through a survey first of the views of predecessors (Alfarabi and Avicenna) as well as his contemporary (Averroes). One useful conclusion of that inquiry is the one already underscored by Leo Strauss that Maimonides does not view metaphysics as something apart from theology—rather identifying the two with the characteristically medieval Arabic "divine science (*ʿilm ilāhī*)."[14] As we will see, even Pines does not seem adequately attuned to this fact, since he seems to draw distinctions between metaphysics and theology that seem dubious. Unfortunately, Altmann spends little time exploring what Maimonides actually argues about the limits of knowledge in 1. 31 through 34.[15]

[12] Herbert A. Davidson, "Maimonides on Metaphysical Knowledge," in *Maimonidean Studies* 3, Arthur Hyman, ed. (New York: Yeshiva University Press, 1992–93), 49–103.

[13] Barry Kogan, "What Can We Know and When Can We Know It?" in *Moses Maimonides and His Time,* Edited by Eric C. Ormsby, ed. (Washington: Catholic University of America Press, 1989), 121–37.

[14] Cf. Altmann, "Maimonides on the Intellect and the Scope of Metaphysics," 106 with Strauss, "Literary Character," 46.

[15] Cf. Altmann, "Maimonides on the Intellect and the Scope of Metaphysics," 110–114.

Although Altmann addresses Maimonides's focus in part 2 on the lack of a satisfactory causal explanation for the motions of the planets, he focuses most of his attention on the Active Intellect, its relation to the Acquired Intellect, and the status of the separate intellects.[16] As is somewhat typical among many of Pines's interlocutors and even Pines himself, Altmann turns back from part 2 of the *Guide* to the account of the negative theology in 1.50 through 70 to acknowledge that it seems to circumscribe what human beings can know about God, if not about the separate intellects. Although Altmann's conclusions are more reasonable and measured than Pines's, they don't give sufficient attention where attention is due, namely, especially to 1.31 through 34 and 2.19, 22, and 24, which we will rectify below.

When we turn to Davidson, we find some of the same issues, though we also find in section three[17] a very helpful direct confrontation with the relatively small amount of evidence on the limits of knowledge from the *Guide* that Pines musters, almost none of which gives a precise sense of where the limits might lie. Davidson begins by placing the smoking gun material from Ibn Bajja in context. We will not present Davidson's detailed analysis of relevant material from Alfarabi, Ibn Bajja, and Averroes on Alfarabi or his critique of Pines on same, which we consider convincing. We agree that Pines has made too much out of one passage. We need not look at this here both because we also showed from Pines's related articles that Pines has likely misinterpreted this isolated passage from Ibn Bajja's comments on Alfarabi's commentary on EN bk. 1 and because as was mentioned earlier this aspect of Pines's argument has not garnered much continued interest among scholars. However, Davidson's survey of Pines's seven passages supposedly indicating the limits of knowledge in the *Guide* is worth considering, if only briefly:

---

[16] Altmann, "Maimonides on the Intellect and the Scope of Metaphysics," 115–19.

[17] Davidson, "Maimonides on Metaphysical Knowledge," 68–87.

(a) part 1, introduction's account of prophecy, which Pines takes to indicate that prophecy must exceed the limits of the knowledge of the philosopher (as Altmann insinuated in his article, this is a dubious line of argument);[18] (b) 3.9, matter as a "powerful veil"—this preoccupies Stern greatly—and we will offer a different way of viewing 3.9, especially in relation to 3.10, later; (c) 1.37-38 on God's *face* and *back* originally in Ex. 33-34, which is complicated greatly by Maimonides's extremely complex portrait of Moses; (d) 2.3, the claim that what is argued about the separate intellects is conjectural—which also will influence Stern greatly; (e) 2.24, which Davidson will add an appendix on, and we will discuss soon and more than once over the course of this chapter; (f) 1.68, since Pines takes the earlier parts of 1.50 through 70 or the negative theological material as laying out Maimonides's "epistemology," he then views 1.68 as "merely theological," which seems like a bizarre inversion of the philosophical and the revealed; (g) 1.54 and 3.54, not surprisingly, Pines views 3.54 especially as affirming the primacy of the practical or what he designated from Ibn Bajja on Alfarabi as "political happiness." Of course, there have been endless debates about how to interpret these closing chapters.[19] It will have to suffice to say here that we don't share the view that God's actions should be interpreted literally as inspiring direct imitation of God's actions, but rather human imitation of God's actions figuratively interpreted. To interpret God's actions practically is to view Him as a father who cares for His own child, but our arguments will support the view, in keeping with the meaning of 1.54, that God provides by providing for the species character of the fetus.[20]

---

[18] See Altmann, "Maimonides on the Intellect and the Scope of Metaphysics," 129.

[19] See, for example, Menachem Kellner, *Maimonides on Human Perfection, Brown Judaic Studies* 202 (Atlanta: Scholars Press, 1990), esp. the notes to chap. 3.

[20] Cf. 1.54, 125.

Sections four and five of Davidson's "Metaphysical Knowledge" follow the pattern set by Altmann and supplemented by Kogan, namely, to focus on the meager statements about intellect in the *Guide*, with one great advantage: Davidson rightly focuses the reader's attention on the Active Intellect. Davidson argues that Maimonides relies on the Active Intellect throughout key arguments of the *Guide*, which is undeniable. We recall that in (d) of section two Davidson scrutinized the passage in 2.3 that acknowledges the conjectural character of claims about the separate intellects. Pines, as will Stern later, reads the key passage in 2.3 as the cup half empty, while Davidson reads it as half full. In other words, Pines and Stern take Maimonides's comments about the separate intellects to indicate serious doubts about separate intellects, while Davidson shows that Pines has disambiguated a translation issue in the *Guide* improperly. And the proper translation would make Maimonides less dubious about the separate intellects. Stern will go on to devote a chapter of his 2013 book to trying to prove that Maimonides is abandoning the separate intellects.[21] Why so much is made out of so little should already be obvious: that Maimonides makes use of the Active Intellect or any of the other separate intellects runs contrary to the claim that there is a clear limit of knowledge at the sphere of the moon.

Here a brief digression on the sphere of the moon is in order: when we use this as shorthand throughout this chapter and book, what we mean primarily is that when Maimonides claims that Aristotle is correct about everything up to the sphere of the moon, he is referring to Aristotle's physics. Of course, the primary problem for which Maimonides critiques Aristotle is his rough attempts at a causal explanation for the apparent disorder in the motions of the planets.

[21] See Stern, *Matter and Form*, chap. 7.

Although the Active Intellect is associated with the sphere of the moon and in both Alfarabi and Maimonides seems to exercise some sort of mediating generally providential rule over the earth does not mean that the claim about Aristotle's account "up to the sphere of the moon" includes the Active Intellect. Indeed, as Stern will try to argue, the absence of reference to the Active Intellect from Maimonides's summary account of the whole in 1.72 shows that Maimonides is dubious of not only the other separate intellects but also of the Active Intellect. It is pretty obvious that all of this is meant to serve Stern's reading of Maimonides as a skeptic. In view of the central importance of the Active Intellect (AI) in prophecy (and by implication in providence), one wonders why Maimonides would make so much use of the AI there if he intended ultimately to deny any role to the Active Intellect—not only in prophecy but also simply in thinking.

Although we side with Davidson in this debate, we still wonder whether piecing together Maimonides's scattered comments on the human intellect, the AI, and the other separate intellects is the most useful approach here. What we find most surprising in these efforts to nail down Maimonides's views on the human and other intellects is the inattention to context. Leaving aside Stern's speculations about why the AI is missing from 1.72, it seems to me that the context for Maimonides's few statements about the separate intellects (mainly 2.3 through 12) has been aptly characterized by Strauss as concerning the angels.[22] The obvious effect of this section is to naturalize all talk of angels, that is, to reduce angels to "forces," which Maimonides does by claiming "all forces are angels" (2.6, 263)—after having already characterized "forces" as natural in 2.intro, 10th premise. Whatever the details of Maimonides's views on the human and other intellects might have been, Maimonides gives little

[22] See A', I, 5, in Strauss's outline, "How to Begin to Study *The Guide of the Perplexed*," in Pines ed., p. 12. See Appendix.

evidence of abandoning the naturalizing tendency of Aristotle's account of the unmoved movers. As we will see later, it is undeniable that Maimonides is at pains to modify elements of Aristotle's arguments about God as the Prime Unmoved Mover. Yes, he must subordinate even the PUM to God as Necessary Existent. None of this suggests, however, that he is simply skeptical regarding what will ultimately be known about what is "above the sphere of the moon."

Before looking at Davidson's critique of Pines's approach to 2.24, let us turn briefly to Alfred Ivry's "Logical and Scientific Premises of Maimonides' Thought." That Ivry presented this article as part of the Festschrift he co-edited in honor of Alexander Altmann already says quite a bit about similarities one might expect to find in it, in addition to the fact that Ivry thought of it as adding whatever difference in perspective he might have to offer.[23] Ivry begins in section one with a strong emphasis on the opposition between the two accounts of God, with which we agree, but it seems to us that he takes this a bit too far. Although there are two accounts of God, it is questionable to associate the one with the Mutakallimun and the other with Aristotle simply. Once again, Strauss is instructive here. The *kalām* that Maimonides adopts in the *Guide* is what Strauss refers to as "intelligent *kalām*." Maimonides does definitely offer a searing critique of the Mutakallimun in 1. 73 through 76. What he makes use of from the dialectical theologians in his own particularization argument (in 2.19) in defense of creation, however, is only superficially similar to that of the Mutakallimun. It seems potentially misleading then to characterize one of his accounts as "scientific" and

[23] Alfred L. Ivry, "The Logical and Scientific Premises of Maimonides' Thought," in *Perspectives on Jewish Thought and Mysticism* (Amsterdam: Harwood Academic Publishers, 1998), 63–97.

the other as "non-scientific."[24] What Ivry argues about the two accounts, or as he calls them "images," is true, however, if what he means is that the God of Aristotle and the God of the Bible and Maimonides's negative theology are as radically opposed as this. It seems to us that Ivry is much closer to accurately characterizing that opposition than Stern, whom he focuses quite a bit of attention on.

In section two of Ivry's article, it is difficult for us to see what is being added to the already extensive forays into what Maimonides argues about the human intellect in the articles by Altmann, Kogan, and Davidson. In section three, however, Ivry offers a promising avenue by which to respond to Stern's attempts to show that the limitations of language preclude us from knowing anything immaterial. As we have already argued in chapter 1, because we share Ivry's rough contrast between the Aristotelian account in 1.68 and 69 in opposition to the negative theology elsewhere, we believe that Stern and other scholars have either ignored or mistakenly understated the differences between the intuitive knowledge possible regarding the philosophic account of God in contrast to the biblical.[25] In sections three and four, Ivry tries to show that Pines and Stern have overstated the implications of the negative theology. Even if we don't agree with every detail of Ivry's argument, we share the primary trend of the argument, which questions the extent of Maimonides's skepticism.

Let us turn now to the kerfuffle over *Guide* 2.24. We will not inquire into this in detail for the following reason: we agree with Tzvi Langermann that this is much ado about nothing. No matter what the translation of the offending passage, given the context, it is inferring too much to say that Maimonides thinks that no one else

---

[24] Ivry, "The Logical and Scientific Premises of Maimonides' Thought," 71.

[25] Stern argues ultimately that where it counts in 1.71 and 2.2 Maimonides is not appealing to two different visions of God. See Stern, *Matter and Form*, 158.

will ever uncover a causal explanation for the apparent disorder in the motions of the planets (or for the uneven distribution of stars in the sphere of the fixed stars). Indeed, shortly after the offending passage, Maimonides states that someone else might "find a demonstration by means of which the true reality of what is obscure for me will become clear to him." This one sentence alone, it seems to me, should have prevented this kerfuffle.[26]

Here is the offending passage in Pines's translation: "For it is impossible for us to accede to the points starting from which the conclusions may be drawn about the heavens; for the latter are too far away from us and too high in place and in rank. And even the general conclusion that may be drawn from them, namely, that they prove the existence of their Mover, is a matter the knowledge of which cannot be reached by human intellects" (2.24, 327). Samuel Ibn Tibbon was so troubled by this passage that he queried Maimonides about it and altered his own translation into Hebrew. Since as Davidson notes, this is in obvious contradiction of the proofs of God's existence from motion in 2.1,[27] Ibn Tibbon attempted to remove this obvious contradiction by translating it roughly, as Davidson renders it in English, "the general proof from the heavens [is] that they prove to us [or: show us] their mover, [whereas other things regarding the heavens] are something unknowable to human minds." It seems to us that Ibn Tibbon is sensing something that contemporary scholars seem to forget: Maimonides never questions the overall accuracy of Ptolemy's calculations.[28] What he objects to is that Ptolemy's calculations depend on an account that no matter how mathematically accurate it is does not comport with Aristotle's (or any other philosopher's) physics or causal explanation. The motions are mathematically predictable. That alone prevents Aristotle's

[26] Y. Tzvi Langermann, "My Truest Perplexity," *Aleph* 8 (2008): 301–317, esp. 306.

[27] Davidson, "Maimonides on Metaphysical Knowledge," 101.

[28] *Guide* 2.24, 326.

argument from motion from simply being abandoned—that is, even if Aristotle was wrong to try to reduce all motions to circular ones, that does not mean that his overall claim that God is a necessary being who stands as the final cause is wrong. Similarly, even if separate intellects don't explain those motions (though surely forces of some kind do), that does not take away from the mathematically predictable nature of the motions.

Davidson offers the following translation because he finds Maimonides's sentence to be a grammatical trainwreck: "The subject of the sentence whose predicate is 'something, to the knowledge of which human minds cannot attain' must be 'the heavens.' ...[It may then be translated as] 'The causes [i.e., the logical principles] from which proofs can be drawn up (*asbāb al-istidlāl*) regarding the [nature of the] heavens are beyond our grasp. The [i.e., the heavens] are at a distance from us and exalted in place and in rank—the general [enterprise of] drawing up a proof from them consisting [solely] in this, that they show us [or: prove to us] their mover—indeed they [i.e., the heavens] are something to the knowledge of which human minds cannot attain."

So far as we can tell, in his 1997 article, "Maimonides' First Commandment, Physics, and Doubt," W. Z. Harvey seems to have opened a new chapter in his reading of Maimonides.[29] Rather than going along with Davidson's or Ibn Tibbon's suggestions regarding emendations to Maimonides text, Harvey is provoked by the seriousness of Ibn Tibbon's objections to the passage. Harvey claims that Maimonides's recourse to the assumption of eternity in his legal works, announced in 1.71 and exemplified in the opening of the *Mishneh Torah*, is the first of two scandals, an exoteric one. The esoteric scandal is that the 26$^{th}$ premise assuming the eternity of the

[29] We say this because in another significantly earlier article—Harvey's "A Third Approach to Maimonides' Cosmogony-Prophetology Puzzle," first published in 1981, which we will draw on later—Harvey does not seem at all skeptical in his reading of Maimonides.

world is not itself proven. In this sense the unproven character of this premise warrants the claim in 2.24. Here, Harvey seems to embrace the radically skeptical arguments of Pines as well as Stern. Harvey, in contrast to Stern, makes his argument all the more provocative by combining the claim of esotericism with skepticism.

We can barely scratch the surface of Joel L. Kraemer's erudite 2006 "How (Not) to Read *The Guide of the Perplexed*." Although its title is especially directed at Harvey's 1997 paper, he does devote considerable space to Davidson's conjectured emendation. In connection with his criticisms of Harvey, Kraemer enters into the details of Maimonides's exchanges with Ibn Tibbon, as well as cautioning all readers not to infer too much from a single passage, especially given the deplorable state of the Arabic texts we have. His criticism of Harvey is that it is a "stunning overinterpretation." In particular Kraemer goes on to suggest that Ibn Tibbon's translation is likely the result of an exchange he had with Maimonides rather than a freelance conjecture.[30] It seems to us that Kraemer and Langermann have gotten the better of this whole argument. This one sentence in *Guide* 2.24 is hardly decisive. To treat one sentence as this decisive is to ignore the fact that Maimonides often makes statements without argument, some of which he not only does not believe but often about which it seems apparent he believes the opposite. We will see examples of this in what follows in 1.31 and 3.15.

Having lingered too long over the early stages of the dialogue initiated by Pines's 1979 "Limitations" article, we will demur regarding a discussion of *Aleph* 8. More than any other piece in that issue, we recommend not only Langermann's "My Truest Perplexities" but also his reference back to his first published article, which as it happens was on 2.24.[31]

---

[30] Joel L. Kraemer, "How (Not) to Read The Guide of the Perplexed" *Jerusalem Studies in Arabic and Islam* 32 (2006): 350–409.

[31] Y. Tzvi Langermann, "The True Perplexity: *The Guide of the Perplexed*, Part II, Chapter 24," in *Perspectives on Maimonides: Philosophical and Historical*

There are a few things that our survey of the history of responses to Pines's article suggests: less attention should be focused on what little Maimonides says about the intellect and how it cognizes—with reference to the Active Intellect and the stages the human intellect goes through—and far more attention should be focused on what he argues about the objects of knowledge. Although the debate about the key passage near the end of 2.24 comes closest to engaging seriously with this question, it is too little to go on and seems to have been misguided from the start. *Pace* Davidson, Maimonides not only does not always say what he means, he often says the opposite. Here some obvious facts about the nature of the *Guide* are worth emphasizing. Very little of the *Guide* consists of arguments. The most obvious exceptions being 1.73 through 76 and 2.intro and 2.1. A great deal of the *Guide* consists of conclusions, usually opposing ones, for which the reader is expected to supply the arguments from her own study of other more narrowly philosophic works. Given these facts, it is extremely dangerous to build one's whole interpretation of a given problem around one assertion by Maimonides. I argue this despite being well aware of and granting Strauss's observation that sometimes a single statement, especially if it runs contrary to the popular view, is likely the view Maimonides holds. The simple admission of human insufficiency in 2.24 is very far from a heterodox statement. On the contrary, it leaves the reader supposing the limits of human knowledge are so great that she should, as Maimonides guides the reader to do in the very next chapter, accept the view of creation and side with the Law. I realize that Harvey in his 1997 "First Commandment" article claims that he is bidding the reader to face the hard life of living with doubts. Still, that life of doubts is highly compatible with obedient belief in revelation. After all, historically skepticism was one of the greatest tools used by the Church

*Studies*, Joel L. Kraemer, ed. (Oxford: Oxford University Press, 1991), 159–74.

Fathers. By the time he writes "Maimonides' Critical Epistemology and *Guide* 2:24," Harvey has introduced so many layers and levels of doubt that no weighing of doubts is possible. We will start to show in our next chapter that Maimonides recommends a different approach to doubts in the immediately preceding chapter, *Guide* 2.23.

## From Prohibitions to Limits: 1.31 through 34

In part one, chapters 31 through 34, Maimonides discusses intermittently the limits of knowledge. The motive of this discussion is not revealed until chapter 32: it is that the Talmud (B. T. Ḥagigah 11b, 13a) appears to forbid inquiry into what is above, below, in front, and in back. Although Maimonides does not enumerate these four things, he quotes the reference in the Talmud to "four things." He mentions the later passage from Tractate *Ḥagigah* first: "Do not inquire about things that are too marvelous for you; do not investigate what is hidden from you; inquire into things that are permitted to you; you have no business with marvels." The earlier passage from the Talmud says, as quoted by Maimonides: "Whoever considers four things, and so on"—and he omits the chilling—"does not deserve to have come into the world"! The similarities between this prohibition of inquiry and the charges against Socrates are both readily apparent and striking—namely, the more dangerous charges leveled against Socrates, the first accusations brought by Aristophanes in the *Clouds*: inquiring into what is above and what is below and making the weaker argument the stronger. These charges are more damning perhaps because more penetrating than the later accusations of not believing in the gods of Athens and corrupting the young. For both Aristophanes and the Talmud, it is evident that the forbidden investigations concern inquiring into what is above, that is, the divine, and what is below, that is, the afterlife. In the Talmud, what is in front seems to refer either to prophetic prediction of the future or foreknowledge of the ways of providence; what is in back could, perhaps, refer to efforts to undo the effects of one's actions through bribery of the divine.[32] These prohibited inquiries are what came to be called in the Jewish tradition the Account of the Chariot and the Account of the Beginning (part 1, intro, p. 6). Although Maimonides does not claim in the *Guide* to teach these two accounts, he certainly inquires into their relation to the Law, especially insofar as he identifies them with metaphysics and physics.

The Talmud at least in this tractate seems to be trying to forbid inquiry into God and the afterlife, at least for the young. As strong as the prohibition at the earlier *Ḥagigah* 11b appears to be, the later passage seems to permit inquiry into the Account of the Beginning and of the Chariot for those with sufficient preparation. Coloring our inquiry into this part of the *Guide* is the suspicion that the Talmud's understanding of the Account of the Beginning and of the Chariot are not likely to be what Maimonides refers to as physics and metaphysics.[33]

Leaving that aside, our focus must be on why Maimonides takes over what appears to be a prohibition (if not an absolute prohibition) of inquiry into the most elevated philosophic matters and transforms it merely into limits of knowledge. Before we try to determine why, we ought to consider at least briefly the transformation of meaning he achieves. He interprets the passage regarding the need to limit your inquiries to that into which you are "permitted" as permitting that your "intellect move about only within the domain of things that man is able to grasp. For in regard to matters that it is not in the nature of man to grasp, it is, as we have made clear, very harmful

---

[32] Cf. *Apology* 23d, 26c, 29b.

[33] Comparison of *Guide* 3.1 through 7 comes closer to what the Talmud has in mind. There we see Maimonides drawing the biblical Account of the Chariot in the direction of philosophic views, but the suspicion that what the Bible and Talmud have in mind are closer to mystical views of *Pardes* is difficult to gainsay. Here, it would be worth comparing the discussion of *Pardes* and its study in Maimonides's *Mishneh Torah*, *Book of Knowledge*, Laws concerning the Foundations of the Torah, 2.11, 4.10–13; Laws concerning the Study (*Talmud*) of the Torah, 1.10–12.

to occupy oneself with them" (1.32, pp. 69–70). In this and the previous chapter, chapters 31 and 32, Maimonides discusses the limits of knowledge or apprehension (*idrak*). He discusses those limits primarily based on an analogy between sensory apprehension and intellectual apprehension. Just as there are limits to what can be sensed, so there are limits to what can be known. At the same time, he underlines that there are "great differences in capacity [or capability] between the individuals of the [human] species" (a point that he underlines even more strikingly in 2.40 when he notes that the difference between human individuals is like that between different species among other animals). The analogy between sensation and intellection has quite limited value. As it happens, we know that Joseph ben Judah is not as well read in physics, which would typically have included Aristotle's *De anima*, as he should be at this point in his studies. Any reader well enough versed in Aristotle's physics would have known how problematic this analogy is. The most striking difference is one Aristotle uses, itself problematically, to prove that the intellect is immaterial, namely, the fact that the intellect does not seem to be overwhelmed by thinking challenging things in the manner that the sense of sight is overwhelmed by too much light or the sense of touch by excessive heat or the like.[34] All this leaves one wondering whether Maimonides intentionally undercuts his own example claiming to persuade us not to investigate too much.

More importantly, the necessity of forbidding inquiry suggests that the intellect has not reached its limit. As Maimonides argues in chapter 31, when the intellect reaches the limits of its knowledge, that is, once it becomes evident that it is "impossible to apprehend" something, then our desire to know it ceases (p. 65). Prohibitions of inquiry should be required only with respect to things we either can know or don't know we cannot know, in other words, prohibitions of inquiry are unnecessary where the limits of knowledge are evident.

---

[34] *On the Soul* 3.4, 429a30–b10.

Ironically, this is the very matter on which so much energy is being expended. Where exactly are the limits that Maimonides alludes to? The examples he gives of things we cannot know are all the sorts of things that we would still today say that we could not know—indeed, even supercomputers might well never know: "the number of the stars of heaven and whether that number is even or odd, as well as our ignorance of the number of the species of living beings, minerals, plants, and other similar things" (1.31, 66). The next time that he offers a comparable inventory in 1.34, it is in the context of a discussion of the "causes that prevent the commencement of instruction with divine science" and specifically "the length of the preliminaries." We will survey this whole cause in the next chapter. For now, let us look with some care at the strange example Maimonides uses to get us started thinking about the length of the preliminaries, recalling all along that the focus here is on why one must not *begin* with divine science. The example is of a sleeping individual who has just been awakened from slumber: "If you were to ask him whether he desired at that moment to have knowledge of the heavenly spheres, namely, what their number is and what their configuration, and what is contained in them, and what the angels are, and how the world as a whole was created, and what its end is in view of the arrangement of its various parts with one another, and what the soul is, and how it is created in time (*ḥudūth*) in the body, and whether the human soul can be separated from the body, and, if it can, in what manner and through what instrument and with what distinction in view…and other subjects of this kind…he would undoubtedly answer you in the affirmative" (1.34, 73–74). These examples are more interesting than the highly quantitative examples given in 1.31. Here, however, once again, it is unclear whether we would or would not be able ultimately if we applied ourselves to answer these questions. In the case of the first potential object of knowledge, the number and configuration of the heavenly spheres, we are no longer in the realm of the absurdly large. Indeed, Maimonides foreshadows exactly the bone of contention that will inspire 2.19 as well as 2.24. Of course, 2.3 through 13 will take up "what the angels are." Here we have clear evidence that not all of these difficult matters are beyond the limits of human knowledge. True, "how the world was created" is likely never to be known. What the soul is, however, is something that Maimonides and many others have addressed elsewhere—relatively satisfactorily. But how the soul is created and whether it can be separated from the body, these are likely ultimately to be beyond human ken. What, however, does Maimonides do to follow out his example of the person awakened from slumber? He notes plaintively that though that person would desire to know the answer to these questions, he or she would likely be unwilling to wait more than a week before being informed of the answer. Having lost patience, the person would "be satisfied with deceptive imaginings through which his soul would be set at ease" (1. 34, 74). This is one of the first of a number of factors that will make knowing the limits of knowledge difficult. The strength of the human desire to know, the lack of desire to labor to come to know what one does not, and the willingness to rest satisfied with imaginings all contribute either to making us eager to accept limits, as the skeptics seem eager to, or to rendering the limits of knowledge vague and unclear. In the next chapter, we will take a look at the ways Maimonides uses "authority" and appeals to our concern with what others might say to further cloud the issue of the limits of knowledge—all of which suggests that the limits are likely to be vague rather than clear.

## The Sphere of the Moon as Limit and Disorder or Lack of a Causal Explanation: 2.22 and 24

In *Guide* part 2, Maimonides appears to identify the limit of knowledge as lying between what is beneath the sphere of the moon, which is to say on earth, and what is above the sphere most clearly in chapter 19 in the course of a dialectical argument in defense of creation—as well as in following chapters, especially 2.22 and 24.

He frames this delineation with reference to Aristotle. According to Maimonides, Aristotle has succeeded in bringing order to the existence of everything beneath the sphere of the moon (306)—and he wished to bring the same order to what is above that sphere. He has succeeded in identifying causes of what is beneath the sphere of the moon, namely, that it "derives of necessity from the motion and the powers of the spheres"; however, regarding what is above the sphere of the moon "he has assigned no clear cause" (307). A striking feature of this passage in 2.19 is that it underlines the causal connection between what is beneath the sphere of the moon and what above is one of necessity. It comes as some surprise, then, that he goes on to argue that the apparent disorder of what is above the sphere requires that there be a particularizer, namely, God, who particularizes—variously through "purpose," "choosing freely," or "willing" rather than of "necessity"—the particular order. What is passingly strange is that a willed order could cause an order of necessity. I do not mean that according to no scheme would it be possible for a creator to produce a necessary order directly, as it were, without the benefit of secondary causes, that is, by way of a form of fideism. Rather, I mean to underline the oddity of Maimonides's claim that that particularized order acts as a set of secondary causes, whose effects are necessary. Why the putative disorder among these causes does not give rise to disordered effects is far from obvious—though it may well be because the disorder is merely apparent. After all, how else could one explain the fact that Ptolemy can predict the motions of the heavenly bodies?

The argument regarding particularization refers initially to one thing and then shifts *a fortiori* to another. Initially, Maimonides argues that particularization helps us to cope with the unsatisfactory character of the Ptolemaic account of the motions of the planets—namely, that it can offer more than one mathematically satisfactory account of the motions (eccentrics or epicycles)—which Ptolemy thus labeled "saving the appearances"—but cannot offer a physically or astronomically satisfactory causal account of the motions (306–9).[35] Eventually, however, Maimonides shifts his focus to the particular arrangement or lack of arrangement of the stars in what was taken to be the sphere of fixed stars (309–10): "And it is even stranger that there should exist the numerous stars that are in the eighth sphere, all of which are globes, some of them small and some big, one star being here and another at a cubit's distance according to what seems to the eye, or ten stars being crowded and assembled together while there may be a very great stretch in which nothing is to be found." Maimonides uses the lack of a causal explanation of the motions of the planets and of the placement of the stars to support his dialectical argument in favor of the creation of the world. In chapter 24, he goes on to identify the initial discord between Ptolemy's mathematically predictive account and Aristotle's physics as "the true perplexity" (325–26). Some have gone so far as to insinuate that the perplexity with which the *Guide* begins, the discord between philosophy and Law, is here displaced by physics or the Account of the Beginning as the fundamental concern of the *Guide*.[36] Such a suggestion loses sight of the context of *Guide* 2.19 and 24, namely, the dispute over the creation or eternity of the world. The arguments that Maimonides provides in Guide 2.13 through 31 treat the dispute over creation versus eternity as part of Maimonides's defense of Judaism. In other words, the arguments regarding the motions and placement of the heavenly bodies are pursued not for their own sake but as part of an extended effort to defend creation for the sake of

---

[35] On the difference between a satisfactory mathematical account capable of predicting the appearances and an adequate causal explanation, see especially *Guide* 2.11, 274–75 and 2.24, 322–25.

[36] Cf. W. Z. Harvey's citation of Ibn Tibbon's comment that 2.24, especially the passage that seems to claim that the human intellect cannot even know that God exists, for which Ibn Tibbon proposed an emendation, is the "strongest difficulty in [Maimonides'] book" in "Maimonides' Critical Epistemology and *Guide* 2:24," *Aleph* 8 (2008): 230.

the Law! Once again, apparently clear limits serve the defense of Judaism; however, actually vague limits serve to defend philosophy. Maimonides's ambition to achieve both at once helps to explain why it appears to some that the limits are clear and to others that they are not.

In the introduction to part 2, based on his refutation of the dialectical theologians' attempts to prove creation (in 1.71 through 76), Maimonides demonstrates from the eternity of the world that God exists, is one, and is incorporeal. Creation versus eternity, then, appears to be the bridge between the arguments regarding God and His nature and the arguments regarding prophecy (2.32–48) and providence (3.8–24). Usually, it is assumed to be a theoretical bridge, but I believe that we're starting to see that the indemonstrability of creation or eternity—including the indemonstrability of premise 26 as the ground of the demonstrations of God's existence, unity, and incorporeality—ultimately serve a theologico-political role. Far from being an esoteric scandal, the indemonstrability of eternity seems to insinuate clear limits of knowledge. The indemonstrability of eternity or creation together with the apparent disorder of the heavens all seem to cry out in confirmation of human ignorance and clear limits of knowledge. We know from 2.13 and 2.25 the reason the dispute regarding creation versus eternity is so pressing: as Maimonides puts it explicitly in 2.25, if the world is eternal as Aristotle conceives of it, then it undermines the Law. How does it undermine the Law? It does so by giving the lie to miracles—and not just any miracles—but to the decisive miracles that indicate divine particular providence.

It is often supposed that having been persuaded that Aristotle is correct regarding the physical order on earth, Maimonides accepts that nothing more can be known regarding what is above the sphere of the moon. In effect the limits of knowledge alluded to in part 1 of the *Guide* are identified in this division between what Aristotle gives a good causal account for and what he does not. Yet one thing Maimonides said in the course of his dismissal of Aristotle's account of the heavenly bodies gives us special pause: the order on earth derives necessarily from what is above the sphere of the moon. Can the disorder above give rise to the order below? Or must the order above be only apparently disordered to serve as a necessary cause of the order below?

That apparent disorder can veil underlying order is the oldest story in philosophy, going back to Thales's ability to predict an eclipse. Indeed, the very wellspring of philosophy, namely wonder, is elicited by that which cannot *yet* be explained (*Met.* 1.2, 983a). Those who infer, from Maimonides's arguments regarding what is above the sphere of the moon, not only that Aristotle does not provide an adequate causal account of the motions of what is above that sphere but also that Maimonides believes that the sphere of the moon marks the limit of human knowledge, infer too much from what Maimonides actually states—relying instead on what he seems to imply. A glance at the relevant passages reveals as much (2.19, 306–7, 311; 2.22, 319–20; 2.24, 326). Maimonides never explains why the sphere of the moon should mark permanently the limit of human knowledge; rather, as much has been inferred for the following loosely affiliated reasons: (1) Maimonides's affirmation of the truthfulness of Aristotle's causal account beneath that sphere, (2) the discord between Aristotelian physics and Ptolemaic mathematics regarding the motions of the planets—and therefore the inadequacy of Aristotle's causal explanation of their apparent irregularities, (3) Maimonides's indications in part 1 that limits of human knowledge—rather than that the Talmud intends to prohibit inquiry into knowledge of what is above, below, in front, and in back—exist, and (4) his assertions that neither eternity nor creation can be proven, consequently, we're able to side with creation and should do so because to do otherwise would undermine the Law.[37] We have already explored the implications of the first point in this part of this chapter, namely, causal knowledge of what is beneath the sphere of the moon; we have touched on here and in the previous part on the third point, namely, the limits of knowledge as a substitute for prohibited inquiry. We have also started to get an inkling of the limited significance of the second point, the discord between Aristotelian physics and Ptolemaic mathematics—namely, that this indicates, and Maimonides would have been well aware of this, not that no causal account is possible but that we have not yet arrived at one. This brings us to the fourth point regarding creation and undermining the Law (2.13 and esp. 2.25). This is the true crux of the matter. And it does not take the turn we expect it to take at first.

## Counterindications to the Limits of Knowledge in Maimonides's Treatments of Prophecy and Providence: 2.32, 3.17 through 18, and 3.51

Because we will return in detail to the passages treated in this section, here strictly with respect to the limits of knowledge, the reader should take the following account as a merely preliminary glance at what we will argue about prophecy and providence in part 2 of this work.

When Maimonides declares that Aristotle's view destroys the Law in its foundation, Maimonides cannot mean that Aristotle is an opponent of law as such. Rather he means that Aristotle is an opponent of the Law as given to one people at one time in history. That this is what he means will be confirmed not only in the prophetology section (2.32–48, esp. in 2.40) but also in the providence section of part 3 (3.8–24). The crucial thing that creation makes possible for

[37] This four-point list should be compared with the three-point list near the beginning of this chapter.

prophecy is the right kind of miracles. As I put it in a lecture at St. John's College in Santa Fe,

> Although in 2.13 philosophers are accused of all effectively believing the same thing, namely, one or another version of the eternity of the world; here in 2.25, Plato's position is presented as potentially more in harmony with revelation than the position of Aristotle. Maimonides subtly distinguishes between Aristotle who undermines "every miracle"; Plato who does not give the lie to "miracles"; and our position on creation, that of the Law, which upholds "all the miracles." It appears that Plato makes room for some but not all miracles. Maimonides proceeds then to set forth all the miracles made possible by belief in creation, among which he includes most notably that God could give the Law to this people at a given particular time.[38]

When we turn to the prophetology section in 2.32,[39] the relevance of particular providence is immediately apparent, even if Maimonides's own views on the subject remain opaque. Of course, he gives the reader three options regarding prophecy: (1) a moral man who is an ignoramus can be made a prophet (a miracle of particular providence); (2) someone with the proper nature and training both practical and theoretical, meeting the requirements of Plato's philosopher-king, must become a prophet; and (3) our view, the view of the Law, coincides with the previous view except that God's will can prevent (*manaʿa*) prophecy (2.32, 361). Much as "will" arose amid staggering ambiguity in *Guide* 2.19, it recurs here in connection with "preventing" prophecy with similar ambiguity,[40] leading the unsuspecting reader to assume that this also constitutes an example of the right kind of miracle of particular providence. Is God's

---

[38] Parens, "Maimonides's *Guide of the Perplexed*: Its Genre and Its Three Great Themes," lecture delivered at St. John's College, Santa Fe, on November 16, 2018.

[39] It should be noted that here we will touch on 2.32 only quite lightly since we will return to it later, especially in chapter 5.

[40] We will follow up on this in chapter 5, below.

ability to transform a moral man lacking the philosophic prerequisites into a prophet or God's preventing prophecy more akin to God's giving the Law to a particular people in a particular time? Obviously, the former is more evidently miraculous. In addition, one must begin to wonder how, given all the limitations on the knowledge of God, Maimonides could claim to know that God's will prevents any particular worthy potential prophet from prophesying.

As we, finally, turn to part 3 to address the limits of knowledge, we see the limit of knowledge discovered in part 2 with respect to God's nature and the character of His providence recurring, in a different but related context. If the limits of knowledge show up in part 2 in connection with the paramount matter of particular providence, namely, the giving of the Law via the prophet to the people Israel in the prophetology section; in part 3, we expect the limits to become thematized, given that particular providence is the theme of the second section of part 3, *Guide* 3.8 through 24. The first section of part 3, chapters 1 through 7, if not thematizing these limits does at least reflect their existence by being easily the most cryptic part of the *Guide*, which is also the most direct discussion of the biblical bases of the Account of the Chariot. The initial impression left by this section is surely that the limits of knowledge stop well short of knowledge of God's nature. Furthermore, the second section of part 3 (chaps. 8–24), devoted directly to particular providence, culminates in arguments based on Maimonides's interpretation of Job, which also leave one suspecting that the justice of God's particular providence eludes us. The peak of this section in 3.17 and 18, however, is far more straightforward about that providence, even leading one to wonder whether ultimately Maimonides maintains the limits he seemed to affirm in part 2. It describes a surprising harmony between God's general providence and the particular self-providence of the intelligent actor that reminds one at least as much of Maimonides's characterization of Aristotle's view (3.17, 464–66) as his preferred account of the Law's view (471–74). As Maimonides puts it most clearly in 3.18, "When any human individual has obtained, because of the disposition of his matter and his training, a greater proportion of this overflow [from God via the Active Intellect] than others, providence will of necessity watch more carefully over him than others—if, that is, providence is, as I have mentioned, consequent upon the intellect" (Pines ed., 475).[41] In other words, it leaves one wondering whether particular providence is anything more than the particular effects of general providence. At the peak of the discussion of particular providence, the limits of knowledge are in surprising abeyance.

Why is Maimonides willing to explain particular providence so directly, when he has previously seemed to shroud God's nature in darkness?[42] At least since the negative theology of *Guide* 1. 52 through 66, Maimonides has at times portrayed God as a mystery well beyond human ken. Yet at other times, such as *Guide* 1.68–69, he has presented a quite different account, that is, of a God whose nature though not able to be subjected to human discursive presentation can at least be grasped by intuition. In effect the limits of knowledge would seem to apply to the former but not the latter. The former is the God of revelation and the latter the God of philosophy. Once again, far too often it is assumed that Maimonides presents only one account of God—if only because Maimonides does such a

[41] Cf. the account of overflow in prophecy in 3.32 and 3.36. There God appears to exercise will only in preventing prophecy (or overflow) to some—not in distribution to all.

[42] It could perhaps be objected that particular providence as divine action is separable from the divine nature, as is implied by Maimonides's discussion of the preferability of resorting to God's actions to characterize His nature over any attempt to capture His nature proper (1.54). But careful study of the *Guide* reveals two very different accounts of divine action that parallel the differences in divine nature, which I will characterize shortly.

good job of blending the two accounts together. As we explained in chapter 1, he uses the category of "relation" to hide these differences, suggesting that God lacks relation to creatures in two very different senses, either as belonging to another genus (the philosophic God) or as being the Most High, who transcends human knowing altogether (the biblical *YHVH*) (1.52, 117–18).

The limits of knowledge identified in parts 2 and 3 have deeper connections. In part 2, these limits emerged around whether God is the creator who could give a particular people a Law at a particular time or the ruler of eternity. Given that we cannot demonstrate eternity or creation, we should opt for that which preserves the Law. In part 3, these limits emerge around God's providence less to nations than to individuals—or at least to nations only by way of individuals. Job bemoans the injustice of his plight. Rather than adopt the most common reply that God's justice is not our justice, Maimonides inquires into what accounts for God's providence. Is it Job's moral excellence or is it his intellectual sufficiency or insufficiency? Job suffers when limited to his righteousness; he ceases to suffer once he has grasped his situation intellectually (3.22, 487–8; 3.23, 492–3). Despite the challenge the Book of Job poses to our sense of justice, Maimonides resists the temptation to read it as a confirmation of divine transcendence and mystery. In doing so, he is merely following out the implications of 3.17 and 18. Previously, we noted that there Maimonides reduces particular providence to the particular working out of general providence. When put this way, it might seem innocuous enough. Yet this broad claim has implications for the limits of knowledge supposedly established in part 2.

If particular providence is nothing more than the working out in detail of general providence, then the giving of the Law to a particular people in a particular time begins to appear problematic. After all, the giving of the Law to a particular people requires the mediating role of a given prophet. In effect, the general account of particular providence in part 3 sheds surprising light retrospectively on part 2. Part 2, chapters 32 through 48 provide (1) an account of the psychology of prophecy, especially in 2. 32 and 36; they give (2) hints as to why prophecy might cease, such as the psychological state of the prophet due to the national experience of the people Israel—that is, exile and its attendant depression (2.36, 372); and they reveal (3) the family resemblance of prophecy to kingship (2.37, 374) elaborating on the hints at philosopher-kingship evident from the beginning of the prophetology (2.32, 361). Every one of these elements raises the question whether prophecy is a matter of general or particular providence—whether God transforms individuals into His vehicle for His particular providence, or prophecy is to be understood more naturalistically as the account in 2.32 seems to suggest. True, the account of prophecy that Maimonides ultimately identifies with the Law (1) purports that God can prevent prophecy; however, the giving of the Law as the consummate example of biblical particular providence would seem to require positive divine intervention. And if (3) the prophet is to be understood on analogy to the philosopher-king, one is constantly led to wonder whether the prophecy of the legislating prophet is due to God's speaking through Moses or due to the prudence or, as Maimonides calls it, the "ruling faculty" of Moses (1. 53, 121; 1.72, 190–91; 2.40, 382; 3.17, 465).[43] That prophecy subsequently ceased could be due to God's preventing prophecy; unless that preventing is itself due to naturalistic forces such as the prophet's depression, which is due in turn to Israel's exile (2.32), which itself is due in turn to the people having ceased practicing the arts of war ("Letter on Astrology").[44]

The likelihood that God's purported willing of the prevention of prophecy (2.32) is *not* the indicator of particular providence it appears to be becomes evident in light of two other pieces of evidence:

---

[43] See Parens, *Maimonides and Spinoza* (Chicago: University of Chicago Press, 2012), 170–72.

[44] See Parens, *Maimonides and Spinoza*, 112–13. We will discuss this in greater depth in chapter 5.

his account of particular providence as little more than the particular effects of general providence (3.17–18) and the various hints he drops about God's role in prophecy throughout the *Guide*. Most importantly, God cannot not overflow (1.68, 166; 2.12, 278–9). Although it might be said of the Active Intellect that it might suffer from some impediment (and even that it would appear is due to the receiver of the overflow rather than the AI—2.18, 300), one could not make the same claim about God (1.68, 166). The negation of general providence does not quite rise to the level of being particular providence, much as the particular effects of general providence are not the same as particular providence.

If 3.17 through 18 together with the interpretation of Job in 3.22 and 23 tend to undercut particular providence in favor of mere general providence, *Guide* 3.51 with its last-minute inspiration intensifies the suspicion that as the *Guide* progresses Maimonides undercuts particular providence more and more. We already expressed our doubts that the limits of knowledge, in particular of God, in 2.32 would permit Maimonides to surmise that God's will would prevent the naturally suited and properly educated prophet to prophesy. The suggestion in the closing moment of insight or inspiration in 3.51 that the divine overflow to the fitting receiver, already described in 3.17 and 18, can only be interrupted by the receiver's failure to contemplate God only reinforces the suspicion that the earlier talk in 2.32 of God preventing prophecy could be otherwise interpreted. And if the limits are clearly at the sphere of the moon, on what basis does Maimonides decide between these ways of interpreting God's relation to His overflow?

In conclusion, the limits of knowledge appear initially to be at the sphere of the moon, stopping short of God and perhaps even all His angels. Consequently, human knowledge would be expected to cease well short of knowing enough about God's nature to know whether

He is particularly or merely generally provident. Yet Maimonides gives ample indication in part 3 that what appears to be particular providence is often merely the working out of general providence at the level of particulars or an effect of many countervailing causes. The disproportion between what he implies about the limits of knowledge and how much he seems to know about providence suggests once again that where the limits of knowledge lie is very far from as clear as at least the skeptical interpreters would suggest. More importantly, this vagueness only enhances Maimonides's use of the limits of knowledge as an essential part of his effort to defend philosophy. As we will see in the next chapter, this vagueness opens up what can be described as the "space" of doubts, which Maimonides leaves it to the reader to sort out. He points us to the doubts without leading us there by the hand.

# CHAPTER 3

# THE SPACE OF DOUBTS AND THE PROBLEM OF AUTHORITY

The vagueness of the limits of knowledge discussed in the previous chapter give rise to what we will call the "space of doubts." Obviously, the word "space" is figurative, but we use it because the limits give rise to doubts regarding the things beyond the limit. And all those things are not, as it were, equidistant from the limit of the sphere of the moon. As we will see, there are also ways other than demonstration for adjudicating what appear to be insoluble dilemmas beyond this putative limit. As previously argued, the very predictability of the motions of the heavenly bodies speaks too much in favor of a not-yet-grasped causal explanation to reinforce, as it appears poised to, the limit of the sphere of the moon. The extent of the limitations on what we can know of God depends on whether the God one has in mind is that of the Bible or of the philosophers. In general, the apparent clarity of the limits of knowledge on closer examination proves to be merely apparent—in no small part because Maimonides gives guidance on how to consider dilemmas on the other side of this supposed line.

When we turn to the dispute between eternity and creation, that dimension of the Account of the Beginning that has direct bearing on the Account of the Chariot, we see that Maimonides accrues evidence that even Aristotle didn't hold that eternity could be proven (2.15). Yet Maimonides eagerly asserts that given the lack of a demonstration we must side with the Law, assuming the world has been created (2.25). That the position of Aristotle undermines the Law "in its principle" is little more than to affirm that Aristotle opposes creation. As we saw in the previous chapter, though, denying it in its principle is tantamount to denying particular providence as well. Maimonides's hasty or eager resolution of the dilemma in 2.25 needs to be considered in light of perhaps the most important statement in the *Guide* regarding doubts shortly before it, in 2.23—which of course also precedes the culmination of the conundrums surrounding the heavens in 2.24. More generally, the series of vaguely outlined limits I have referenced give rise to a space of doubts, especially once one takes seriously Maimonides's call in 2.23 to weigh doubts. It is not sufficient to consider passages from Aristotle's *On the Heavens*, as Maimonides does in 2.15, that may indicate that even Aristotle did not consider his arguments for the eternity of the world to be demonstrative. One must weigh the two sides, which Maimonides does not do before his readers. Rather, he leaves this task to them, as he does so many others.

Although Josef Stern is reasonable in suggesting that the *Guide* abounds in dilemmas, I doubt they possess the evenhandedness characteristic of true skepticism. Rather than a sort of skepticism, Maimonides is generating a space of doubts intended to have different effects on different readers. For those who don't care to venture forth, these doubts may drive them into the arms of the Law, but, for the intellectually courageous, it would be difficult to accept with little argument that one should side with particular providence and the Law. To make matters worse, Maimonides not only says in 2.25 that if it were demonstrated that the world is eternal that he would proceed to offer a figurative interpretation of creation much as he did the indications that God is corporeal in the Bible, but he also proceeds however subtly to offer just such a figurative interpretation in 2.30. This fact together with the call to weigh doubts in 2.23 act as catalysts to further inquiry into this space of doubts.

## Doubts, Authority, and Disgrace: The New Post-Alexandrian World

Maimonides breaks new ground in the fitting approach to doubts in 2.23. Near the end of the preceding chapter, 2.22, he draws the reader's attention to the guidance of Alexander of Aphrodisias.[1] Alexander recommends that on either side of a dilemma what one ought to consider is the number of doubts that appear on each side (320). In 2.23, Maimonides modifies this comparison of the quantity of doubts with his suggestion that it should not be the number of the doubts but "rather …how great is their incongruity and what is their disagreement with what exists (*wa-mukhālafat al-wujūd*)." We would simply ignore the role played by "what exists" in the weighing of doubts, if we hadn't had our attention drawn to it back in 1.71. Since then the reader has been led to wonder whether creation is less compatible with what Maimonides sometimes refers to merely as "what exists" and elsewhere as "the nature of existence" (*ṭabīʿat al-wujūd*).[2] In 1.71, the reader was told that the Muslim dialectical theologians tried to defend creation but did so by violating the nature of existence. There and even more so here, Maimonides

[1] Alexander of Aphrodisias (mid-2nd- to mid-3rd-century CE) is one of two Hellenistic commentators that Maimonides cites most often; the other one being Themistius (317–387 CE). See Pines's account of Alexander in the *Guide* on lxiv–lxxv of his translator's introduction.

[2] In chapter 1, I pointed the reader to the passages in 1.71 where Maimonides uses the key phrase "the nature of existence" (*ṭabīʿat al-wujūd*), namely, pp. 179, as the adage of Themistius, and 182 through 183 of the Pines ed.; however, I did not note that he uses simply *al-wujūd* (in the following contexts, "the appearance of that which exists [*al-ẓāhir min amr al-wujūd*]" [178] and "no consideration is due to how what exists is [*bi-mā ʿilayhī al-wujūd*], for it is merely a custom" [179]) in advance of most though not all of those pages, as if to prepare for that larger and more exact phrase. Although the contexts of both these more abbreviated phrasings are highly revealing, the latter is especially so, even in the little we quote here. The opposition is between naturally being or existing as opposed to mere custom (*ʿāda*).

insinuates that unless he can defend creation in such a way as to preserve or comport with the nature of existence, creation should not be defended. The high compatibility of the eternity of the world with the "nature of existence" is obvious given the connection between nature and that which is unchanging.

This Maimonidean departure from Alexander also reminds the attentive reader of a parallel back in Guide 1.31. There, Maimonides reviewed the same Alexander's listing of three causes of disagreement, (1) the love of domination and strife, (2) the "subtlety and obscurity of the object of apprehension in itself and the difficulty of apprehending it," and (3) "the ignorance of him who apprehends" it. Maimonides attends to disagreement at this juncture in 1.31 because the chapter concerns the limits of knowledge, and how those limits are manifest around things about which one cannot arrive at a demonstration. He added to Alexander's causes the following one:

> It is habit[3] and upbringing (*al-ilf wa-l-tarbiyya*)... Man has love for, and the wish to defend, opinions to which he is habituated and in which he has been brought up (*al-ārā' alatī ilfihā wa-rabī ʿalayha*) and has a feeling of repulsion for opinions other than those. For this reason alone also man is blind to the apprehension of true realities and inclines toward the things to which he is habituated. This happened to the multitude with regard to the belief in His corporeality and many other divine subjects as we shall make clear. All this is due to people being habituated to, and brought up on, texts (*al-ilf wa-l-tarbiyya ʿalā nuṣūṣ*) that it is an established usage to think highly of and to regard as true and whose external meaning is indicative of the corporeality of God and of other imaginings with no truth in them, for these have been set forth as parables and riddles. (1.31, 67)

In the lexicographical chapters in which this series of chapters on the limits of knowledge in 1.31 through 34 occur, this argument

[3] *Ilf* here and below might be better rendered as "familiar" or "accustomed."

seems quite innocuous. No one can gainsay the suggestion that Maimonides inveighs constantly against thinking corporeally about God, in a way that reaches something of a peak in 1.35. That the Bible leads its readers to adopt thinking corporeally about God is proven by history. However, when this argument is pieced together with the argument in 2.23, something more challenging begins to emerge. Already here in 1.31 Maimonides is underlining that in these our monotheistic times, texts have taken on unprecedented authority. Alexander wrote from within the pagan world. In that world works about gods do not have the sort of theological authority of monotheistic texts. The claim that one God has created the world makes the scriptures said to be revealed by such a God unprecedented in their claims to authority. This contributes significantly to our habituation in the opinions inculcated by monotheistic scriptures.

In 1.34, the theme of "traditional authority (*taqlīd*)" becomes explicit.[4] As we saw in chapter 2, 1.34 discusses the things preventing "the commencement of instruction with divine science" (72). Of course, this chapter falls within the first and vaguest account of the limits of knowledge. The third and longest cause preventing one from commencing inquiry there concerns the "length of the preliminaries" (73–6). Maimonides's lengthy account of this cause is very rich. We must limit ourselves to a very quick sketch of the topics covered, including some of which we covered in greater detail in the previous chapter, to consider the passage on "traditional authority": he describes the experience of even the dullest of people when asked after awaking from sleep whether he desires to know the highest

---

[4] The following discussion of authority in Maimonides might be fruitfully compared with Y. Tzvi Langermann, "Criticism of Authority in the Writings of Moses Maimonides and Fakhr al-Dīn al-Rāzī," *Early Science and Medicine* 7 (2002) 3: 255–75. Note that Langermann only discusses scientific or philosophic authorities, without referencing Maimonides's broader discussion of the problem of authority that he discusses initially in 1.31 and 34.

things such as what the soul is and how it is "created in time (*ḥudūth*)" in the body. He would express the desire to know but would want that desire allayed quickly. Unfortunately, one can only know Him by way of His works, which then means a great deal of study of other things, including math, logic, natural science, and only after these such high and lofty subjects as are contained in "divine science." It is here that Maimonides invokes a qualified necessity in resorting to "traditional authority," which we will return to momentarily. Another reason for all these preliminaries is that so many "doubts (*shukūk*)" will occur along the way. And many premises are needed for addressing these topics. For those who possess only a longing for quick answers, it would be better that they not inquire. This intention to discourage some from inquiring certainly fits with our suggestion that the limits of knowledge and the space of doubts discourage those lacking intellectual courage and, as the fourth cause will indicate, natural aptitude. This account of the third cause contains one of Maimonides's most memorable distortions of biblical wisdom literature: "For [Solomon] says that the just one among men is he who gives everything its due; he means thereby that he gives all his time to seeking knowledge and spares no time for anything else."[5]

The "traditional authority" passage deserves to be quoted in full.

> Accordingly if we never in any way acquired an opinion through following traditional authority (*taqlid*) and were not correctly conducted toward something by means of parables, but were obliged to achieve a perfect representation by means of essential definitions and by pronouncing true only that which is meant to be pronounced true in virtue of a demonstration—which would be impossible except after the above-mentioned lengthy preliminary studies—this state of affairs would lead all people to dying

[5] This is Maimonides's interpretation of "*[the slothful] coveteth greedily all the day long; but the righteous giveth and spareth not*" (Prov. 21:25–6).

> without having known whether there is a deity for the world, or whether there is not, much less whether a proposition should be affirmed with regard to Him or a defect denied. Nobody would ever be saved from this perdition except *one of a city or two of a family*. As for the few solitary individuals (*al-āḥād*) that are *the remnant whom the Lord calls*, the perfection, which constitutes the end to be aimed at, is realized for them only after the above-mentioned preliminary studies.

This passage is reminiscent of two things at once: on the one hand, the claims of the Muʿtazilite *kalām* that though the rational law is rational, showing that it is rational takes time, and for that reason scripture commands what is rational, which becomes the traditionally authoritative, and, on the other hand, Aristotle's suggestion that in the sciences we rely on the insights of our predecessors.[6] Of course, we know that Maimonides did not agree with the Mutakallimun regarding rational law from EC, chap. 6. Oddly, he almost makes it sound as if for the "solitary," whose presence has been felt since Maimonides's expression of willingness to give "satisfaction to a single virtuous man while displeasing ten thousand ignoramuses" in the introduction to part 1, there might not be the need to rely on "traditional authority" at all. However that may be, what Maimonides says about the need on the part of most for traditional authority is not nearly as surprising as his insinuation that there are some solitaries who have no need for it. As we will see, this passage together with a few others sprinkled throughout the *Guide* paint a picture of a Maimonides who, despite his towering authority in the Jewish tradition, sees little place for authority at least for some. One of the other passages that echoes this account of the solitary appears in its numerological echo, 3.34. This is surely one of the most shocking chapters in the *Guide*. We will not quote it at length here. The Law concerns "the majority of cases" not "what happens rarely." Indeed,

[6] *Met.* 2.1, 993a30–b19.

it pays no attention to the damage that it might do to the "unique human being (*wāḥid*)."

Let us return at last to *Guide* 2.23, we arrived here because we wanted to understand more fully how the discussion of doubts in this chapter, as a modification of Alexander's teaching on doubts in 2.22, might relate back to Maimonides's similar updating of Alexander back in 1.31. What has emerged so far is that Maimonides is engaged in subtle reflections on the novel situation posed by the enormous authority of revealed scripture, as evident in both 1.31 and 1.34. As we will see shortly, his discussion of doubts will invoke the authority of scripture or of the prophets most responsible for it, apart from God—namely, Abraham and Moses. Shortly after announcing that it should not be the number of the doubts but "rather ...how great is their incongruity and what is their disagreement with what exists (*wa-mukhālafat al-wujūd*)," Maimonides takes up again the earlier discussion of Alexander's regarding causes of disagreement: he underscores that there should not be any imbalance between the opposing views on the basis of "upbringing (*tarbiyya*) or for some advantage." He exhorts us to "free [ourselves] of what is habitual (*al-muʿtād*), rely solely on speculation, and prefer the opinion[7] you ought to prefer" (2.23, 321). As in 1.31, upbringing and habit prove to be obstacles to unconstrained inquiry. Echoing somewhat 1.34's reasons that one can't begin with divine science, Maimonides then notes that the inquirer faced with doubts must possess three things: a nature tested by mathematics and logic, "knowledge of the natural sciences,"[8] and character formation that prevents him from

[7] It should be noted here that the world "opinion (*al-ray'*)" does not occur here but has been interpolated by Pines from several lines before: "one of two opinions (*aḥd al-rāy'iyin*)."

[8] Once again, Leo Strauss highlighted that Joseph ben Judah is deficient in his knowledge of natural science, out of an over-eagerness to acquire knowledge of divine science (Strauss, "How to Begin to Study *The Guide of the Perplexed*," Pines ed., xx).

succumbing to lust or anger.[9] Despite these loud echoes of 1.31 and 1.34, Maimonides then tacks in a direction contrary to these. He exhorts the reader not to be deceived by anyone who would lead you to doubt the creation of the world: "For in this opinion is contained the destruction of the foundation of the Law...." Rather than sticking with the plan to weigh doubts, he exhorts the reader to "always be suspicious in your mind as to this point and accept the authority (*muqalladan*) of the two prophets who are the pillars of the well-being of the human species...." What is perhaps most striking about this is how Maimonides provides before the reader's eyes an example of what he has just admonished us to avoid, namely, a failure to resist the push in one's character to prematurely decide such issues. Little wonder then that he goes on to say the reader ought not criticize him for his "rhetorical mode of speech." He purports to justify himself by noting that Aristotle also proffers rhetorical speeches in favor of the eternity of the world—and 2.23 is at the heart of the defense of creation after all.[10] Maimonides impugns Aristotle's use of rhetoric because, according to Maimonides, Aristotle resorts to rhetorical support from the "ravings of the Sabians." At other points in the *Guide*, it is amply evident that while Maimonides impugns these ravings, he more frequently impugns the Sabians for failing to draw the appropriate conclusions from their own assumption that the world is eternal, that is, for their failure to draw the fitting philosophic conclusions from that assumption.[11] Maimonides concludes 2.23 with the promise that in pages to come he will bring out "grave doubts" about the current claims to know the "arrangement of the motions of the sphere" and to account for them on the basis of nature and the "law of necessity." Of course, 2.24 is a tour de force in

---

[9] Cf. a related discussion to come shortly in 2.36, 371–2.

[10] Indeed, given that this section runs clearly from 2.13 through 31, 2.23 is almost at the center of these 19 chapters. The center being 2.22.

[11] Cf. 3.29, 516 and even 2.39, end into 2.40.

uncovering the tensions between Aristotle and Ptolemy on the motions of the heavenly bodies.

Leaving aside the description of 2.23, we are struck by the tension between Maimonides's admonition to weigh doubts with extreme care and his appeal to authority to warn off those who might succumb to the arguments of Aristotle. There is one other element to add to this interplay between doubt and authority, which reaches a peak in 2.23, namely, the suggestion that if one differs with the opinions of one's authority one will experience "disgrace (*shanāʿa*)." As we will see in the next section of this chapter, in a series of chapters leading from 2.14 to 2.22 and then later again in 3.16 through 18, Maimonides repeatedly invokes "disgrace" as the accompaniment of going against one's authority. He does not limit this to the disgrace the Jew should feel in departing from the belief in creation but even imputes to philosophers that they fear disgrace at departing from Aristotle. When compared with the first half or so of 2.23, the appeal to authority and the disgrace felt in disobeying an authority are, as Maimonides himself openly states, rhetorical at best and evidently at odds with the exhortation to weigh doubts. If one succumbs to the feeling of such disgrace, how can one weigh doubts? Surely, Maimonides does not want us to prejudge the weighing of said doubts.

There is one more statement on authority that we will attend to here, which reminds us more of the treatment of it in 1.31 and 34 than of 2.23, namely, 3.51.[12] This chapter is part of a group of

---

[12] Here a minor numerological hint is worth noting: 1+3+1=5, 2+2+3=7, 3+5+1=9. It is as if Maimonides were suggesting that in each passage he is intensifying (increasing by two) the problem of authority. One thing is certain: his evident questioning of authority would be considered anathema in at least some other monotheistic faiths. In chapter 6 on providence, we will consider again the role of authority especially as it appears in relation to the moral moment of Job's journey. I believe that it is not by chance that that chapter is 3.23, indicating some connection to what we've been discussing in 2.23.

chapters that have been considered a sort of coda to the *Guide*, about which there is much disagreement. Some argue that in 3.51 through 54, Maimonides departs from the heavy emphasis on theoretical perfection to an emphasis on practical perfection and fulfillment.[13] This interpretation is at best a reasonable interpretation of the last moments of 3.54—though we consider this a misinterpretation even of the very end of the *Guide*. Nothing could be further from the truth as an interpretation of 3.51. Of course, this chapter contains shocking claims by means of the parable of the king's palace about the different ranks among human beings engaged in different intellectual activities, including some hints that philosophers may well be closer to God than the rabbis, as practitioners of jurisprudence, the queen of the Jewish sciences. One's rank is determined by one's proximity to the king, that is, God. At least for now, I will set aside that debate. After going through these rank orders twice, first as parable and then with reference to specific human types, Maimonides picks up on the importance of turning wholly toward God to contemplate Him. It is at this point that he says, "As for someone who thinks and frequently mentions God, without knowledge, following a mere imagining or following a belief adopted because of his reliance on the authority (*qallad*) of somebody else, he is to my mind outside the habitation [of the King] and far away from it and does not in true reality mention or think about God" (p. 620). If one doubted the intensity of Maimonides's critical view of relying on authority, as, for example, moments in 1.34 and in 2.23 might make one doubt, here he leaves little doubt.[14]

---

[13] See, for example, Menachem Kellner, *Maimonides on Human Perfection* (Atlanta, GA: Scholars' Press, 1990), 63–64.

[14] This passage in 3.51 should also be compared with one in 1.50. It contains a discussion of the difference between saying, opining, and imagining, on the one hand, and knowing and "representing (*taṣawwur*)" to one's intellect, on the other. See Harry Austryn Wolfson, "The Terms *Tasawwur*

## Disgrace before Authority in Greater Detail

As we just saw above, Maimonides muddies the waters in our struggle to weigh doubts by interjecting "disgrace (*shanāʿa*)" often directly or explicitly in relation to "authority (*qallad*)" into the mix. I believe that Maimonides uses such language intentionally not only to throw at least some of his readers off the trail of a clear-headed weighing of doubts surrounding creation and eternity as well as about doubts surrounding the related views on providence but also to bring into relief what is at stake in weighing these doubts. The most useful analogue to this use of moral language and the way Maimonides uses it to cover over somewhat challenging thoughts is the way Maimonides treats the case of Moses our Master. When discussing prophecy, on the one hand, Maimonides makes it amply evident that the prophecy of Moses is unique and incomparable because "there will never be another Law" (2.39, 379); on the other hand, he does more to reveal the blemishes and blots on Moses's character that impede his prophecy than he does perhaps for any other prophet (2.36, 372–73; 2.38, 376–77; 2.45, 397; and *EC* chap. 4).

We will preface this discussion by digressing for a moment to clarify somewhat the meaning of "disgrace (*shanāʿa*)" and to note some variations in Pines's translation of it and related terms. The term *shanāʿa* is very similar to another key term in the *Guide*, namely, *ʿār*.[15] In *Guide* 3.8, Maimonides sets forth one of his most

---

and *Tasdiq* in Arabic Philosophy and Their Greek, Latin, and Hebrew Equivalents," *The Moslem World* 33 (1943) 2: 114–28.

[15] In his *Arabic-English Lexicon*, Edward W. Lane contrasts *shanāʿa*, which he renders as "was, or became, bad, evil, abominable, foul, or unseemly," with *qubḥ*, which could refer to the disgraceful or the morally base, that the latter "imports more." By this, I believe he means that *qubḥ*, like *ʿār*, carries greater moral import than does *shanāʿa*. That *shanāʿa* does not carry the same moral weight is evident in the fact that Pines sometimes translates it as "incongruous." Also see Steven Harvey, "Disgraceful! Maimonides' Use of *Qabīḥ* in the *Guide*," *Oriens* 50 (2022), 280–320.

breathtakingly severe attacks on matter and flesh, that is, the shame (*ʿār*) attaching to them. Much like his invocations of "disgrace (*shanāʿa*)," his invocations of "shame (*ʿār*)" are ultimately far more complicated than they appear at first, which should come as no surprise to any reader who was awake while reading *Guide* 1.2. There the reader sees one of the most breathtakingly open attacks on morality or of its relative importance in the entire Jewish tradition. That attack is so severe that it has led some to claim that Maimonides is a conventionalist. Since we have argued against this interpretation elsewhere,[16] we will leave the matter here at the acknowledgement that Maimonides initiates in *Guide* 1.2 the most concerted effort to elevate intellectual virtue in the history of the Jewish tradition. Returning to our focus here, the contrast between Maimonides's use of these two key moral terms, disgrace and shame, it should be noted that Pines has not always attended as he should have to the difference between them.[17] Pines renders *ʿār* as "shame" when translating some of the passages at the center of Strauss's discussion of Maimonides's hyperbolic mistranslation of Aristotle on the "sense of touch" in 3.8. But on most other occasions he lapses into rendering the term as "disgrace," following Strauss.[18] In addition, at crucial junctures rather than rendering *shanāʿa* as "disgrace," Pines renders it as "incongruity," namely, in the all-important chapter on particular providence, 3.17.

---

[16] See Parens, "Prudence, Imagination, and Determination of Law in Alfarabi and Maimonides," in *Enlightening Revolutions: Essays in Honor of Ralph Lerner*, Svetozar Minkov and Stéphane Douard, eds. (Lanham, MD: Lexington Books), 31–55.

[17] Even in 3.8, Pines is not consistent. He renders *ʿār* as "shame" on pp. 432 and 434 but reverts to "disgrace" on p. 435, and he renders *ʿār* as "disgrace" twice in 2.36 on p. 371, once in 2.40 on p. 384, and once in 3.49 on p. 608, all in a context alluding to the same passage about the sense of touch in Aristotle.

[18] See "Literary Character," in *PAW*, p. 75.

To my knowledge, Maimonides first introduces "disgrace (*shanāʿa*)" into the conversation near the beginning of the section running from 2.13 to 31 devoted to defending creation against eternity. He does so in 2.14. This chapter is notable for a few reasons. First, it provides the philosophers' arguments for eternity in a part of the *Guide* clearly intended primarily to defend creation. Second, it begins in a somewhat atypical manner: the chapter opening highlights Maimonides's relationship to the addressee, with frequent uses of the second person singular personal pronoun "your." Here, the conceit that the *Guide* is addressed to Joseph ben Judah, his talented pupil with a notable gap in physics, comes to the fore. It is as if he were putting the reader most like Joseph ben Judah on notice to be especially attentive. Third, Maimonides emphasizes that he will not flesh out the complete discourses of the philosophers: he will merely indicate "their intentions (*bi-aghrāḍihim*)"—much as he did for the Mutakallimun. Fourth, despite the previous mention of the philosophers, here he adverts to it being his own opinion (first person singular verbal form) that only Aristotle's opinions should be considered.

In keeping with his admonition to attend only to the view of Aristotle, Maimonides begins with four Aristotelian arguments each one enumerated as a "method (*ṭarīq*)." These arguments are about the following: that motion is not subject to coming into being or passing away, matter is not subject to coming into being and passing away, the matter of the whole heaven, above all, could not pass away because it has no contraries, and, finally, an argument about the fact that the possibility of the world's existing (that is, the possibility of creation) would have to pre-exist its being, which is made to segue immediately into the arguments of the latter-day followers of Aristotle. This argument and those that follow, according to Maimonides, are all "derived from [Aristotle's] philosophy." Given Maimonides's own deference to Aristotle in the opening of the chapter, this appears to recommend the following arguments—and even to raise the question whether they might not be more to the point than the preceding because they were conceived as arguments against creation. In contrast, Aristotle's own arguments appear to have been made without serious consideration of the possibility that the world was created after nonexistence.[19] When we return to the doubts regarding eternity in greater detail in the next section, we will return to the method of defending the eternity of the world based on the problem of possibility. For now it will have to suffice to say that it depends on the fact that for something to later exist, its possibility requires a substratum. According to Maimonides, "This [argument as elaborated by the followers of Aristotle] is a very powerful method for establishing the eternity of the world." He also refers to it as the "most important of the methods followed by Aristotle."

In addition to the method mentioned above, the other neo-Aristotelian arguments are four in number. He gives three others without numbering them: (1) if God "produced the world in time (*aḥduth al-ʿālam*)," He must have been in potentia before He created the world. Then something else must have caused Him to be in act. (2) Only an impediment (*al-muwānaʿ*) can prevent a being wishing to act from acting, but God can have no impediments.[20] (3) All of God's actions are perfect. He does nothing "without an object." Perpetual existence is more perfect; therefore, the world perpetually exists. He then notes that all subsequent arguments for eternity are ramifications of these, leaving it somewhat unclear whether that applies only to the preceding. To those seven he adds an eighth, which is where he finally invokes the term "disgraceful (*al-tashnīʿa*)."

---

[19] Although it is true that poets such as Hesiod speak of the gods coming to be out of chaos, there is little evidence that that chaos is thought of as being simple nonexistence. As Maimonides himself points out in 3.29 (p. 516), the eternity of the world is a presupposition of all polytheists. Lacking a single omnipotent God, creation from nonexistence makes little or no sense.

[20] Cf. 1.68, 166 regarding impediments.

> They also say in order to prove that the opposed doctrines are disgraceful (*al-tashnīʿa*): How could the deity, may He be honored and sublime, be idle and not do a thing in any respect whatever or cause a happening to take place in the course of the perdurable pre-eternity, so that whereas He did not do a thing throughout the duration of His existence—which is eternal and unending—He inaugurated that which exists when yesterday came? For if you were to say, for instance, that God created many worlds before this one—their number being that of the mustard seeds required to fill the globe of the ultimate sphere—and that each of these worlds has remained in existence a number of years equal to that of the mustard seeds required to fill it, this, in respect to its status compared to His infinite existence, may He be exalted, would have been as if you were to say that God created the world yesterday. For as soon as we affirm the inauguration of that which exists after nonexistence, there is no difference between one's positing that this happened hundreds of thousands of years since or at a very recent time. Accordingly, this is also a way by means of which those who believe in the eternity of the world prove the incongruity (*sh.n.ʿ*) of the opposed doctrines.

Assuming that God exists eternally—and no one in this dispute would gainsay that assumption—any claim that the world came to be after nonexistence implies that God was for some inconceivably long period of time idle. What is perhaps most noteworthy about this first appearance of disgrace is that the philosophers view the opinion of their opponents as disgraceful. Often in what follows, disgrace is felt before some authority on the part of the person or persons holding the view. The current example of disgrace is not a case of being bullied into one's position by a feeling of disgrace before an authority.

The very next chapter (2.15), however, sets one thinking in a contrary direction regarding Aristotle and those who follow him. Maimonides begins by arguing that even Aristotle did not hold that he had demonstrated the eternity of the world. Indeed, in this chapter he draws evidence from *On the Heaven* to try to prove that. He begins by noting that Alexander of Aphrodisias thought there were fewer doubts attaching to Aristotle's view. The passage invoking disgrace occurs early in this chapter. "Most of the people who believe themselves to philosophize follow Aristotle as an authority (*yuqallidu*) in this question and think that everything that he has mentioned constitutes a cogent demonstration as to which there can be no doubt. They regard it as disgraceful (*yastashniʿu*) to disagree with him..." (p. 290). After this passage he goes on to observe that all but Plato held the view that the motion is not generated and underscores that Aristotle would not be appealing to his predecessors for something he could demonstrate. This is an interesting case because it reminds us of 1.34 where "traditional authority (*taqlid*)" was said to be needed for all but the solitary. There I noted that Aristotle himself underscores the way one depends on the opinions of the wise in getting started in science. So which is it here? Is this that kind of reliance on the opinion of the wise, or is it merely paying obeisance before the authority of Aristotle? We will have to see where subsequent appeals to disgrace take us, but, at least so far, it seems dubious that the followers of Aristotle were really as submissive before authority as this passage might make one think. After all, the followers of Aristotle in Maimonides's time have the authority of the religions of the communities in which they find themselves to contend with as well.

In the same chapter (2.15), Maimonides invokes Alfarabi in a rare role apparently opposed to his—or at least so it seems. Maimonides begins by citing a passage from Aristotle's *Topics* in which he uses the world's eternity as an example of something we would like to know but that seems like something that is too vast or too great (1.10, 104b15ff.). Given that the *Topics* is a logical work, this example cannot be considered a strong indicator of Aristotle's own view on the matter of eternity. Leaving that aside, Maimonides goes on to observe that Alfarabi considered it "disgraceful (*istashnaʿa*)" that Galen thought there was no demonstration possible regarding eternity. Alfarabi held that it was possible to prove such eternity by proving the eternity of the heavens. It is worth observing that although Maimonides is indebted to Galen as a physician, he has little respect for him as a philosopher.[21]

Maimonides opens 2.16, by announcing that he will explain "what I believe with regard to this question [of creation v. eternity]." He begins by noting still in the first person that he does not approve of anything in the attempts of the Mutakallimun to demonstrate the "newness of the world (*ḥudūth al-ʿālam*)."[22] When a point cannot be proven, it is better that it "remain a problem or that one of the contradictory propositions simply be accepted." Of course, he will go on to accept the creation of the world in 2.25. But here he gives us no guidance as to why one might accept one of two unproven contradictories. At this point, he wishes to emphasize that the only bar he need meet to defend creation is to show that it is "not impossible." But given that neither position has been proven, creation ought to be accepted "because of prophecy." Of course, it is worth noting that in the logic of the *Guide* it would seem that believing creation is possible is crucial for understanding prophecy aright—at least from the biblical point of view. The exhortation to accept prophecy then appears to be circular. With this preparation, Maimonides then turns to appeal to disgrace. Given that by this point the reader has not yet read the chapter on doubts, 2.23, it seems premature to sway

---

[21] See, for example, *Eight Chapters,* chap. 1, in *Ethical Writings*, pp. 61–2nn1 and 3. Also see Pines, "Translator's Introduction," pp. lxxvii–viii and Y. Tzvi Langermann's passing reference to Maimonides as usually viewed in the study of the history of science as a "'hostile' source" regarding Galen in his "Islamic Atomism and the Galenic Tradition," *History of Science* 47 (2009): 277–95, esp. 278.

[22] Why Pines decides to translate this as "newness" here rather than his typical "creation in time" is unclear. By the time we reach the bottom of the page he translates the adjectival form as "newness" but when the form is nominal he renders it as "created in time."

the reader by appeals to "disgrace." Be that as it may, Maimonides writes simply, "I shall make it clear that just as a certain disgrace (*shanāʿa*) attaches to us because of the belief in creation in time (*al-ḥudūth*), an even greater disgrace attaches to the belief in eternity." By the time we reach 2.25, it will become amply evident that the disgrace attaching to eternity is that it undermines the Law as given to a specific people at a specific time and place. We will need to dig deeper to find the disgrace attaching to creation. One thing is certain: based on 2.23, we should not take Maimonides's word (authority) for it when he declares the disgrace attaching to eternity is greater. Disgrace deriving from authority is a problem characteristic of "our times," as Maimonides makes so amply evident in 1.34 and 3.51.

After the brief 2.16, part two, chapter seventeen is the first clear salvo in Maimonides's defense of creation. This chapter contains Maimonides's rhetorical defense of creation, based on the example of the orphaned child. Chapter 19 will contain his most serious dialectical defense of creation, the particularization argument. Between these two chapters, Chapter 18 will oscillate strangely between eternity and creation, consumed by the problem of will and impediment, one of the central topics of our chapter 7. Be that as it may, 2.17 starts the defense of creation off on a relatively weak foot. In brief, the example is that of a child who was born of a mother who "died after she had suckled him for several months." A man raises the child alone on an "isolated island." This child will ask how he came to be. And the man will answer that all of us are "generated in the belly of an individual belonging to our species." But the child will wonder how something could live in the belly of a woman without doing what he does as a grown child: eating, drinking, breathing, excreting. Maimonides goes on to argue that the Aristotelian position is like that of the child who won't believe that things could be different when he was growing in the mother's belly than when he is a child living outside his mother. Here, Maimonides claims that

Aristotle infers too much from the "nature of what exists." All that is required is that one acknowledge that what was before the world came into being could be different from the "nature of what exists (*ṭabīʿat al-wujūd*)," which has achieved a stable existence. Here, as mentioned in chapter 1, Maimonides appears to allude to the Half-and-Half Teaching. When he goes on to defend the position of creation he writes, "For we [the followers of *Moses our Master and Abraham our Father*] maintain that after motion has come into existence with the nature characteristic of it when it has become stable, one cannot imagine (*lā yatakhayyalu*) that it should come into being as a whole and perish as a whole, as partial motions come into being and perish" (2.17, 297). Although some might suppose this appeal to imagination might be casual, we should not. Despite what Maimonides will argue in 3.15, he made it amply evident in 1.73, in his explication of the Tenth Premise that imagination is a fitting judge of the reality of little or nothing. Leaving that aside, according to Maimonides, this limitation in our thinking is merely because we haven't considered something "created from nothing (*mubdiʿa*)."[23] Elsewhere in this chapter he invokes the possibility of something being "brought into existence from absolute nonexistence (*al-ʿadam al-maḥḍ*)" (2.17, 296).[24] That this view is not disgraceful is then stated

[23] See Pines's note on this participle, 297n6.

[24] As Pines puts it at 296n3, "other possible translations [of nonexistence] are 'privation' and 'nothingness.'" Cf. the opening of *Guide* 3.10, "Those Mutakallimūn, as I have made known to you, do not imagine nonbeing other than absolute nonbeing (*al-ʿadam al-muṭlaq*); but they do not consider the privations of all the habitus as privations." The Arabic term in each case here is the same *ʿadam* (s., or *aʿdām*, pl.). As argued earlier, the Mutakallimun place existence and nonexistence on a par—each equally the product of divine will. On this passage, cf. Sara Klein-Braslavy, *Maimonides as Biblical Interpreter* (Boston: Academic Studies Press, 2011), 73; an earlier version of this chapter appeared under roughly the same title, "The Creation of the World and Maimonides' Interpretation of Gen. i-v," in *Maimonides and Philosophy*, S. Pines and Y. Yovel, eds. (Dordrecht, Boston: Martinus Nijhoff, 1986), 65–78.

in the following manner: "The essential point is, as we have mentioned, that a being's state of perfection and completion furnishes no indication of the state of that being preceding its perfection. It involves no disgracefulness (*lā shanīʿ*) for us if someone says that the heavens were generated before the earth or the earth before the heavens or that the heavens have existed without stars or that a particular species of animals has existed without another species being in existence. For all this applies to the state of this universe when it was being generated" (2.17, 297–298). Rather than invoking authority to make us feel disgraced, here Maimonides denies that what an Aristotelian might deem disgraceful really is so. The low bar Maimonides is trying to meet in this chapter is evident from the ensuing mini-dialogue. All Maimonides wants to show is that creation is "possible." Given the connection between necessity, possibility, and impossibility established in 1.73–76, one cannot help but wonder what sort of possibility is being defended here. About the possibility of "creation in time (*al-ʿālam muḥdath*)" Maimonides concludes strangely, "Now this contention cannot be proved to be impossible by inferences drawn from the nature of what exists (*bi-ṭabīʿat al-wujūd*), which we do not set at nought (*lā nunākiru fīhā*)" (2.17, 298). It is as if Maimonides acknowledges while denying it that he is putting the nature of existence at risk. This is the gravest doubt on the side of creation. That Maimonides sometimes says the opposite of what he means is one of the more challenging facts of the *Guide*. No single declarative statement can be taken on its own.[25]

[25] These last two sentences highlight facts that can be easily shown about the *Guide*. They alone raise questions about two things: Herbert Davidson's renowned view that Maimonides writes sloppily and the kerfuffle Davidson initiated with his article "Maimonides on Metaphysical Knowledge," in *Maimonidean Studies,* vol. 3, Arthur Hyman, ed. (New York: Yeshiva University Press, 1992–93), 49–103, esp. 99–103. That piece led eventually to issue 8 of *Aleph: Historical Studies in Science and Judaism* on *Guide* 2.24.

If 2.14 offers ways that the philosophers argue for eternity, 2.18 begins to set forth ways to undercut the defenses of eternity offered by the philosophers. At times, in defending a position, one cannot help but reveal the weakness of one's own position. This is what we characterized as "oscillating" between eternity and creation. Since we will return to 2.18 to address will and impediments in chapter 7, we will give an even rougher sketch than usual to bring out the role of "disgrace" in this chapter. The "First Method" here overlaps with what were the Fourth and unnamed Fifth Methods, which served as a bridge between the arguments of Aristotle himself and the arguments of his followers in 2.14. Proponents of eternity reject creation because it requires God changing from potentiality to actuality if He creates the world. First, Maimonides argues that for immaterial beings, which are purely actual, acting in time does not entail potentiality as it does for material beings. Second, he uses Alfarabi's discussion of the Active Intellect (AI) in his "Letter on the Intellect" to try to argue that when the AI has an effect in time, it is due to the recipient not the agent. As we will see later, this builds on, or rather modifies, the previous argument about impediments and the AI in 1.68 (p. 166). Although Alfarabi uses the language of "impediment" in the "Letter on the Intellect" in this very connection, that is, to deny the possibility of even the AI, let alone God, being impeded, Maimonides touches only lightly on it until the "Second Method." While he led the reader to believe that through recourse to Alfarabi, he would find the means to resolve the challenge posed by this issue of changing from potency to act, the Second Method, which uses the language of "impediment (*al-māniʿ*)" perhaps more than in any other passage in the *Guide*, is prefaced with an acknowledgment that "it is difficult to resolve this doubt, and the solution is subtle. Hear it." The solution here will end up leading us more or less directly into 2.19, that is, into whether God should be viewed as purposive in particularization or not. It is striking that this method mentions impediments only to reference their absence, while the preceding method references obstacle or impediment lightly. As Pines explains, Maimonides's subsequent argument in defense of purposeless will is highly reminiscent of Alghazali's.[26] The Third Method of arguing for eternity herein challenged is characterized early on as "very feeble (*ḍaʿīf jiddan*)." Anything in God's eternal wisdom comes forth without delay with His wisdom because His wisdom like his essence is eternal (p. 301).[27] The repudiation of this "feeble" method is used rhetorically to pave the way for the particularization argument of 2.19. It is said to be feeble because we cannot plumb the depths of God's wisdom, as is evident from our inability to "know what was His wisdom" in making the number of spheres or planets what they are or the number of stars or in bringing the world into existence when he did, namely, "at a recent period (*mundhu madda*)." Here Maimonides says that God's "volition (*al-mashī'a*)" is opaque for us. It is indistinguishable from His attribute-less essence. Here is where he denies that disgracefulness attaches to the view of creation in the following way: "You shall hear much about this notion, when we shall speak of providence. By looking at matters this way, this disgracefulness (*al-shanāʿa*) is thus abolished." Presumably the disgracefulness that has been removed is the suggestion that God's creation means that God is somehow changeable or deficient with respect to actuality. The second appearance of disgracefulness (*al-shanāʿa*) anticipates the point at which the disgracefulness can be pushed to the other side of the scale. Maimonides writes of the opinion of creation "outweighing the other in the scales." Recalling that all this talk of disgrace precedes our methodological touchstone, 2.23, we are struck by the way Maimonides works to tip the balance of the scale rhetorically even while promising that ultimately it will be tipped by means (only) of "speculation (*al-naẓar*)."

---

[26] Pines, Translator's Introduction, cxxviii.

[27] Pines appears here to insert the word "decision" to capture the effect of the redoubling of the relevant verb (*b.r.z.*) and the particle *qad*.

After 2.18, Maimonides suspends the drumbeat about "disgrace," which recurred at least once in every chapter from 2.14 through 2.18, until he reaches 2.22, the crucial chapter before the presentation of the methodological guidance in 2.23. As we will see in a later chapter, the chapters running from 2.18 through 2.21 are the most important in the *Guide* for defending creation. Aside from the start framed in 2.18, Maimonides will drop the talk of "disgrace" throughout these chapters.

Part two, chapter twenty-two marks a return to direct criticism of the claim of eternity. Yet the criticism here is strange and challenging indeed. Maimonides invokes none other than Aristotle and those who follow him to take to task the possibility that our world of multiplicity could have "proceeded" from the One or a First Cause. The criticisms he levies are the criticisms of the philosophers themselves. The talk of "proceed" and "process" surely conjures up Neoplatonism—though as we have already noted in chapter 1, Neoplatonists do not treat such procession as temporal.[28] When Maimonides then turns around the critique on Aristotle, it lands rather lightly since Aristotle doesn't think of the First Cause as a cause from which other beings proceed, even in the case of the other unmoved movers, each of which is one. After linking this attack on procession from the One, Maimonides reiterates the reasonableness of his preceding arguments in 2.19 and following regarding purposing and particularizing. It is here that "disgrace" arises. Maimonides attacks Aristotle for the impotence of the God he envisions. We should not be surprised then that the next series of invocations of "disgrace" will have to wait until the discussion of divine foreknowledge and potency in the section on providence running from

[28] It must be underscored here that what Pines renders as "proceed" in 2.22 is, in Arabic, literally "necessitate." See chapter 7 below. Of course, Pines uses this translation because the problem highlighted in this chapter is the renowned problem in Neoplatonism of how more than one immaterial being could "proceed" from another.

3.16 through 18. Here, Maimonides's attack on the Aristotelian God is uncharacteristically hyperbolic, despite concluding on an important conciliatory note:

> This is an opinion that does not agree with the order of that which exists (*niẓām al-wujūd*), an opinion in favor of which no cause and no new persuasive proof have been brought forward. Withal very disgraceful conclusions (*shanāʿāt*) would follow upon it. Namely, it would follow that the deity, whom everyone who is intelligent recognizes to be perfect in every kind of perfection, could, as far as all the beings are concerned, produce nothing new in any of them; if He wished to lengthen a fly's wing or to shorten a worm's foot, He would not be able to do it. But Aristotle will say that He would not wish it and that it is impossible for Him to will something different from what is; that it would not add to His perfection but would perhaps from a certain point of view be a deficiency.

Immediately following this, Maimonides anticipates the partisan attacks of his opponents and, once again, uncharacteristically acknowledges his own potential limitations. More importantly, it is exactly here that he reiterates what he has mentioned a number of times previously, namely, Aristotle is correct about everything up to the sphere of the moon. Leaving those subsequent, framing remarks aside, Maimonides presented Aristotle's arguments against the notion that an inability to will novelty indicates a deficiency in God back in 2.13. We will revisit this issue shortly when we turn to 3.16 through 18. This labeling of an Aristotelian view as disgraceful may be a fitting conclusion to the hard push to argue for creation in 2.18 through 21. Whether it is minor or consequential, it is worth noting that, despite the appeal to "existence" or "what is" (*al-wujūd*) in this passage, it is not preceded by "nature (*ṭabīʿa*)" but "order (*niẓām*)." One of the most confusing features of Maimonides's argument about God as particularizer is whether his argument suggests God produces order or disorder. If order, then why God as intellect could not be thought to be the cause of it is unclear. If disorder, then such would seem to be unworthy of God. Even if we argue that it is an order we cannot fathom, what would indicate that that inability is an in-principle impossibility of fathoming for human beings, given that Maimonides has none of the reasons in-principle that, say, Kant has?[29]

The next occasion on which "disgrace" is invoked is the series of chapters on particular providence running from 3.16 through 18. As with the chapters running from 2.18 through 21, we will be taking a closer look at the discussion on particular providence in a later chapter. For that reason, our survey of the references to "disgrace" in these chapters running from 3.16 through 18 will necessarily be somewhat cursory.[30] *Guide* 3.16 discusses philosophic views on providence as presented in Alexander of Aphrodisias's *On Governance* or *On Providence,* which are strikingly similar to the account in Plato's *Laws,* book 10.[31] We will discuss this more later. Suffice it to say that Maimonides treats Alexander and the philosophers whom he treats so respectfully elsewhere with great severity. Perhaps in the spirit of 3.15, in which almost anything goes, including the possibility that intellect may not be more dependable than imagination(!), Maimonides opens with the following salvo: "An aberrant opinion

---

[29] Kant's in-principle limits are determined by the limits of the forms of sensibility and the categories of the understanding. For Kant, human beings are in-principle incapable of understanding anything but what we experience through sense experience in our limited lifetimes. It almost goes without saying that Maimonides's account of human being does not indicate any such in-principle limits. All the limits Maimonides indicates are indicated based merely on experience. They are, in other words, merely empirical not transcendental limits. Of course, where the limits lie in what experience can teach us is what is contested in the *Guide.*

[30] There are also at least two references to *sh.n.*ʿ in 3.14, one of which Pines renders as "absurdity." The link of 3.14 to 16 through 18 requires further explanation, which we'll have to wait until chapter 6 to provide.

[31] Cf. Pines, Translator's Introduction, pp. lxv–vii. Pines notes Alexander's reference to Plato (lxv) in his original work, though Pines does not seem to connect Alexander's account to *Laws* 10.

is professed by the philosophers concerning God, may He be exalted, with respect to his knowledge of what is other than He; and it is a very great aberration, and they have stumbled in such a way that neither they nor those who follow them with regard to this opinion can find absolution" (3.16, 461). From this moment forward the chapter is a pitched battle between "us" and "them." In the opening, he continues, saying of the philosophers that they have "evil and incongruous [or shameful] (*al-shanīʿa*) opinions" about God's knowledge. After laying out the three opinions on providence, which cannot help but involve the problem of divine knowledge, Maimonides goes on to argue that to avoid "imputing negligence to God" or what we have referred to elsewhere as impotence, they decided it was reasonable to claim that God is ignorant of everything in "this lowly world" (3.16, 462).[32] After alluding to the role of the human individual in evil, as discussed in 3.12, Maimonides goes on to write, "After having established this foundation that destroys every good foundation and deforms the beauty of every correct opinion, they tried to eliminate its disgracefulness (*shanāʿatahā*) through thinking that the knowledge of these things is impossible for the deity for various reasons." Presumably by "this foundation that destroys every good foundation," he means the philosophic view that God thinks either only of himself or of the species, which was effectively confirmed in 3.12.[33] Amid a field of battling opinions of "us" and "them," Maimonides goes on to allude in a very compressed fashion to various positions that believers in revelation must take if they are to address the evils experienced in human life, evidently without warrant. He writes, "Because we, the community of those who adhere to Law, claim that He had known them before they came about, they charged us with two disgraceful (*shanāʿatayin*)

[32] What Alexander and Maimonides have in mind here are either Aristotle's account of the Prime Unmoved Mover as thinking only of him or itself or the related medieval suggestions that God thinks only the species.

[33] See 3.12, 442, and cf. 2.13, 283.

opinions [or things],"[34] namely, that there can be a science of pure nonbeing and that knowledge of a thing in potential and in act are the same. Of course, both attributing a similar status to nonexistence as one attributes to existence, as we know from 3.10, and the tendency to collapse potency into act, as we know from chapter 1, are the result of the views of the Mutakallimun. As we will see later, the intensity of Maimonides's rhetorical vituperation toward the philosophers in 3.16 fits well with the vacillation surrounding intellect and imagination in 3.15. Both chapters appear in shocking contradiction to the all-important 3.17, as we will see in the chapter on providence.

For now, we must finish our survey of the moments in 3.17 and 18 when "disgrace" is used either alone or in conjunction with explicit reference to "authority" to be able to see past disgrace to the proper weighing of doubts. In the vast and complex 3.17, "disgrace" crops up twice: in conjunction with the view regarding animals of the Muʿtazilite *kalām* and also in a comparative treatment of positions of the Muʿtazilites and Ashʿarites. As we have argued elsewhere, Maimonides presents the positions of the Muʿtazilites and Ashʿarites in the reverse of their historical order in 3.17.[35] That is, he presents the positions of the Ashʿarites first and of the Muʿtazilites second. He characterizes the earlier position as suffering from both "incongruities (*shanāʿāt*)" and "contradictions (*tanāquḍāt*)," while he characterizes the later position as suffering only from "incongruities (*shanāʿāt*)" if from "great incongruities (*shanāʿāt ʿaẓīma*)." In other words, the later or Ashʿarite position has escaped certain contradictions inherent in the Muʿtazilite position, though the resulting more consistent teaching is even more incongruous or disgraceful than the earlier position. Since Maimonides's own position (471–4) appears at least at first to partake of elements of the

[34] There is no explicit reference to "opinion (ray')" here. Pines interpolates it from earlier in the paragraph.

[35] Parens, *Maimonides and Spinoza*, 120–22.

Muʿtazilite position, he goes out of his way (by reversing the historical order) to not make too obvious how the earlier position led to the later one.[36] Maimonides follows this initial account of disgracefulness with an added disgracefulness in the Muʿtazilite position. Since the Muʿtazilites are so intent on God's justice, they wonder, "Why has this particular animal been killed? Whereupon they assumed the burden of the following disgraceful (*al-shanāʿa*) answer: This is better for it, so that God should compensate it in the other world." In other words, their obsession about justice became so acute that they could not help but view the death of even animals as the result of sin. In a couple of pages, Maimonides will go on to assure the reader that no one in the Jewish community has ever adopted this view, except for a handful of the "latter-day *Gaonim*" who were under the influence of the Muʿtazilites (147). As it happens, not two pages earlier it appeared that confusion about the difference between animals and human beings is nothing peculiar to the Muʿtazilite *kalām*.[37] When Maimonides summarizes the three positions he set forth before turning to the Law of Moses our Master, "Aristotle followed what is manifest in the nature of that which exists (*ṭabīʿat al-wujūd*). The Ashʿariyya tried to avoid ascribing to Him, may He be exalted, ignorance with regard to anything.... The Muʿtazila also (*ayḍan*) tried to avoid having to ascribe to Him, may He be exalted, injustice and wrongdoing." This unguarded comment about Aristotle is very revealing.

When finally Maimonides turns to what he characterizes as his belief regarding providence, he says of it, "As for my own belief ...I am not relying upon the conclusion to which demonstration has led me, but upon what has clearly appeared as the intention of the book

[36] As we will see in chapter 6, through mapping of the positions of the Bible, the Muʿtazilites, and the Ashʿarites onto the positions of the characters in the Book of Job, Maimonides will reveal the historical order, even though here he suppresses it.

[37] Cf. p. 469 and 1.14's reference to Eccles. 3:19.

of God and the books of our prophets. This opinion, which I believe, is less disgraceful (*aqall shanāʿa*) than the preceding opinions and nearer than they to intellectual reasoning (*al-qiyās al-ʿaqlī*)" (p. 471). Uncharacteristically, Maimonides here claims a traditional basis for an approach to providence which, though it might appear at first to be traditional, proves ultimately to be anything but traditional. When he contrasts his position with "the preceding opinions," he seems to be referring only to the preceding two opinions of "the multitude of our scholars" and of our "latter-day scholars,"[38] that is the scholars who sought to interpret the Law of Moses our Master, the first without the benefit of the teachings of the Mutakallimun and the latter with that benefit.

Maimonides brings to a close this especially revealing series of comments on what is disgraceful, which began in 3.16, at the end of 3.18. Although his surprising views on providence are already given terse expression in 3.17 near the end, in 3.18 he argues unusually forthrightly, invoking Alfarabi in his now lost Commentary on Aristotle's *Nicomachean Ethics*, as well as Plato to support intellectualist views on providence. This philosophical conclusion to what started in 3.16 as something of a diatribe against the philosophic view of providence, concludes as follows: "Consider this chapter as it ought to be considered; for through it all the fundamental principles of the Law will become safe for you and conformable for you to speculative philosophic opinions (*ārā naẓariyya falsafiyya*); disgraceful views (*al-shanāʿāt*) will be abolished; and the form of providence (*ṣūra al-ʿināya*), as it is, will become clear to you" (476). Despite the introduction of his view as conforming to scripture (471), when all is said and done, it is the unusually characterized "speculative philosophic opinions" that prevail—and in doing so, they capture the very "form" of providence.

[38] See p. 469.

I have sometimes been accused by reviewers of my books of not providing arguments: I believe this is because some of my readers do not see the necessity of careful and extended analysis of the writings of authors as rhetorically complex as Maimonides and Spinoza. I beg to differ. The purpose of this extensive survey and rhetorical analysis of Maimonides's many uses of "disgrace" is intended to show the reader just how difficult it is to ferret out what Maimonides considers the relevant doubts on each side in the dispute between philosophy and Law. Not only does Maimonides not spell these doubts out explicitly, but also, he conceals them under layers of recrimination with morally loaded words like "disgrace." Our purpose here is to attune the reader to these rhetorical layers that it is our job to peel back.

## Doubts regarding Creation and Eternity

Having lingered over the "disgrace" attached to various views regarding eternity and creation as well as providence, we turn now to a preliminary look at the doubts, especially attached to eternity and creation respectively, but also briefly to those attached to the opposing positions on prophecy and providence. Much of the remainder of this book will explore in greater detail these doubts. When considering the doubts attaching to creation and eternity, we are not surprised to note that Maimonides is much closer to revealing openly the doubts associated with eternity. After all, the defense of Judaism requires that Maimonides press down hard on the side of the scales that would place eternity in an unpromising position. Whatever doubts attach to creation are much more difficult to see. This unequal visibility of the doubts on these two sides has only been intensified by the recent tendency among scholars to show that Maimonides could only side with creation.[39]

---

[39] I refer here not only to Kenneth Seeskin's *Maimonides on the Origin of the World* (Cambridge: Cambridge University Press, 2005) but also to

The doubts on the side of eternity are, as we have already indicated, that to side with eternity as Aristotle does is to undermine the principle of the Law, namely, creation. As *Guide* 2.25 reveals Aristotle's position eliminates all miracles; Plato's position preserves some; however, no position besides creation *ex nihilo* or creation after absolute nonexistence preserves what is needed to uphold the Law. What is required to uphold the authority of the Law fully is assurance that God has the power to give the Law to a particular people at a particular place and time. And for God to possess the power to intervene in the particulars, God must be capable of creation *ex nihilo*. It is worth underscoring here that eternal creation along Neoplatonic or Avicennian lines would not be sufficient for particular providence.[40]

Kenneth Seeskin has argued that creation has the immense advantage over eternity that creation accounts for why beings exist. He

---

arguments as divergent from Seeskin's as W. Z. Harvey in "A Third Approach to Maimonides' Cosmogony-Prophetology Puzzle" and Howard Kreisel in "Maimonides on the Eternity of the World." Both of the latter two authors argue for some version of eternal creation. In doing so, they claim to have preserved everything that need be preserved to uphold the view of the Law. The result is some form of Jewish philosophy or "Torah/philosophy" as Stern puts it. Or to put the matter differently, none of what is at stake in the dispute between philosophy and Law is preserved—and one imagines that one has upheld creation sufficiently to uphold divine omnipotence and particular providence. Cf. W. Z. Harvey's much more recent account of Isadore Twersky's "integration" of philosophy and Law in "Twersky on Integration of Law and Philosophy in Maimonides," unpublished remarks delivered for a symposium at Harvard University on the 25th anniversary of Twersky's death on January 19, 2023. See especially his closing comments on the views of Maimonides himself.

[40] See chapters 5 and 7 below, especially our discussion of Herbert A. Davidson in chapter 5, "Maimonides' Secret Position on Creation," in *Studies in Medieval Jewish Literature and History*, Isadore Twersky, ed. (Cambridge: Harvard University Press, 1979), 16–40 and, in chapter 7, Seymour Feldman, "The Theory of Eternal Creation in Hasdai Crescas and Some of His Predecessors," *Viator* 11 [1980]: 289–320.

makes the animus of his book *Maimonides on the Origin of the World* amply evident by opening his book with Leibniz's phrasing, which so pleased Martin Heidegger, why is there something rather than nothing? One wonders, though, whether there was a reason that Aristotle did not ask this sort of question, and whether he was truly at a disadvantage for not having asked it. It seems to me that this question is necessarily a post-revealed or post-monotheist question. Only once one seriously entertains the possibility that the world might have come into being after absolute nonexistence would one entertain the question, why is there something rather than nothing? Aristotle has reasons for not entertaining such a possibility seriously, which we will consider shortly.[41]

This brings me to the doubts on the side of creation. Here we must emphasize that we are referring only to the coming into being of the world after absolute nonexistence (2.17, 296). One of the main reasons that Maimonidean scholars have recently retreated to eternal creation is that they realize that creation *ex nihilo* lacks coherence.[42] Maimonides points this out himself in 2.13 (281–2). However, that lack of coherence rests on accepting Aristotle's claim that time cannot exist without motion—or that at least the eternity of which God partakes exists apart from the accident of time. Presumably, one must entertain the possibility that Aristotle misunderstood time on the assumption of eternity. Let us then grant, as Maimonides at least seems to grant in 2.17 that absolute nonexistence can pre-exist the created world—or to be more precise that God

[41] See Aristotle, *Physics* 1.8, 191b13–15. What would become the Latin adage *nihil ex nihil fit* is usually traced back first to Parmenides.

[42] Also consider Norbert Samuelson, "Maimonides' Doctrine of Creation," *Harvard Theological Review* 84 (1991): 249–71. Samuelson is so impressed by Maimonides's initial attack on creation that he asserts that the creation or revealed view agrees with Aristotle that no time pre-existed creation. Indeed, they agree that "both claim that the universe has always existed."

could exist without the world, since absolute nonexistence could hardly be said properly speaking to exist.

Even if one were to grant that time could pre-exist the world and motion, this only leads to the most pressing question related to God, creation, and time. In *Guide* 2.14, the chapter following the one in which the pre-existence of time is made a problem (2.13), Maimonides voices one of the more important objections to creation raised by proponents of eternity. Although Maimonides refers to it only as "another method," it is the Sixth Method listed in 2.14 and is one of the purest expressions of one of the most significant doubts connected with creation. It will recur in 2.18 in a more elaborate form in preparation for the most dramatic proof for creation provided in 2.19. "Another method. They say: An agent acts at one time and does not act at another only because of the impediments (*al-mawāniʿ*) or incentives that may supervene upon them. For the impediments (*al-mawāniʿ*) may render necessary the nonaccomplishment of a certain action that the agent wishes to accomplish.... Now as the Creator, may His name be sublime, has no incentives necessitating the alteration of a will, nor hindrances or impediments (*ʿawāʾiq...mawāniʿ*) that supervene and cease to exist.... His action exists...permanently in actu." In other words, if the world came into being after absolute nonexistence, precisely because a created world is not eternal or has existed only for a limited time, it implies that God was somehow impeded from bringing the world into being sooner. Even if God transcends time, the problem of impediment to creation is implied by the limited existence of what He has created.[43]

Leaving all the conundrums associated with time aside, the doubts associated with creation may have less to do with time than what creation implies about God's being or nature or essence and about His relation to all that exists. It is worth noting that the entire

---

[43] We will return to the more elaborate discussion of the problem of impediments in relation to creation found in *Guide* 2.18 in chapter 7.

section 2.13 through 31 on eternity and creation focuses more on mustering arguments on behalf of (if not proving) a creator than it does directly on behalf of creation. As Maimonides knows all too well from having thought this through back in 1.71, it makes little sense to try to prove God's existence from the assumption of creation because it always presupposes what it has to prove. The peak of all of these arguments is surely 2.19, and that chapter is devoted more to proving the necessity of a particularizer than proving creation directly. Or to put matters differently, what Maimonides argues is that the superlunary order or disorder evinces a particularized effect. To prove this, Maimonides is compelled to argue for God as particularizer as both purposive and possessed of will. We will address these arguments in the final chapter in greater detail. For now it will have to suffice to say that a being of will who brings the world into being out of absolute nonexistence poses certain risks regarding the "nature of existence." What one gains from claiming a will brings the world into being out of nonexistence is to justify every imaginable claim on behalf of particular providence. Yet, once again, one must wonder whether what one gains for particular providence isn't had at the expense of the "nature of existence."

Of course, the issue we allude to here is evident in the history of all three of the monotheistic faiths. It is the problem of the relation between God's goodness and God's power or omnipotence, as Descartes frames it in his *Meditations*. Maimonides reveals it in the dialectic between the philosophers and the Ashʿarite *kalām*. It appears similarly in the dialectic between Thomas Aquinas's tethering of the divine will to the overarching Eternal Law, on the one hand, and the subsequent attacks on the constraints Thomas permitted God to submit Himself to, which of course eventuated in the voluntarist reactions of an Ockham, on the other.

Although Maimonides may appear to come close to granting will sufficient place in his defense of creation, above all, in 2.19, to fall prey to the same dynamic, we believe that he is well aware of it.

And rather than succumb to this dynamic or dialectic, he airs it so that the prudent reader might draw the correct conclusion. Although this dialectic is sometimes presented as that between goodness and power or intellect and will and although they appear in this guise in the *Guide* as well, there is a less obvious contrast that seems perhaps intended to veil this dialectic or conflict: I refer to the contrast between will and impediment. The place of "impediment" (*ʿāʾiqa*) is amply evident in the case of prophecy and providence. It is less obvious in the case of creation and eternity. At the end of the next chapter and in the following chapters, we will bring out the striking place of impediment in the *Guide*—and especially focus on how it appears at first as a strange doppelganger of will.

# PART II

# OBSTACLES TO BEING AND ACTION

## CHAPTER 4

# PRIVATION, PARTICULARIZED, AND ABSOLUTE

This chapter might appear at first a bit out of place. After all, we promised to focus on the doubts on either side in the debates between philosophy and Law regarding prophecy, providence, and creation. As it happens, there is a *motif* that runs throughout these greatest themes that proves to be the key to understanding the status of these doubts, namely, privation. In every instance, the opinion Maimonides advocates for each of these greatest themes involves some element of privation. Consequently, this *motif* will serve as both puzzle and clue as we attempt to weigh the doubts on each side of these three themes. If at times it seems that we discuss privation more explicitly than doubt, that is because Maimonides has so steeped these themes in this odd *motif.*

Recent scholarship on the *Guide* has emphasized the centrality of the parable of female and male, matter and form. That emphasis risks missing the central importance of privation to the *Guide.* Our purpose here is not to suggest that Maimonides is some sort of crypto-nihilist; rather, we seek to make sense of why privation plays such a prominent role in the *Guide.* To begin with, confusion abounds between matter and privation. Some interpreters blame matter for things that privation should be held responsible for. This is not by accident: Maimonides both highlights and takes advantage of this confusion, especially in connection with his relatively rare forays into morality in the *Guide.*[1] Not only will we attempt to clarify

---

[1] Here, it is worth reviewing Maimonides's observation at the end of 3.8, perhaps the most apparently ascetic chapter in the *Guide*, that in it he has "turned aside from the purpose of this Treatise to deal with moral and also religious matters (*umūr khalqiyya wa-dīniyya*)." Since 1.2, if not the

the relation between matter and form, but also we will try to clear up what is to my knowledge a neglected mystery of the *Guide*: what exactly is "particularized privation (*al-ʿadam al-makhṣūṣ*)"? There are so many difficulties and challenges in the *Guide* that no one should be scolded for neglecting this fact, but it is a fact that Maimonides drops this phrase at a key early moment of the *Guide*: in 1.17, he acknowledges "Plato and his predecessors" as having made human beings aware of the distinction between matter and form by riddling about them, much as Maimonides sees riddles about matter and form in the Bible's references to female and male.[2] When he goes on to add "particularized privation" to the pair to make a threesome, he does not identify the author who had this insight. Of course, any reader with even a smattering of knowledge of Aristotle recognizes this threesome.[3] However, I am unaware of any reference in Aristotle to the modifier "particularized." Given that "particularization" (*takhṣīṣ*) plays such a prominent role at key moments in the *Guide*—namely, at the peak of the arguments of the Mutakallimun for the creation of the world (1.74, Fifth Method) and in the peak of Maimonides's defense of creation in his own replacement for the *kalām* argument (2.19)—it is somewhat surprising that, to my knowledge, this passing reference to "particularized privation" has not been taken more seriously. Reminding ourselves of Maimonides's

introduction to the first part, it has been evident that the *Guide* is not primarily concerned with morality.

[2] *Guide*, introduction to part 1, pp. 13–14. Cf. Joseph Stern, *The Matter and Form of Maimonides' "Guide,"* esp. pp. 356–60. For a book centering on Maimonides's understanding of the whole in light of the matter-form distinction, so far as I can tell *Matter and Form* says surprisingly little directly about introduction to part 1, pp. 13–14, with its extended quotation from Prov. 7:6–12. Stern seems to prefer to focus on 3.8 where the parable of the married harlot reappears.

[3] *Physics* 1.9 and *Met.* 9.9.

exhortation to take seriously every word of the *Guide*,[4] this juxtaposition of privation and particularization cries out for clarification.

Yet other matters also related to privation call out for clarification or explanation. Why does Maimonides so frequently resort to impediments to action rather than action as evidence for particular providence? As it happens, the three greatest themes of the *Guide*—creation, prophecy, and providence—are all touched in one way or another by impediments. Obviously, the connection between particularized privation and particular providence is not merely a matter of the link between "particularity" in both phrases.[5] Indeed, it is less the common term "particular" or "particularity" than the negativity or privation that links them. In other words, Maimonides's reference to "particularized privation" may well be linked to impediment by virtue of the air of privation about them both. After all, it is a curiosity of the *Guide* that at the peak of his arguments in defense of his preferred versions of purportedly biblical views on creation, prophecy, and providence that each is haunted by the specter of impediment. God's particular care seems evident only in His refusal of care where it would otherwise appear to be deserved or natural. This repeated trope cannot be accidental.

This chapter will open only the first page in the story of impediments in these highest themes. Subsequent chapters will take each in turn in the order of the accessibility of their references to impediment: prophecy, providence, and creation. We will begin this chapter, however, by attempting to get at least a preliminary sense of

---

[4] Introduction to part 1, p. 15.

[5] Strauss helpfully highlights Maimonides's distinction between general and particular providence as that between the genus (*nawʿ*) and the particular (*shakhṣ*) in "The Place of the Doctrine of Providence," 539-540n9, citing 3.17, 472 [36b] and 473 [37a] and 3.18, 476 [39a]. Unfortunately for the English reader, Pines renders "particular (*shakhṣ*)" and its cognates with the term "individual" in phrases such as "individual providence" or "providence concerning the individual" or even "providence watching over human individuals."

what the phrase "particularized privation" might refer to, especially by comparison to the misunderstanding of privation exemplified by the Mutakallimun, who hold that the only privation is "absolute." Then we will turn to the confusion of matter and privation in moral matters not only in 3.8 but throughout the *Guide* and even in *Eight Chapters*. Then we will slow down to take an even closer look at one of the more provocative series of chapters of the *Guide,* 3.8 through 10. This will give us an opportunity to plumb the depths of Maimonides's claim in 3.10 that the Mutakallimun view all privation as absolute. Finally, we will turn to privation as impediment, perhaps the most interesting sort of "particularized privation." There, we will set the stage for the rest of the book.

## The Differences between Particularized and Absolute Privation

It is worth considering the likely effect on Joseph ben Judah of reading about "particularized privation." Let us recall Leo Strauss's observation that Joseph ben Judah's Achilles's heel is his ignorance of natural science or physics.[6] Given this gap in his education, the *Guide* is written in such a way as both to take advantage of it to hide things in plain sight and to point the way to how one might fill this gap. The phrase "particularized privation" appears to be a clear case of hiding something in plain sight. If Joseph is unfamiliar with Aristotle's *Physics* and the relevant commentaries on it, then he is not likely to notice when something as unusual as this phrase is used in the *Guide*. Based on my personal experience, I can say that it has taken many readings for me to become sufficiently interested in this phrase to pursue it further. One could imagine that Joseph might

[6] As we noted in chapter 3, Strauss makes this observation in "How to Begin to Study *The Guide of the Perplexed*" (Pines ed., p. xx). This observation is based on a comparison of 1.34 (p. 75 on the proper order of study of logic and the theoretical sciences) with Maimonides's sketch of what Joseph had studied in the Epistle Dedicatory (p. 4).

not be aware of what a puzzle this phrase is until he had read the *Guide* and related works many times.

Given that Maimonides hopes that the intellectually curious student of the *Guide* will inquire further about this phrase, we must begin to search for other clues to piece together with "particularized privation." Both particularization and privation become significant themes in Maimonides's critique of the Mutakallimun's arguments for God's existence (actually for creation), unity, and incorporeality, running from 1.73 through 76. We already touched on this part of the *Guide* in chapter 1. There we saw that the Mutakallimun's premises come together in premise 10 on admissibility as opposed to possibility or potentiality. And we saw that in turn the admissibility premise culminated in the Fifth Method to prove creation/creator, that is, the particularization argument.

Already in the long discussion of the 10th premise, the admissibility premise, particularization comes up. After all, the very essence of the admissibility premise is to underscore that any particular thing can come to be anything, an elephant the size of a flea, etc. (206). Because form and nature are out of the picture, anything goes. In a world in which anything goes,[7] it will prove to be indispensable that there be an omnipotent being who oversees every particular thing in every particular detail. Much as beings lack any fixity, so the power of perceiving them is similarly compromised: not intellect but imagination grasps what is admissible. Having set the stage for admissibility and its centrality in the thought of the Mutakallimun, Maimonides turns to a dispute between a Mutakallim and a philosopher, which he presents as his means of "reveal[ing] to you the secrets of these matters" (207): the dialogue or dispute begins with the Mutakallim asking the philosopher why some things have some characteristics and why others have others. He includes in the question

[7] Everything, that is, except the principle of non-contradiction, which the Mutakallimun are unwilling to compromise. See 207 top.

somewhat indiscriminately both essential and accidental characteristics. The philosopher responds by drawing the distinction between "two species of accidents (*nawʿān min aʿrāḍ*)" or attributes, namely, those connected with form and those connected with matter. To translate it into more precise philosophic parlance, the former are properties, and the latter are accidents.[8] "Now the various kinds of matter found in bodies that are in the stage of ultimate composition differ greatly because of the forms, which particularize (*al-ṣūr al-makhṣuṣa*) these various kinds of matter, so that the substance of iron becomes different from that of cream and so that each of these substances has attached to it the differing accidents that you see." The Mutakallim's response is predictable. He begins by denying that there are forms necessitating that there be different kinds of beings or "a variety of substances." As I explained in chapter 1, he follows up with eight of the other premises set forth in this chapter, including one that Maimonides has not touched on yet, premise 12. As I argued there, the upshot of all these premises which comes across most clearly in the denial of form is to establish a sort of equipoise between existing and not existing or being and non-being. This clearly is connected with the fact that the Mutakallimun hold that all privation is absolute privation. What else would be the consequence of supposing that non-being has the same status as being?

The question remains: what is the point that Maimonides is having the philosopher make in relation to "particularization"? Given that for Maimonides as for his contemporaries, matter is the principle of individuation, it isn't immediately obvious what he means when he claims that the form "particularize[s]" these various kinds of matter. One clue, however, is that it is form that is the

---

[8] Although Pines renders the plural of *aʿraḍ* as "accidents," this Arabic term is probably best rendered as "attribute" here. Like the Greek *sumbebekos*, the Arabic *aʿraḍ* covers both the broader "attribute" and the narrower "accident." See Soheil M. Afnan, *A Philosophical Lexicon in Persian and Arabic* (Beirut: Dar El-Mashreq, 1968), pp. 172–73.

contrary to privation rather than matter. In other words, when Aristotle discusses matter, form, and privation, we find him establishing a sort of triangle, in which matter is the starting point as potency and matter can become either the good actuality, that is, it can either achieve the form, or it can become the bad actuality, which is any number of privations of the form.[9] In keeping with Aristotle's use of the target in connection with virtue,[10] the matter is similar with form: although there is only one way to hit the target there are an indefinite number of ways to miss it. If the form selects or elects[11] the matter to be a kind of being, then privation means the failure to fulfill that for which it is selected. Review of the rest of 1.17 confirms this way of thinking about 1.73, 10th premise. After noting that privation is always conjoined with matter, Maimonides writes, "For, were it not for this conjunction with Privation, Matter would not receive Form. It is in this sense that Privation is to be considered one of the principles [along with Matter and Form]. However, when a form is achieved, the particular privation in question,[12] I mean the privation of the form that is achieved, disappears, and another privation is conjoined with matter, and this goes on forever, as has been made clear in natural science." Matter (the female principle) is portrayed as promiscuous (that is, as a "married harlot") because it is

---

[9] *Met.* 9.9.

[10] EN 2.6, 1106b30–34.

[11] One of the meanings of *kh.ṣ.ṣ.* is to select or elect. And indeed this root is linked by Afnan to the "proprium" or the property. It is worth noting that another root is translated with cognates of "particularize," namely, *j.z.'.*, which usually refers to a particular as a part of some greater whole. See, for example, the long quote in chapter 1 from 2.29, p. 346. As we will see in chapters 6 and 7 on providence and creation, respectively, this difference over particularization is the key to seeing the large gap between the way the dialectical theologians use the term in 1.73, 5th method, and the way Maimonides uses it himself in 2.19.

[12] Lit. "that privation (*dhālika al-ʿadam*)." No reference is made to *kh.ṣ.ṣ.* here.

constantly changing forms as well as privations. Strikingly, though, it is not matter but form that takes the lead in particularization. The character of the privation attached to matter is dictated by the form that determines what the matter will become.

In brief, the issue of particularization takes a number of unexpected turns. Form is what guides particularization rather than matter. The disagreement over particularization between the philosopher and the Mutakallim concerns nothing like the particularity of a member of a species but rather that matter cannot but become a certain kind of being or fail to fulfill the form of said being. However the possibility that matter could become just any kind of being is precluded by form. The Mutakallim is not able to see that even if a potential being such as an acorn fails to become a healthy, mature oak, it would not have been able to become an elephant. A sickly and deformed oak is still an oak.

Let us consider briefly both 1.74, Fifth Method and 2.19 to see whether they have anything to add about particularization that might clarify what Maimonides is pointing to with "particularized privation." When we discussed 2.19 earlier, we were especially interested in the fact that even there Maimonides pointed to particularization not only of beings but of the time at which something would come to be. It was evident at the time that the mention of time was included to support the creation of the world "after" absolute nonexistence.[13] Here, I quote the references to things other than time that I omitted in chapter 1. "It is admissible that this should be endowed with the shape, size, and accidents it has...and it is also admissible that it should be bigger or smaller, endowed with another shape or with other accidents....Accordingly its particularization in respect of a certain shape or a certain size or place or accident...is a proof of the existence of someone who particularizes, who has

[13] I place "after" in scare quotes because surely temporality is absent from the world without beings, except for God.

freedom of choice, and who has willed one of two admissible possibilities" (1.74, Fifth Method, 218). Initially, it is difficult to see what new light this sheds. However, a few things begin to surface when one recalls the Mutakallim's refusal of any distinction between properties and accidents. That same lack of distinction is expressed here. The Mutakallim's blindness to the presence of form is evident in size and shape acting as the only residue of form. Although it is true that for an Aristotelian size and shape are typically viewed as accidents, that is because form limits the range of possibilities of size and shape. Maimonides indicates for the Mutakallim the lack of this distinction by adding "accident" to the list. Seen in relation to the discussion of the 10th premise this method reminds us that we go wrong when we suppose that particularization refers primarily to the distinctive accidents of an individual. The real locus of our attention in thinking about "particularized privation" should be between form and privation of form rather than between matter and privation. One more observation is worth mentioning. It is noteworthy that Maimonides refers to the being with choice willing "one of two admissible possibilities." If this had been proposed by an Aristotelian, she might have suggested something more along the lines of "hitting the target of actuality or missing it in any number of ways." The world of the Mutakallim is a world of ones and zeroes: the on-off between being and non-being. The equipoise between being and non-being seems implied by this choice between two admissible possibilities.

Let us turn now to take another look at 2.19, which we will also return to in chapter 7 from yet another angle. Early on in 2.19, Maimonides confirms our reading of 1.73 and 74. That is, he notes the Mutakallimun's inattention to the particularization that is attributable to form. He puts it as follows: "In their opinion there is no difference between plants particularized through being red rather than white or through being sweet rather than bitter or between the heavens being particularized through having the shape they have instead of having been made square or triangular" (303). Although in his treatment of particularization in 1.73 and especially 1.74 Maimonides does not bring into the mix matters regarding the heavens, most readers of the *Guide* know that the order or disorder of the heavens is the key marker of particularization in 2.19. If by this point in the argument the reader is not yet aware that Maimonides will build his whole argument about particularization as evidence for a creator who wills rather than the God of Aristotle around the order or disorder of the heavens, it still is obvious to almost any reader that there is something more important about the order of the heavens than a mere accident in an individual plant. The difference between the colors of plants, which are viewed by Maimonides as accidental, and the order of the heavens is not only large, but also, as we see in subsequent pages, at least from the Aristotelian point of view that which Maimonides is able to explain about the heavens stems from form rather than matter. Those accidents in plants are due merely to matter. Indeed, in the next couple of pages, through an imaginary dialogue with Aristotle (much as the Mutakallim engaged in a dialogue with the philosopher in 1.73, tenth premise), Maimonides goes on to explain by way of this dialogue that the order beneath the sphere of the moon derives from the mixture of the four elements, which though they are elemental, have their places or the places they tend toward connected directly to their form. Maimonides then turns from the order beneath the sphere of the moon to that which is above it, in the heavens. Maimonides makes this move from sub- to superlunary by asking whether the matter of things superlunary is the same as things below. Aristotle answers that they are obviously made of different matter since the superlunary are subject to circular rather than linear motion (305). Although Maimonides argues for a difference between the matter of the planets and the stars because of differences in the kinds of motions they appear to undergo, the differences in the motions of the planets are due to differences of form that are "particularized." Far from abandoning "form," together with the philosopher back in 1.73, according to Maimonides it is form that particularizes—even if it is God who must endow each planet with its form. Now, there is one difference between the way form particularizes beneath the sphere of the moon as opposed to above, namely, form and matter are, in keeping with the eternity a parte post that Maimonides presupposes,[14] together eternally. As a result, there would appear to be no necessity that privation play a role in this marriage of matter with form. However, as my stated ambivalence about whether to refer to the superlunary as ordered or disordered was meant to suggest, there is evidence of negativity or privation linked to Maimonides's account of the superlunary similar to what we have seen so far in 1.17 and 1.73–74. Indeed, the argument overall could be boiled down to the following: the justification for claiming that God is a creator who wills the purpose of the superlunary—including both the apparently disorderly motions of the planets as well as the apparently pattern-less distribution of the stars in the sphere of same—is less order than, at least, apparent lack of order. In other words, the driving force behind Maimonides's particularization argument in 2.19 is either that the superlunary is disordered or at the very least appears to be disordered because we have not yet fathomed the underlying causes of order. Although privation is not joined to particularization as it was described back in 1.73 by the philosopher, particularization in 2.19 is still haunted by negativity or privation. When we return to 2.19 in chapter 7, we will have more to say about this joining or linkage.

For now, we must turn to 3.10 briefly (because we will return in greater depth to it as part of a broader analysis of 3.8 through 12, in the third section of this chapter) to confront Maimonides's deeper insight into the *kalām* misunderstanding of privation as absolute. In a book filled with one gem-like chapter followed by another, there is something extraordinary about 3.10. This will be even more

---

[14] See 2.26 through 28.

obvious when we look at it in its context later in this chapter. For now, we merely hope to shed some light on the difference between Maimonides's understanding of privation, including particularized privation, and the *kalām* view. At first glance and in a book filled with perplexities, it is especially perplexing. To experience that perplexity fully, I will quote liberally from Pines's translation.

> Those Mutakallimun, as I have made known to you, do not imagine nonbeing other than absolute nonbeing; but they do not consider the privations of all the habitus as privations. For they think that every privation and the corresponding habitus—as for instance, blindness and sight, death and life—have the status of contraries, like the warm and the cold. For this reason they say in absolute parlance that nonbeing does not need an agent, for only an act calls necessarily for an agent. This is correct from a certain point of view. Though they say that nonbeing does not need an agent, they say, according to their principles, that God makes blind, makes deaf, and causes that which moves to rest. For these privations are to their mind existent things.

Before we interpret this passage, it is worth observing that this is the chapter in which Maimonides goes on to explain what at first glance might appear to be contradictory claims. On the one hand, he states what has led some interpreters to suppose that he has a view of good and evil that is as relativistic as that of Spinoza, namely, "evils are only evils in relation to something; and that everything that is an evil with reference to one particular existent, that evil is the privation of this thing or of one of the states of this thing....All evils are privations" (439). On the other hand, he claims, "Accordingly the true reality of the act of God in its entirety is the good, for the good is being." Against the backdrop of the Mutakallimun's avowal of the absoluteness of privation, the claim about the relative character of privation comes into focus. Maimonides also here sheds light on "particularized privation." For Maimonides as for Aristotle, the proper way to think of privation is that it is always attendant on form. Privation does not have an independent existence that could warrant the name "absolute." That the dialectical theologians do not understand the relative character of privation is evident from their inability to recognize things like death and deafness as privations. As a result and in the interest of making God directly responsible for everything, not only the good but also the evil, they treat these privations as if they had an equal status with the habitus of which they are the privations. In the quoted passage, the reader is thrown back on her heels by the statement that according to them "nonbeing does not need an agent." If death requires an agent, as they claim, shouldn't absolute nonbeing? However, when we piece together this passage with 1.73, seventh premise, in which Maimonides notes that for the Mutakallimun privations like death and deafness must be created anew in every moment, we see further confirmation of the argument Maimonides here makes. The dialectical theologians are exceedingly literal minded. Since they do not view death as nonbeing in absolute parlance, the only thing that, according to them, deserves the name nonbeing or is nonbeing in "absolute parlance" is the void. A dead or deaf human being still consists of atoms, until it decomposes, and in this sense is from their point of view something. Only if one sees God solely as the cause of good, and understands privation properly as relative to a being's possession or lack of possession of a form, can one place privation in its proper place. With Aristotle and (to my knowledge without Maimonides's knowing of his writings) Augustine, and many others, Maimonides affirms the connection between God and being and denies God any causal role in privation.[15] The relativization of privation is part and parcel of the strange talk of "particularized privation." Neither privation nor evil are absolute things. A focus on "absolute nonbeing" is something neither Maimonides nor Aristotle shares with the Mutakallimun.

Our inquiry into "particularized privation" has taken us from 1.17 to 1.73 and 74 to 2.19 and then to 3.10. Our survey of these

---

[15] Aristotle, *Met.* 9.9; Augustine, *Confessions* 7.18.

key moments has given us a far greater sense for what can be lost if one focuses only on matter and form. In this case, as we will see shortly, matter especially gets short shrift. For now, we have been surprised to see that privation is joined in striking ways with form. Indeed, it is form that is responsible for the particularization of privation—not matter. Despite the fact that privation can bring with it great suffering, we are already on the way to coming to appreciate more fully what Maimonides goes on to argue in 3.12, that in the grand scheme of things the evil that is the privation of life or death is necessary for the greater good of the whole. Although the dialectical theologians stop short of claiming that God is the cause of the void, they do go so far as to suggest that God causes what the philosophers call privations. In contrast, Maimonides sticks with Socrates in claiming that God is the cause only of good.[16]

## Matter, Touch, and Shame[17]

In chapter 3, we touched on one of the themes we will discuss now, "shame (*ʿār*)," to distinguish it from what was then our focus—namely, "disgrace (*shanāʿa*)." The crux of our argument is that Maimonides appears at first glance to intend to inflame our sense of shame and to excoriate the sense of touch along with matter as the root of all evil. Closer examination of the relevant passages reveals important shifts from the attack on matter to subtler acknowledgments that matter is not itself evil, rather evil is a privation. Now that we have attended as carefully as we have already to 1.17, none of this should come as a surprise. What is surprising, however, is just how changeable is Maimonides's rhetoric regarding matter. Ultimately, we will be able to reconcile the attacks on matter with the

[16] Plato, *Rep.* 379b.

[17] This whole section should be compared with Stern, *Matter and Form*, chap. 9, as well as with Aviram Ravitzky, "The Balanced Path and the Path of Asceticism: The Unity of Maimonides' Ethics," *Tradition* 47 (2014) 1: 28–47.

subtler finger-pointing at privation by distinguishing when Maimonides argues in a biblical mode and when in a philosophic mode.[18] Although it has often been argued that Maimonides grew more ascetic in the *Guide*, the asceticism that appears here manifests biblical asceticism. That this asceticism manifests itself more strongly toward the end of the *Guide* in part 3, starting as early as 3.8, will fit well with the fact that the *Guide* concludes with a survey of the Law and its purposes in 3.36 through 49. As early as 3.33, Maimonides indicates the biblical basis of this ascetic trend in his argument.

Beginning at the beginning of the *Guide*, however, as we have already mentioned before gives the reader the opposite impression. It is there in 1.1 with its clearly Aristotelian anthropology in which man is said to be made in the image and likeness of God insofar as he has an intellect, followed by the chillingly intellectualist account of the Garden of Eden in 1.2, that we receive the animus and spirit of the *Guide* as a whole. Never before in the history of the Jewish tradition has any author called for such a profound demotion of morality. If the Law has as its foremost aim the moral formation of the Jewish people, Maimonides is here to make room for emphasis on the intellect. Otherwise, it would be difficult to explain the shocking suggestion that Adam was intellectually perfect before eating of the fruit of the tree of knowledge of good and evil and was thereafter misled into an obsession with moral matters. That Maimonides is not an immoralist can easily be shown by the sheer volume of the writing he devoted to halakhic matters. His most obvious concern must be for the well-being of the Jewish people. Yet he also understood that because he knew better than anyone else that human perfection is not moral perfection, that it must be his job, for better or worse, to serve the well-being of that one in ten thousand, whom he

[18] Also see my "Maimonidean Ethics Revisited: Development and Asceticism in Maimonides?" *Journal of Jewish Thought and Philosophy* 12 (2003) 3: 33–62.

alludes to on more than one occasion. These two poles serving the greatest good of the whole of society together with the greatest good of the most perfectible part of society is something that has rarely been attempted with comparable success in the history of human endeavor. Unfortunately, some interpreters fail to take adequate stock of the tensions between these goods—and rush to suggest that Maimonides failed because his *Mishneh Torah* did not simply displace the Talmud. Could Maimonides really have imagined such a sea change in a community so steeped in tradition? Or did he instead intend with a work like the *Mishneh Torah* to provide a means of summarizing the Talmud for a few and a lens for interpreting the Talmud for the rest?[19]

Leo Strauss has done more in a few pages of his "Literary Character of the *Guide for the Perplexed*" to reveal the limits of Maimonides's moralism in the *Guide* than any other interpreter. And this he does merely in the interest of providing an example of how Maimonides uses silence, or as he says, "an omission of something which only the learned, or the learned who are able to understand on their own, would miss."[20] His example is Maimonides's repeated reference to Aristotle on the sense of touch, that is, that it is a shame or disgrace to us. The original Greek phrase is *doxeien an dikaiōs (hē aphē) eponeidistos einai.*[21] As Strauss explains, when Maimonides references this phrase he omits the parenthetical remark, which amounts to "it is said" or "they say," that indicates this is an *endoxon*—a generally accepted opinion. By so omitting this

---

[19] *Guide* introduction to part 1, p. 16; 1.34, 75; and 3.34, 534. Compare this view with Aviezer Ravitzky, "Maimonides: Esotericism and Educational Philosophy," in *The Cambridge Companion to Maimonides*, Kenneth Seeskin, ed. (New York: Cambridge University Press, 2005), 300-323; also cf. Isadore Twersky, *Introduction to the Code of Maimonides* (Mishneh Torah), (New Haven: Yale University Press, 1980), chap. 6, esp. 538.

[20] "Literary Character of the *Guide for the Perplexed*" in *Persecution* (Chicago: University of Chicago Press, 1980), 75.

[21] EN 1118b2.

qualification, Maimonides turns it into a moralizing trope on the part of Aristotle. Or as Strauss puts it, Maimonides's "citation from Aristotle actually reflected popular rather than philosophic opinion."[22] Although Strauss does not explain further, we believe that Maimonides here attributes to Aristotle what he takes to be the upshot of the biblical view regarding the sense of touch. As Strauss notes, this phrase about Aristotle on the sense of touch recurs four times in four different chapters of the *Guide*, indicating that it is "something like a *leitmotif*."[23]

Although it would be useful to consider this passage in all four contexts, we will have to limit ourselves to Maimonides's treatment of it in 3.8 with an eye to our theme about matter and especially privation. This will lead us eventually to Maimonides's discussion of the human faculties involved in action in *Eight Chapters*. Even before looking more closely at these passages, we need to consider what, according to Strauss, is a retort to this *leitmotif*, namely, Maimonides's clear pronouncements that no sense is any more shameful than any other. This he states forcefully in 1.46 and 1.47, as Strauss notes.[24] In 1.46, Maimonides insists, "In truth, the status of all the organs is the same" (101), and in 1.47, he clarifies, "Now the status of all five senses—with regard to the fact that He, may He be exalted, is high above them—is one and the same....For the status of the apprehension of all of them is one and the same" (104). The opening of 1.47 points to the reason that the senses of taste and touch are not ascribed to God in the "books of the prophets," namely, because the Bible has avoided ascribing to God "anything that the multitude imagine to be a deficiency" (104). It almost goes without saying that the imagination of the multitude is not a good

---

22 PAW, 75.

23 PAW, 75n104, citing 2.36, 371; 2.40, 384; 3.8, 432 and 435 (Strauss refers to this fifth time only with "cf." or "compare" perhaps because no reference is made in this instance to Aristotle); and 3.49, 608.

24 PAW, 76n106.

ultimate moral guide. Whatever doubts interpreters might have of Strauss's interpretation of the relevant passage from Aristotle—for example, that Maimonides might have had access to a version of Aristotle's Ethics that did not retain in Arabic the remark about "they say"—this passage seems to provide strong confirmation of Strauss's interpretation that the supposed pronouncement of Aristotle on the sense of touch is far from philosophic.

Let us turn now to take a closer look at 3.8—not only the references to the *leitmotif* about touch—but especially to distinguish further the differences between the biblical and philosophic views of matter and privation. The movement of the chapter as a whole is *from* a harsher treatment of matter which reaches a peak of sorts at the first reference to the sense of touch and Aristotle's supposed view of it *to* a milder and more circumspect treatment framed by the second reference to the shame associated with the sense of touch. The chapter as a whole concludes with one of the most humorous moments in the *Guide* in which Maimonides underscores the asceticism of the Bible by noting what words for sexual and excretory organs, their actions, and emissions are wholly absent from it, giving one of the clearest indicators in the *Guide* as a whole what is the source of the asceticism that appears periodically in this book.

Although the chapter opens by linking all generation and corruption of bodies to their matter, in contrast to the permanence associated with form, Maimonides quickly mentions in passing without further clarification that "the nature and true reality of matter are such that it never ceases to be joined to privation" (431). This with an eye to reminding us that matter acts like a married harlot, constantly taking on one form to put on another. From that point forward until roughly the middle of the chapter, the finger points squarely at matter. A few sentences later in the same English paragraph, after repeating the taking on and putting off motif, Maimonides writes, "It has become clear that all passing-away and corruption or deficiency are due solely to matter." The link between privation and form that was so crucial in part 1's account of particularized privation is here just a memory. Everything good and noble in humankind such as our ability to think and control our passions are linked to our form, and everything bad and base such as our desires for food, drink, sex, and our tendency toward anger are linked to matter. Eventually, Maimonides goes so far as to speak of the "impulses of matter (*dawāʿī al-māda*)" as if our flesh were wholly responsible for impelling us "toward the dirt and the generally admitted shame (*ʿāriḥā al-mashḥūr*) inherent in matter." One can hardly imagine an account more redolent of the Garden of Eden and the play on the name of our father, Adam, whose name of course also means "dirt."[25] In the spirit of Genesis 3:19, we are borne of dirt or dust or the earth and to dirt shall we return. The strong link to matter is a biblical trope. Maimonides modulates this trope somewhat by noting there are different human types who act differently in relation to "the dirt"—some revel in it, others are properly ashamed of it. Near the peak of his apparent vituperation, the Aristotle trope appears. The fitting response to the dirt is to limit one's partaking of it to "only that which is indispensable." The human end is not these things but rather the contemplation of the Account of the Chariot. (Given the close proximity of this chapter to the mystifying presentation of the biblical Account of the Chariot in 3.1 through 7, one gets a better sense of why this most moralistic of chapters is placed where it has been.) Despite the intensity of Maimonides's moral vituperation, it is all used here toward the end of intellectual perfection. Even when Maimonides runs contrary to the intense demotion of moral virtue in the opening of the *Guide*, he uses biblical moralizing with an eye to such intellectual perfection.

---

[25] Although the word Maimonides uses for "the dirt" here is *qaḍāra*, which can also mean uncleanness or filth, the resonance of all these words—Adam, dirt or dust or earth—and even "privation" (*ʿadam*) is at least worth mentioning. Of course, the first letter of Adam and dust is *aleph* and the first letter of the word for privation is *ʿayin*.

After citing a series of proof texts from Isaiah, Genesis (3:16 rather than 18), Jeremiah, and Proverbs, confirming the biblical animus against the flesh, Maimonides sums it all up: "Also the commandments and prohibitions of the Law are only (*innamā*) intended to quell all the impulses of matter."

An almost unnoticeable moderation of the vituperation in 3.8 comes when Maimonides focuses on "drinking" among the traditional triumvirate of food, drink, and sex. Rather than focus as the conclusion of the chapter will on sex (which he anticipates on this same page [434] by noting the animus against copulation in our "wise and pure Law"), Maimonides focuses on drink as intoxicating drink. Here, Maimonides is able to distinguish the need to retain intellectual virtue from the general animus of the chapter in focusing on moral virtue or moral asceticism. While the "disapproval of the uncovering of the private parts" is merely "a generally accepted opinion," getting drunk is wholly unnecessary and more importantly "is an act committed by a bad man in virtue of his free choice…[which is] shunned by the intellect."[26] Here we see hints of the nuance we associate with factoring privation into the equation above and beyond mere matter and form. A tiny toehold for that was given at the beginning of the chapter, though Maimonides does not here connect the dots. In the next section of this chapter, we will take a closer look at 3.8 in context. For now, we must turn for some guidance to *Eight Chapters*, chap. 2.[27]

After presenting an Aristotelian account of the faculties of the soul in chapter 1, Maimonides turns in chapter 2 to explore what causes disobedience in the soul. In this chapter, he presents two subtly different accounts of the causes of disobedience. The first refers to what things in the soul are held liable for obedience and

---

[26] Also see my discussion of this passage in *Maimonides and Spinoza*, 173–74.

[27] The following discussion expands on insights captured in my "Maimonidean Ethics Revisited," pp. 49–50.

disobedience of the Law. They are, using the Aristotelian terminology set forth in chapter 1, "the sentient part and the appetitive part." The "nutritive or imaginative parts" are not held responsible for obedience or disobedience. The second account explains the locus of "the moral virtues," returning to Aristotelian parlance. They are found "only in the appetitive part" because the "sentient part" is merely the "servant of the appetitive part." Similarly to the view of the Law, the nutritive and imaginative parts are not considered responsible for virtue and vice. The clear and obvious difference between the view of the Law and the philosophic view is that the former makes the sentient part responsible while the latter does not. Although the sense of touch is only one sense among the usual five, it seems obvious that this subtle distinction between the revealed and the philosophic views regarding action or obedience and disobedience to the law or morality is essential to the Law—namely, pointing the finger at matter by way of touch—which the philosopher does not do. It also seems likely that there is a direct connection between the Law's emphasis on the flesh or dust or matter and the philosophic emphasis on appetite. As we know from Socrates, perhaps the most important appetite, *erōs*, is less a god to be celebrated than a lacking for or of something. In this sense, it is not too far a stretch to say that philosophy connects human action with privation. As we will see when we take a closer look in the next section of this chapter at *Guide* 3.8 through 10, especially 3.10 Maimonides moves in 3.8 from a biblical emphasis on matter to a philosophic emphasis on privation.

For now, it is worth surveying *Guide* 3.33 as well as 3.36 through 49 for a few key moments that make it clear that the asceticism of the *Guide* is ultimately that of the Bible. One way of thinking of 3.33 is as a gateway to the following treatment of the Law, which starts with a summary in 3.35. The juxtaposition of 3.33 with 3.34 is startling. If 3.33 encapsulates the Law, 3.34 encapsulates philosophy.

Leaving that aside, 3.33 anticipates the central focus of 3.36 through 49. Two times in this chapter, Maimonides encapsulates the animus of the Law: "To the totality of purposes of the perfect Law there belong the abandonment, depreciation, and restraint of desires in so far as possible, so that they should be satisfied only in so far as this is necessary." True, he goes on, over the course of chapter, not only to reiterate this point about the Law but also to note that when human beings follow their base appetites "the longing for speculation is abolished" and other more obvious harms result (532). Maimonides concludes the chapter by acknowledging that the Law appears at times to emphasize bodily cleanliness, but he underscores that its primary concern is with the "purification of actions and the purification of the heart" (533). Stated differently, one might mistakenly imagine that outward appearances are all that count; however, "this is not the purpose of the Law, for the first purpose is to restrain desire." This sums up the matter nicely.

When we turn then to 3.36 through 49, we turn to a very complex account of an entire tradition of Law. Here, we merely acknowledge the complexity of the topics treated and point to the most useful work on the subject of which we are aware that has compared this division of the Law into fourteen parts in the *Guide* with similar accounts of a division of the Law into the same number of parts (14) though into different parts in the *Mishneh Torah* itself and in the *Book of Commandments*.[28] Near the end of this fourteen chapter section of the *Guide* (3.36–49), Maimonides encapsulates the Law in the following formulation reminiscent of what we have just considered in 3.33: because God calls on you to sanctify yourselves to be holy as God is holy, "for this reason, transgression of the *commandments* is called *uncleanness*. This expression is used with regard to the mothers and roots of the *commandments*, namely, [the

[28] Lawrence V. Berman, "The Structure of the Commandments," in *Studies in Jewish Religious and Intellectual History*, S. Stein and R. Loewe, eds. (Tuscaloosa, AL: University of Alabama Press, 1979), 51–66.

*commandments* concerning] *idolatry*, *incest*, and *shedding of blood*" (3.47, 595). It is not by chance that these three things, identified as the mothers and roots of the commandments are earlier identified as *the* things for which the death penalty is sought (3.41, 562). The ultimate status of these laws is borne out by the fact that 3.41 is devoted to a discussion of what appears in the last book of Maimonides's *Mishneh Torah*. Focusing, however, on the matter of desire, Maimonides encapsulates in a surprising formulation the ultimate character of the incest prohibition. Prohibited sexual relations have an unusual importance in Jewish law, though their importance is emblematic of Judaism's heavy emphasis on both respect for the old (and thus the Law) and an enormous emphasis on the atomic family. It seems to me that in this connection one sentence encapsulates the centrality of restraining desire, announced in 3.33, "Not all *incestuous and adulterous sexual intercourse* is punished by *death by court of law*; only such as is easy to engage in or most shameful or has the strongest attraction." Far from being squeamish, Maimonides is more than capable of confronting the spirit of the Law. The Law punishes severely not only great crimes but also crimes that are liable to be easy or likely to be committed if the gravest punishments aren't established. One more thing needs to be added. The closest to an adjustment of this emphasis appears at the end of this section in 3.49. I refer to Maimonides's appeal to Aristotle's Ethics on the importance of friendship. He goes on to state that "lov[ing] one another, help[ing] one another, and hav[ing] pity on one another …the attainment of these things is the greatest purpose of the Law" (3.49, 601–2). He immediately pivots to infer: "Hence *harlots* are prohibited." The prohibition of harlots is the flipside of the prohibition of forbidden sexual relations. Both relate to the obvious matter of knowing who is whose father and mother, and who is whose son or daughter. In other words, who will inherit what from whom? And to whom is obedience due? Unless these things are known, one can expect such a society, which places respect for what is old at its center, to descend into disorder and disunity. Biblical asceticism is driven less by a desire for individual moral perfection than for communal well-being.

## Re-thinking the Relation between Matter and Privation: 3.8 through 10

Although we have just devoted considerable attention to 3.8, now that we have put matter and privation into some perspective in morality, it is important to begin to turn to the focus of the rest of this book, namely, the important role of privation in more theoretical terms. In the fourth section of this chapter, we will look at "impediment" and its theoretical role in creation, prophecy, and providence. For now, though, we need to slow down to take a much closer look at another cluster of chapters in the *Guide*.

We will not repeat our look at 3.8. We will, however, tie 3.8 by way of 3.9 to 3.10 to bring out the shift we have already anticipated. 3.10 represents a shift away from the emphasis in 3.8 on matter. 3.9 both echoes the spirit of 3.8 and offers a link to the new approach in 3.10. Part three, chapter nine opens with the following: "Matter is a strong veil preventing the apprehension of that which is separate from matter as it truly is. It does this even if it is the noblest and purest matter, I mean to say even if it is the matter of the heavenly spheres. All the more is this true of the dark and turbid matter that is ours." Here we see already a pivot away from morality toward intellectual perfection. However, the tone is not only essentially the same as what we saw in 3.8, but also the choice of the word "veil" (*ḥijāb*) resonates with other discussions of impediments to intellectual perfection. We refer to *Guide* 3.51 where Maimonides has a sudden insight, when someone who has the right nature and has received the right education does not receive divine intellectual overflow as it should, that is due to a "veil" in them resulting from their failure to focus continuously on God. We will return to this later in our chapter on providence (3.51, 625–26). For now we turn briefly to consider another "veiling" moment, which marks a shift from the moral to the intellectual, namely, *Eight Chapters*, chap. 7. Like *Guide* 3.9, almost the first word of the chapter is the "veils" that interpose themselves between prophets and God. To make a somewhat complex story simple, according to Maimonides, "vices are veils." Although he acknowledges as he did earlier in EC, chapter 4 that no one possesses all the moral virtues, here he singles out "irascibility" or "anger" as one of the vices that "prevent[s] prophecy entirely." And although we know from EC, chapter 4, as well as from *Guide* 2.38 (376–77) and 2.45, first degree (397), that it was precisely this vice that Moses suffered from,[29] Maimonides engages in the sort of hyperbole about Moses we find elsewhere here near the end of EC, chap. 7: he claims that no prophet was ever closer to God. Despite the troubling claims about anger, Maimonides here claims that only one veil existed between Moses and God, that is, the lowliness of the "unseparated human intellect"—in a rare moment of apparent promotion of separation from the body in death.

Leaving aside the contradictory accounts of Moses, what interests us here is the way that Maimonides uses veils to refer to vices or moral failings but is interested less in their moral impact than in their intellectual impact. Veils impede overflow to the intellect. Maimonides's use of this language of veiling both in the *Guide* and EC likely has its origin in the veil hadith, which provided a great deal of fodder for Islamic mysticism.[30] I do not know whether Maimonides's use of this image for straddling the moral and intellectual realms has been remarked on. Having mentioned the veils, Maimonides goes on to reference the more familiar biblical images of God's being hidden from us by a "heavy cloud, or by darkness or by an enveloping cloud" (3.9, 437). This chapter like 3.15 is crucial for interpreters who wish to claim that Maimonides is clear about the

[29] *Ethical Writings*, pp. 73–74.

[30] See al-Ghazālī, *The Niche of Lights*, David Buchman, trans. and ed. (Provo, UT: Brigham Young University Press, 1998), 44.

limits of our knowledge. It includes such notable statements as that the talk of "*a thick cloud*" in the Bible "draws attention to the fact that the apprehension of His true reality is impossible for us because of the dark matter that encompasses us and not Him, may He be exalted; for He, may He be exalted, is not a body." And he concludes the chapter by alluding to all the smoke and impediments to seeing God that are presented with reference to the theophany at Sinai, despite the fact that from God overflows "no darkness, but perpetual, dazzling light." In brief, 3.9 is one of the clearest examples of the identification of the impediment or hindrance or veil between us and God as matter itself. As we turn to 3.10, Maimonides will shift his explanation of such hindrances.

We recall that Maimonides opens 3.10 with the contrast between the Mutakallimun's view that privation is absolute (that is, void) with the philosophic view that privation is a contrary of form. The privation of a habitus is not thing-like, rather it is a lack of something. One of the consequences of the Mutakallimun's view is that they also reify things like death. Death is not viewed as the lack or an absence of life but as a reality that God must make anew at every moment. Much as Maimonides identifies faulty views in Judaism about providence by referring the reader to the mistaken views of the Ashʿarite *kalām* (3.17), comparison with 3.9 suggests that Maimonides is drawing a similar parallel here. It is the tendency to absolutize or reify privation that leads to the view that matter is a veil. Despite or perhaps because of the pretty Sufi resonance of this claim that matter is a veil, Maimonides ultimately disagrees with the view espoused in 3.9. In 3.10, after arguing against the absolutization of privation, Maimonides acknowledges biblical passages that seem to make God an agent of evil—most notably the passage from Isaiah that God is He "who forms the light and creates darkness, who makes peace and creates evil" (Isa. 45:7).[31] By tying the Hebrew

[31] Cf. Thomas Aquinas, *Summa theologiae*, prima pars, q. 49, a. 2.

biblical term "creation (*bara*)" to privation, Maimonides insinuates that to say God creates darkness or evil or any other privation is not to say that he "makes (*oseh*)" them. It almost goes without saying that the uses of "form," "creation," and "make" in this passage were not likely originally intended to indicate differing activities with any sense of philosophic precision.[32] As we recently noted, by the end of 3.10, God is presented as the cause only of good. Maimonides here uses a critique of the Mutakallimun to put as much distance between his view and the idea that God causes evil as possible.[33] At this point, though, we are less interested in what this tells us about God than what it reveals about privation.

There are two things that Maimonides declares about privation in 3.10 that require additional consideration to clarify further the character of privation. After insinuating his rejection of the *kalām* notion that "privations are…existent things," Maimonides goes on to claim, "It behooves us to let you know our opinion about this, according to what is required by philosophic speculation. Now you know already that what removes an impediment (*ʿāʾiq*) of motion is, from a certain point of view, the mover" (438). And then roughly a page later, he claims, "It has thus become clear to you that, according

[32] Despite that creation of the world (that is, being or beings) out of absolute nonexistence (2.17, 296) would appear to be a unique kind of creating and making, when it comes to privation (cf. absolute nonexistence) it is unclear what sense it makes to speak of a distinctive activity of creating. All this should be compared with Maimonides's casualness in the use of create vs. make in 1.68 and 69 as well as in 1.74, fifth method.

[33] Cf. Harry Blumberg's brief but insightful treatment of Maimonides on evil or privation in his "Theories of Evil in Medieval Jewish Philosophy," *Hebrew Union College Annual* 43 (1972): 149–68, esp. 152–53 with the underappreciation of Maimonides's appeal to privation in mounting his arguments about providence in Moshe Halbertal, *Maimonides: Life and Thought*, trans. J. Linsider (Princeton: Princeton University Press, 2014), p. 332, as cited in Robyn Ashworth-Steen, "How Satisfactory Is Maimonides' Solution to the Problem of Evil," *European Judaism: A Journal for the New Europe* 50 (2017) 1: 113–122, esp. 114n7.

to every opinion, the act of an agent can in no way be connected with a privation; the agent can only be said to have produced the privation by accident, as we have explained." We linger over these passages because they will resonate throughout the rest of our inquiries into privation, specifically our next section and following chapters on "impediment." In the first passage, Maimonides is acknowledging that when a being removes an impediment it is in a sense the mover. He goes on to specify this abstract suggestion by reference to producing a privation by removing a certain habitus. And the example he gives of this is of "one who destroys sight...[as having] made blindness...even though...blindness [as a] privation[]...do[es] not need an agent." Obviously, the second passage claiming that an agent cannot be connected with privation is the conclusion drawn from this claim regarding acting as a mover. An agent that produces a privation can only do so "by accident." We linger over this because the indicators we receive in the *Guide* that God wills things in connection with creation, prophecy, and providence is His being said to impede or prevent them. For a being, who is the cause only of good, this is strange from every angle: (1) How can the only indication that God acts be this accidental form of acting? (2) Indeed, does it make sense to think of any action of God as affecting something merely accidentally? (3) Why would a being who causes only good be responsible, for example, for depriving the prophet with the fitting nature and education of the great good of prophecy?

## Toward Impediment as the Leading Example of Privation

Pines renders two Arabic terms, sometimes within the same paragraph—namely, *ʿāʾiq* and *māniʿ*—as "impediment," "obstacle," and "hindrance" as well as in verbal settings, usually in the passive, as "prevented."[34] These are hardly technical terms. The common thread running through them is, of course, privation. Given that the closing three chapters of this book will concern "impediment" in relation to creation, prophecy, and providence, one might have thought that the following chapters would follow the order of their appearance in the *Guide*. The order of the *Guide* regarding these three greatest themes follows the order typical in works of Jewish *kalām*. It almost goes without saying that the *Guide* is anything but a typical work of such *kalām*.[35] That order is roughly speaking genetic, that is, creation comes temporally before all else. Another option would have been to treat providence first. The rationale for that would have been that in a sense both creation and prophecy are examples of God's providence.[36] The reason, however, we have decided to treat prophecy first is that it is the one setting among the three in which "impediment" or "prevention" is most obviously a *motif*. In other words, we are following the order that Aristotle refers to as what is "first for us." We will work from the most obvious to the most challenging and least obvious: from prophecy to providence and finally to creation.

Here we will merely anticipate very briefly where we are headed in the next three chapters. Although "impediment" or "privation" stands out most clearly in the case of prophecy, the sort of

---

[34] As we will see when we turn to providence in chapter 6, he also uses, as we already saw in passing, "impediment" to render the more powerfully metaphorical "veil" in 3.51. I believe that Pines's translation decision reflected his sense that this unusual use of veil was in the context a follow up to prior discussions of "impediment."

[35] Leo Strauss, "The Place of the Doctrine of Providence according to Maimonides," *Review of Metaphysics* 57 (2004): 537–49.

[36] That providence has priority matches what Seth Benardete has identified, at least in connection with Plato, as the "eidetic" order. At the risk of offending some, one might even call providence ontologically prior to creation and prophecy. This could be considered anathema by some because of the perceived (not merely temporal) priority of creation.

"impediment" involved is in some respects less direct. In the cases of providence and creation, the possibility arises that some impediment exists between God and the recipient. The impediment involved in prophecy is less direct because there is no suggestion that God is impeded. Rather, God is the one putting up the hindrance or obstacle. As has already been hinted, the more one thinks about it the less plausible it becomes that God should impede, especially in the case of a prophet who according to philosophy it is necessary or at least only natural that he should become a prophet. When we turn to providence, we will discover that there is a sense in which Maimonides views the case as almost wholly analogous to prophecy. After all, they are both the result of "overflow" from God to the prophet or recipient of providence, in accordance with the capacity of the receiver and in harmony with the detailed psychological description of prophecy in 2.36. Furthermore, that overflow appears to be due solely to the intellectual perfection of the recipient. Whether God could impede someone from receiving His overflow, although divined by many readers, does not seem to be seriously entertained by Maimonides. Instead, the only possibility seriously considered is that lack of overflow to a worthy recipient is due solely to the recipient having lapsed in the contemplation of God (3.51). If in the case of prophecy we move from the consideration of a recipient whom God has somehow impeded to providence in which case only the recipient could impede overflow, then when we finally turn to creation, here, in the context in which "impediment" appears most frequently, we are confronted by the suggestion that God could be impeded. Of course, we know from more than one place in the *Guide* (esp. 1.68) that such an idea is dubious. Impediment comes up in arguments made against the revealed position. Will is used as the answer to the suggestion that God could be impeded. These alternatives "will" and "impediment," however, may not be as different as they appear at first.

# CHAPTER 5

# PROPHECY, GOD'S WILL, AND IMPEDIMENTS

Among creation, prophecy, and providence, prophecy displays the role of impediment or obstacle or prevention most obviously. It is for this reason that we begin these three chapters with the case of prophecy. At the same time, prophecy does not raise the possibility that God's will should be impeded, which appears at least initially to be a more likely possibility in the case of creation and providence. Rather, it is God's will that does the impeding. In light of chapter 4, and especially our discussion of 3.10, this cannot but appear strange indeed. Yet, why Maimonides has recourse to impediment as the sole indicator of the difference between the philosophic opinion and the "opinion of our Law and the foundation of our doctrine" seems relatively obvious: to make the distinctive feature of the revealed view that God can will whom He wishes to be a prophet, regardless of their nature and education, is to fall back to the first view, identified with that of the ignoramuses among the Pagans and some of the multitude among the Jews. This view is the miraculous view. As we already saw in chapter 1, Maimonides studiously avoids leaving real room for miracles, at least after the six days of creation. Although resorting to the prevention or impediment of an action appears to be Maimonides's only option, it is worth underscoring that the prevention of an action isn't properly speaking an action. We have already grazed this topic lightly in our previous consideration of 3.10; however, we will return here to take an even closer look.

Since prophecy is the second of the three great themes of the *Guide*, we will begin our inquiry into prophecy and its relation to impediments with a consideration of the debate regarding what W.

Z. Harvey has called the "cosmogony-prophetology puzzle." Near the opening of *Guide* 2.32, Maimonides notes the parallel at least in the number of opinions on creation and prophecy. This link between creation and prophecy has exercised interpreters greatly since almost the moment Maimonides finished the *Guide.* Since our purpose is to clarify why impediment keeps popping up in Maimonides's treatment of all three of these greatest Jewish themes, we believe it would be helpful to consider the contemporary debate at least about how creation and prophecy are linked or related. Harvey's "A Third Approach to the Cosmogony-Prophetology Puzzle" is the third in a series of articles by Lawrence Kaplan, Herbert Davidson, and Harvey on the puzzle of these two sets of three. When we consider this scholarly debate, it will become apparent that at least these three scholars do not consider the divide between eternity and creation to be emblematic of the divide between philosophy and revelation. Indeed, they deny that any such divide exists. Foremost among their reasons is the surprising view that the biblical account of creation and Plato's account of "creation" are for all intents and purposes equivalent. We will question this view not only in this chapter, but perhaps especially in chapter 7, the chapter on creation.

After this introduction to the scholarly debate, we will digress very briefly to consider the curious question: whom would God impede in preventing prophecy? It is necessary to at least consider the only alternative to the prophet himself, namely, the Active Intellect. Although we know ultimately that Maimonides will deny the AI can be impeded (in 2.18), it is still worth considering however briefly this strange question that Maimonides does nothing to raise.

In the third section, we will consider the impediment of prophecy by looking closely at the uses of the relevant key terms in chapters other than 2.32, namely, 2.36 and 2.39, so that we might return later in the chapter to a careful consideration of 2.32. *Guide* 2.36 and 2.39 reveal things not only about the psychology of prophecy in general but also about perhaps the most special case of impediment, that of Moses. Despite Maimonides's frequent denials that he will talk about Moses, he proves incapable of sticking by his denials.

In the fourth section, we will turn to 2.32 to consider it in some detail and in relation to the *Letter on Astrology*. This brief but potent letter casts additional light on the significance of the focus on impediments, largely by dwelling on the largest example of God's impeding prophecy, namely, the *Galut* or Exile. That the Exile figures prominently in Maimonides's account is already evident from the references to impediment or prevention of prophecy in the *Guide*. Although in 2.32 Maimonides clearly states that God's will prevents or impedes the reception of prophecy in the third opinion on prophecy, it is ultimately quite difficult to see how this could fit with his ultimate insistence in 3.10 that "the true reality of the act of God in its entirety is the good, for the good is being" (440).

## The Creation-Prophetology Puzzle Expanded

Although W. Z. Harvey refers to the "cosmogony-prophetology puzzle," for the sake of comprehensiveness, I will refer to the "creation-prophetology" puzzle because, in keeping with the *kalām* character of the *Guide,* its three great themes are creation, prophecy, and providence. Ultimately, I will argue that though Maimonides explicitly links his discussions of creation and prophecy, he intends the reader also to connect these two themes to providence. While there appear to be three opinions on creation and prophecy, but innumerable opinions on providence, that appearance is deceiving. One of the keys to this whole puzzle is that on all three of these great themes ultimately there are only two opinions, flowing from the basic opposition between creation and eternity or revelation and philosophy. Why we argue this in connection with providence will have to wait until chapter 6. In the meantime, we will begin to join the argument by focusing on a scholarly debate that reveals that many scholars do not recognize the depth of the opposition between creation and eternity, at least in the thought of Maimonides. In the debate about the creation-prophetology puzzle that misunderstanding has contributed mightily to general confusion about how to approach this puzzle. Connected to misunderstandings of the place of Plato in the *Guide* is the less surprising suggestion that the eternity-creation divide can be finessed by solutions such as so-called eternal creation.

When Maimonides first sets forth his account of the three opinions on creation in 2.13, he begins by opposing the account of creation with the view of the philosophers. He refers to the opinion of the latter as the second opinion. Only after explaining the implications of the denial of creation out of nothing, does he turn to consider the case of Plato's opinion. In a long paragraph in Pines's translation (283), Maimonides sets forth all the most important claims about the philosophic view, namely, that nothing comes from nothing is the shared opinion, that the impossible has a fixed nature, and God's inability to alter what is impossible does not detract from his power. When he adds Plato's view, he includes this as part of the "second opinion."[1] The importance of these statements has often been neglected because they seem to be upended in 2.25. Through careful attention to exactly what Maimonides writes, I believe that other scholars have exaggerated what Maimonides could have meant, in part as a result of backreading from subsequent thinkers such as Moses Narboni and Hasdai Crescas.

At this point, let us bring into the discussion Lawrence Kaplan, Herbert Davidson, and Warren Zev Harvey.[2] Kaplan published a

---

[1] See Munk-Joel on 28a, line 10 and 28b line 8. Although Maimonides's comments about impossible things is often pointed to as crucial for understanding Aristotle's view of the possible, necessary, and impossible, he seems here to be attributing the very same view to Plato.

[2] Lawrence Kaplan, "Maimonides on the Miraculous Element in Prophecy," *Harvard Theological Review* 70 (1977) 3–4: 233–256. Herbert Davidson, "Maimonides' Secret Position on Creation," in *Studies in Medieval Jewish Literature and History,* Isadore Twersky, ed. (Cambridge: Harvard University Press, 1979), 16–40. W. Z. Harvey, "A Third Approach to Maimonides' Cosmogony-Prophetology Puzzle," originally in HTR 74 (1981): 287–301;

quite comprehensive and immensely useful exploration of what Harvey dubs the "cosmogony-prophetology puzzle" first in 1977. Even more useful than his own argument is his survey of the relevant literature among the medieval commentators on the creation-prophetology puzzle, especially the commentaries of Ibn Kaspi, Shem Tob (or Shem Tov Ibn Falaquera), Efodi (that is, Profiat Duran), and Abravanel. Ultimately, he defends a view first fully formulated after these commentators by the Polish scholar Mordecai Jaffe (or Yoffe),[3] which comes to be shared by Yosef Kafiḥ. With all this legwork under him, Kaplan sets the stage for Harvey who goes on to enumerate three opinions: Kaplan's (Jaffe's descending from Shem Tob and Efodi), Davidson's (descending from Abravanel), and his own. Stating the view on creation or cosmogony first and the view on prophecy second, the following is Harvey's recapitulation of the affiliations of views on creation with views on prophecy.[4] We will spell out Harvey's use merely of numbers, translating his numbers in the following ways. The three views on creation/eternity will be referred to as 1. Creation, 2. Plato's view on creation, 3. Aristotle's view on eternity. And the three views on prophecy will be referred to as 1. The ignoramuses' view of prophecy, 2. The philosophic view of prophecy, and 3. Our Law with prevention (that is, the same as the philosophic view with the caveat that God can will to prevent prophecy).

*Kaplan – 1:3, 2:1, 3:2 – that is, creation : our Law with prevention; Plato's view on creation : the ignoramuses' view of prophecy; Aristotle's view on eternity : the philosophic view of prophecy*

reprinted in *Maimonides: A Collection of Critical Essays*, Joseph Buijs, ed. (Notre Dame, IN: University of Notre Dame Press, 1990), 71–88.

[3] Whose dates were 1530–1612 CE.

[4] See W. Z. Harvey, "A Third Approach to Maimonides' Cosmogony-Prophetology Puzzle," 72.

*Davidson – 1:1, 2:3, 3:2 – that is, creation : the ignoramuses' view; Plato's view on creation : our Law with prevention; Aristotle's view on eternity : the philosophic view of prophecy*

*Harvey – 1:1, 2:2, 3:3 – that is, creation : ignoramuses' view; Plato's view on creation : the philosophic view of prophecy; Aristotle's view on eternity : our Law with prevention*

Although Kaplan is pretty scrupulous in quoting the relevant passages of Maimonides's accounts of the three opinions on creation in 2.13 and on prophecy in 2.32 from the Pines translation, he does not attend to the differences between 2.13 and 2.25.[5] In contrast, Herbert Davidson does attend to some but not all the differences. Davidson's attention to detail is significantly greater than Harvey, who treats the various opinions as so well worked over—which I grant is reasonable given the amount of commentators' ink spilled over especially Maimonides's account of the third opinion on prophecy—that he need pay little attention to the details. Given that his is the third piece in not so many years stating a somewhat but not hugely different position, he seems to want to avoid repeating any more than is absolutely necessary. The obvious difference between the presentation in 2.13 and in 2.25 is that, in the former presentation, Maimonides underlines the fact that the differences between Plato's view and Aristotle's view are irrelevant, while, in the latter presentation, he seems to make something out of the differences. Davidson underscores the denial of differences in 2.13 between the two views by referring the reader to the following passage, which Pines renders as, "It is useless for us to wish to prove as true [the opinion of Plato, because]…there is no difference between those who believe that heaven must of necessity be generated from a thing and pass away into a thing or the belief of Aristotle who believed

[5] See Kaplan, "Maimonides on the Miraculous Element in Prophecy," 233–35.

that it is not subject to generation and corruption."[6] Davidson describes this, Maimonides's first statement, as "strange," and he goes on to note that in 2.25, Maimonides changes his tune. For Davidson, this is worth noting since he has argued so often that Maimonides's contradictions are inconsequential or merely the result of mistakes. We should not be surprised to see Davidson then go on to argue that the first statement in 2.13 is sloppy and wrong and the second statement in 2.25 is correct and a revision based on things learned from 2.13 through 24. To sum up the second statement in 2.25, according to Davidson, is tantamount to claiming that there is little or no significant difference between the Platonic view and that of the Bible. In other words, creation out of pre-existing matter is equivalent to creation ex nihilo for all intents and purposes. They are effectively equivalent because, according to Davidson, "After completing his entire discussion of creation [2.13 to 2.24], after weighing the diverse arguments for and against the scriptural and Aristotelian opinions, and after determining that the scriptural opinion is philosophically more plausible, Maimonides adds a sort of epilogue. There he acknowledges that in its theological implications the Platonic opinion is as fully acceptable as the scriptural opinion. The Platonic opinion, unlike the Aristotelian opinion does not destroy 'the foundations of the Law'; it is wholly compatible with revelation, miracles, and providence." I do not exaggerate when I say that here Davidson seems to have overread one sentence in 2.25, while ignoring not only 2.13 but especially the greater context in 2.25. The relevant sentence from 2.25 out of which Davidson culls so much is the following, according to Pines's translation: "If, however, one believed eternity according to the second opinion we have explained – which is the opinion of Plato—according to which the heavens too are subject to generation and corruption, this

[6] Davidson, "Maimonides' Secret Position on Creation," 20–21n27. Davidson's translation differs only slightly from Pines's.

opinion would not destroy the foundations of the Law (*qawāʿid al-shariʿa*) and would be followed not by the lie being given to miracles (*al-muʿjiz*), but by their becoming admissible." Let us begin with the obvious: Maimonides does not say that Plato's view is compatible with revelation, providence as the Bible sees it, or even *all* the miracles. In contrast, he goes on to state in the next paragraph,

> Know that with a belief in the creation of the world in time (*ḥudūth*), all the miracles (*al-muʿjizāt kulluha*) become possible and the Law becomes possible, and all questions that may be asked on this subject vanish. Thus it might be said: Why did God give prophetic revelation to this one and not to that? Why did God give this Law to this particular nation (*li-umma mukhaṣṣaṣa*), and why did He not legislate to the others? Why did He legislate at this particular[7] time, and why did He not legislate before it or after it? Why did He impose these commandments and prohibitions? Why did He privilege the prophet with the miracles mentioned in relation to him and now with some others? What was God's aim in giving this Law? Why did He not, if such was His purpose, put the accomplishment of the commandments and the nontransgression of the prohibitions into our nature? If this were said, the answer to all these questions would be that it would be said: He wanted it this way, or His wisdom required it this way. And just as He brought the world into existence, having the form it has, when He wanted to, without our knowing His will with regard to this or in what respect there was wisdom in His particularizing the forms of the world and the time of its creation—in the same way we do not know His will or the exigency of His wisdom that caused all the matters, about which questions have been posed above, to be particularized (329).

The question then arises whether creation proper makes possible miracles that Plato's view does not. Based in part on 2.13's account of the fixed nature of the impossible, there is reason to believe

[7] Here, Maimonides merely uses "this (*hādhihī*)" without adding an adjectival from of the root *kh.ṣ.ṣ.* to emphasize particularity.

that, when Maimonides presents this list of the things that creation proper makes possible in 2.25, he might be indicating miracles that Plato's opinion does not make possible. In effect, the earlier part of the passage on Plato in 2.25 that reads "would be followed not by the lie being given to miracles" should be interpreted as meaning "would be followed not by the lie being given to [some] miracles." The most noteworthy feature of the rhetorical questions listed above from 2.25 is their particularity with respect to place, time, and people. These are some of the markers of particularization we already noted in 1.74, Fifth Method and 2.19. Yet they are even more particular than in 2.19 in certain respects. The notion of particularization in 2.19 references only the particularity of the apparent disorders of motions of the planets and apparent disorder of the specific placement of heavenly bodies—but those particularities are subject to eternal regularity. It seems relatively clear that Maimonides is not going as far in defending particularization in 2.19 as did the Mutakallimun in 1.74. The sort of particularity identified in 2.25 concerns God's entering into history to affect changes specific to a particular people. This sort of particularity, which of course is precisely what is at stake in particular providence of a biblical sort, is something that a creator who willed the world into being out of nothing would be capable of. Over the course of chapters 6 and 7, we will return to argue that these are not things that, according to Maimonides, the Platonic opinion makes possible.[8] If this argument is true, then, contrary to Davidson, the implied distinction between the Aristotelian and Platonic opinions in 2.25 is more misleading than the lack of distinction in 2.13.

Ultimately, the most striking feature of this still widely influential and studied debate about the creation-prophetology puzzle is the extent to which all three interpreters, Kaplan, Davidson, and W. Z.

---

[8] See Leo Strauss, "How to Begin to Study *The Guide of the Perplexed*" in Pines ed., pp. liv–lv, especially his comment on the Platonic view of providence.

Harvey, agree that the Platonic opinion is compatible with revelation. This is obvious in the case of Davidson, based on the quote we already provided about Plato's opinion being compatible with "revelation, miracles, and providence," in the biblical senses. Let us glance for a moment at the arguments of Kaplan and Harvey. As Kaplan's resolution of the puzzle (1:3, 2:1, 3:2) indicates, ultimately, he holds that the Platonic view of creation is compatible with the ignoramuses' view of prophecy. Kaplan starts to build the case for this based on Mordecai Jaffe's commentary on Maimonides.[9] Jaffe presents prophecy before creation, arguing that just as Maimonides describes God as being able to make whomever He wishes into a prophet, so Plato argues that God can make whatever He wishes out of eternally pre-existing matter. Furthermore, Jaffe argues that Plato does not prepare the matter for its reception of form. The twentieth-century translator of the *Guide* from Arabic into Hebrew, J. Kafih, disagrees with Jaffe on this one point, noting that Maimonides says nothing about preparation or the lack thereof of the matter. With this caveat, Kaplan assents to this interpretation, "Kafih's assertion that according to Maimonides's interpretation of Plato's view 'there is no fixed nature existing at all' is, undoubtedly, correct." By connecting 2.13 to the admittedly impressionistic account of the order of the whole in 1.72, Kafih and Kaplan draw the inference that unless the heavens exist eternally as they are "there is no causal natural order." Indeed, Kaplan goes on to infer that for Plato prophecy could only be the result of "the special divine will."[10]

It would appear that this way of interpreting Maimonides's presentation of Plato all goes back to the one sentence alluded to by Davidson, "If, however, one believed eternity according to the second opinion we have explained—which is the opinion of Plato—according to which the heavens too are subject to generation and

[9] Kaplan elaborates Jaffe's interpretation with his corrections, starting on p. 249 of "Maimonides on the Miraculous Element in Prophecy."

[10] Kaplan, "Maimonides on the Miraculous Element in Prophecy," 250.

corruption, this opinion would not destroy the foundations of the Law (*qawāʿid al-sharīʿa*) and would be followed not by the lie being given to miracles, but by their becoming admissible." Once again, a trend in interpretation seems to have developed that the Platonic opinion is effectively the same as the revealed, at least for Maimonides. We need not concern ourselves with the rest of Kaplan's argument here, except to note that ultimately regarding prophecy he views Maimonides's account of the third opinion ("the opinion of our Law and the foundation of our doctrine") as consisting of the philosophic view (effectively the second opinion) however with the "logical entailment" from creation that God can miraculously withhold prophecy.

When we turn to Harvey, we should perhaps not be surprised to see that he agrees with Davidson and Kaplan in seeing little difference between the Platonic opinion on creation and the revealed opinion; however, Harvey combines this with the view that Maimonides ultimately holds to some notion of "eternal creation."[11] I do not mean to suggest that Harvey agrees with Davidson that Maimonides adopted a Platonic view. Rather, Harvey denies this, implying, in harmony with Kaplan's interpretation of Jaffe, that creation proper and the Platonic view are equally hostile to "'a fixed natural order.'"[12] Precisely because Maimonides is committed to "a fixed natural order," according to Harvey, he must side with Aristotle regarding eternity. Furthermore, according to Harvey, Aristotle's view on eternity is compatible with the third opinion on prophecy.

Harvey is in respectable company with Moses Narbonne (or Narboni) in claiming that Maimonides adhered not only to Aristotle's view but in thinking that Aristotle's view is compatible with "eternal creation." We do not intend here to deny the evidence

---

[11] W. Z. Harvey, "A Third Approach to Maimonides' Cosmogony-Prophetology Puzzle," 76.

[12] W. Z. Harvey, "A Third Approach to Maimonides' Cosmogony-Prophetology Puzzle," 75n19.

Harvey musters that Maimonides sides with Aristotle regarding eternity;[13] however, we are not ultimately convinced by Harvey's efforts to show that Maimonides thinks eternity is ultimately compatible with the Bible by way of something like "eternal creation." His evidence, for example, that Maimonides attributes "volition" or "will" to the Aristotelian God proves little or nothing. Indeed, Harvey here does little more than trust Maimonides's word choice. What Harvey does not explain is why we should accept the finessing of the most essential divide in the *Guide,* that between eternity and creation.[14] It hardly seems sufficient to argue as he does, "First, to avoid a common misunderstanding, it should be emphasized that to conclude that Maimonides held Aristotle's theory of eternity is *not* to say that he denied creation, and it is *not* to say that he denied religion; rather, it is to say that he denied what he considered to be the vulgar notion of creation and the vulgar notion of religion."[15] This disclaimer is the way he sets the stage for his affirmation with Moses Narbonne that Maimonides ultimately adheres to what amounts to "eternal creation." Eternal creation made strange bedfellows in the Jewish tradition: Moses Narbonne, the recognized Averroist interpreter of Maimonides, Abraham Abulafia, and Hasdai Crescas.[16] We will return to consider eternal creation in chapter 7. Some might be, but I for one am not convinced by Harvey's assurances that Strauss was wrong about the centrality and significance of the opposition between philosophy and Law, eternity

---

[13] W. Z. Harvey, "A Third Approach to Maimonides' Cosmogony-Prophetology Puzzle," 76–78.

[14] Cf. Leo Strauss, *Persecution and the Art of Writing* (Chicago: University of Chicago Press, 1980), 121, 124n92.

[15] W. Z. Harvey, "A Third Approach to Maimonides' Cosmogony-Prophetology Puzzle," 75–76.

[16] W. Z. Harvey, "A Third Approach to Maimonides' Cosmogony-Prophetology Puzzle," 76n23.

and creation.[17] One thing of which I am certain is that a careful rereading of 2.13, especially p. 283 in Pines's translation should give anyone pause who holds that Plato and revelation are on the same page—a view espoused by all three of the interpreters we have considered here.

## Who or What Might God Impede?

This section is a brief digression on a matter that is almost wholly conjectural. For that reason we will consider it wholly apart from a careful consideration of 2.32. Our conjecture concerns whom God would impede or prevent in prophecy in the third opinion on prophecy described in 2.32. It is natural to leap to the conclusion that He would directly impede the prophet. However, another possibility is that God would impede the Active Intellect (AI). After all, God's overflow is not directly to the prophet, assuming that Maimonides's account of the psychology of prophecy in 2.36 is accurate. Until one reaches 2.18, which we will not do in this series of chapters on impediments until chapter 7, it is still within the realm of possibility that the AI might be impeded. Neither form of prevention, of the human recipient of divine overflow or of the AI, is especially promising, though.

Not only will Maimonides deny the claim that the AI can be impeded in 2.18 but also there is nothing in Maimonides's account of overflow that suggests that overflow is anything but constant and unimpeded. Indeed, everything about Maimonides's imagery about overflow in 2.12 suggests that it is wholly impersonal and constant or natural. Indeed, this is why we and others describe his account of prophecy as "naturalistic" (in a suitably medieval sense of the word).

[17] W. Z. Harvey, "A Third Approach to Maimonides' Cosmogony-Prophetology Puzzle," 74n14. Also cf. this account with Harvey's later account, "Twersky on Integration of Law and Philosophy in Maimonides," unpublished remarks delivered for a symposium at Harvard University on the 25th anniversary of Twersky's death on January 19, 2023.

Although it will ultimately appear to be more plausible that the human recipient should be impeded, it is not much more convincing. After all, since in 2.32 the one who is prevented from prophesying has the correct nature and education. Once again, it appears to be anything but natural that such a recipient should be prevented from prophesying. This mystery will reach its apex in 2.18 when Maimonides entertains the Ghazalian suggestion that God also could not have a purpose or end in impeding the potential prophet.

## Prevention or Impediment in the Prophetology

As we noted near the end of the previous chapter, prevention, impediment, hindrance, or obstacle are all translations of the two relevant Arabic terms, *ʿāʾiq* and *mānīʿ*. Of course, these are not technical terms. So far, we have not been able to detect a significant difference between them. And they are sometimes used in the same passage with little apparent, if any, difference in meaning. One could reasonably argue that these are such generic terms that they should not be tracked as if they were a significant indicator of anything. Let us see. No one would gainsay the importance of trying to figure out what Maimonides means when he speaks of God's will to prevent prophecy. Why God would do such a thing has puzzled interpreters for centuries, arguing largely on the basis that it seems to contradict a later claim in the *Guide* (3.17, 470) in which Maimonides seems to cite favorably the following Talmudic saying: "*The Holy One, blessed be He, does not withhold from any creature that which it has deserved.*"[18] By considering some notable uses of prevention and hindrance in the prophetology section, we will be given further evidence with which to consider how we might interpret Maimonides's third opinion on prophecy.

---

[18] According to Kaplan, Shem Tov, Efodi, and Ibn Kaspi all agree that this passage must mean that though it is logically possible for God to withhold that He would never withhold the good of prophecy from someone worthy. Kaplan, "Maimonides on the Miraculous Element in Prophecy," 241, 257.

Although we will return eventually to consider 2.32 in detail, we begin with the other passages in the prophetology involving prevention or hindrance or impediment. That next occurrence is in 2.36. If 2.32 lays out the three opinions on prophecy, 2.36 explains the psychological mechanics of prophecy. It builds on the earlier discussion of overflow from God via the Active Intellect in the significantly numbered 2.12, which, given the way 2.12 follows 2.6, which underlines that all angels are, in effect, natural forces, all contribute to the widely accepted inference that Maimonides's account of prophecy is highly naturalistic.[19] As Kaplan acknowledges, despite his insistence that miraculous prevention is for Maimonides a "logical requirement" flowing from his supposed doctrine on miracles, Maimonides's account of prophecy is essentially that of the philosophers, as he himself states.[20]

In 2.36, this account which Maimonides calls the "true reality and quiddity of prophecy" is that overflow should proceed from God to the Active Intellect and from there to the intellect of the prophet, followed eventually by overflow to the imagination. Now as we already know from 2.12, "overflow (*fayḍ*)" is merely a metaphor for what appears to be a continuous process. Despite his eventual vigorous insistence that it is merely a simile to which we resort because this action is apart from matter, it is worth observing the detail with which he first describes this simile:

---

[19] Of course, chapters 36 and 12 are both multiples of 6. Apparently, there is some connection in the *Guide* between nature and six. In 2.6, see p. 263. Cf. Nasser Behnegar, "Reading 'What Is Political Philosophy?'" in *Leo Strauss's Defense of the Philosophic Life: Reading "What Is Political Philosophy?"* Rafael Major, ed. (Chicago: University of Chicago Press, 2013), 41n5, on Strauss's identification of the link between the number 17 and nature, which is of course hinted at by the subject matter of *Guide* 1.17, citing Leo Strauss, *On Tyranny*, Victor Gourevitch and Michael S. Roth, eds. (NY: Free Press, 1991), 275.

[20] Cf. Kaplan, "Maimonides on the Miraculous Element in Prophecy," 252 with 2.32, 361.

> Hence the action of the separate intellect is always designated as an overflow, being likened to a source of water that overflows in all directions and does not have one particular direction from which it draws while giving its bounty to others. For it springs forth from all directions and constantly irrigates all the directions nearby and afar....For its action is constant as long as something has been prepared so that it is receptive of the permanently existing action, which has been interpreted as an overflow (3.12, 279).

This passage seems to leave little or no room for, as it were, a turning off of the fountain that overflows, pointing instead to any obstacle being in the receiver.

Returning to 2.36, the main task of this striking and colorful chapter is to describe the preparation of the receiver of prophetic overflow. Rather than focus on the intellect of the receiver, Maimonides dwells especially on the imagination of the potential prophet. When he states the prerequisites of prophecy, we hear not only what we might have expected from 2.32—namely, allusions to what amounts to the philosopher-king as prophet teaching, which Maimonides knows from Alfarabi[21]—but he also adds this focus on the imagination. Although I said earlier that this chapter concerns the "psychological mechanics," it might be more accurate to describe it as providing an account of the embodied psychology of the prophet. Given the importance of the imagination in prophecy, Maimonides dwells at length on the necessity that the bodily substratum of the imagination be of the greatest perfection with respect to temperament, size, position, and matter.[22] He explores the powers

---

[21] The way that Maimonides puts the matter is that it is not sufficient for the prophet to be perfect in the "speculative sciences" nor merely prepared by "improvement of moral habits." Alfarabi, *The Principles of the Opinions of the Inhabitants of the Virtuous City*, in Walzer ed., *Al-Farabi on the Perfect State* (Oxford: Clarendon, 1985), chaps. 13 through 15, esp. 15, §10.

[22] Contrary to the doctrine apparently widely accepted among Aristotelians that the intellect must not be rooted in a bodily substratum, Maimonides

of the imagination at some length, including its powers in sleep in dreams and while awake. The comment regarding hindrance comes more or less in the middle of this chapter. Before returning to focus on it, I want to note that much of the rest of the chapter focuses on the sense of touch. Indeed, this is one of the chapters that includes Maimonides's distorted report of Aristotle's claim that the sense of touch is a "shame" or "disgrace" to us. Although Maimonides jokes about how some philosophers haven't taken to heart the need to curb their passions, he seems to be admonishing Joseph ben Judah about the necessity of curbing one's passions if only to avoid falling prey to the harm that his passion for honor might do to him.[23] This then is followed by the striking account of an exemplary case of impediment to prophecy, namely, the case of Moses. Without specifying here in the *Guide* that Moses fell prey to his anger,[24] Maimonides underscores that sadness and anger were often responsible for causing prophecy to "cease"[25] and proceeds to describe how prophecy ceased for Moses in the desert. Here, we leave aside the confounding

---

appears to accept the bodily basis of the intellect. Cf. 3.17, p. 465 with Aristotle, *De anima* 3.4, 429a23–b5 and the immense commentary tradition that reaches its peak in Averroes's *Long Commentary on the "De Anima" of Aristotle* (see the translation from the surviving Latin as well as Arabic fragments by Richard C. Taylor with Thérèse-Anne Druart [New Haven: Yale University Press, 2011]) and in Thomas Aquinas's discussions in both his commentary on *De anima* and in more apologetic works such as *De unitate intellectus* and both the *Summa theologiae* and *Summa contra gentiles*. For a fulsome discussion of Averroes in relation to the preceding tradition and in relation to Thomas, see Stephen R. Ogden's *Averroes on Intellect* (New York: Oxford University Press, 2022).

[23] Cf. Maimonides's *Letter to Joseph* regarding his relation to the Exilarch in *The Ethical Writings of Maimonides*, Weiss and Butterworth, trans. (New York: Dover, 1983), 113–123.

[24] Of course, we recall from EC, chap. 7 that irascibility or anger is Moses' peculiar "veil."

[25] *ʿ.ṭ.l.*

account of how imagination played no role in the prophecy of Moses (2.36, 373).

About hindrance, Maimonides underscores the role the body can play in hindering or impeding prophecy. His account of imagination and its bodily basis, which he states directly only near the end of the chapter while discussing Moses, serves as the context of his account of its impediment. Just as the account of Moses and the impediment or, should I say, cessation of prophecy that occurred due to his anger highlights the role of the recipient in impediment, so does this passage on hindrance remind us of the same thing: "After these preliminary propositions, you should know that the case to be taken into consideration is that of a human individual the substance of whose brain at the origin of his natural disposition is extremely well proportioned because of the purity of its matter and of the particular temperament of each of its [that is, the brain's] parts and because of its size and position, and is not affected by hindrances (*ta'aqhu 'awā'iq*) due to temperament, which derive from another part of the body. Thereupon that individual would obtain knowledge and wisdom until he passes from potentiality to actuality and acquires a perfect and accomplished human intellect and pure and well-tempered human moral habits" (2.36, 371).The sort of hindrance Maimonides alludes to here was discussed in 1.34 in his account of the fourth cause why inquiry cannot begin with divine science, namely, the natural aptitudes. There Maimonides alludes to the connections of a hot heart with anger and a hot and humid temperament with lasciviousness (1.34, 77). At least in the case of such bodily obstacles or impediments or hindrances, they seem to come from almost any direction. That is, it is not just the bodily substratum of the imagination that is a potential obstacle. Indeed, almost any aspect of the body has the potential of posing an obstacle to intellectual perfection, that is, prophecy. Obstacles, impediments, and hindrances appear to possess the opposite of the regularity of the overflowing source of prophecy. That source appears to be utterly regular and continuous.

We turn now to consider another example of prevention or obstacle or hindrance or impediment in 2.39. This chapter follows 2.38, which contains the second salvo in the mystery of Moses in the *Guide*. In 2.38, Maimonides discusses the powers or faculties of the soul required for prophecy. It is an interesting addendum to 2.36. These powers are not comparable to Aristotle's faculty psychology, drawn on for the previous account in 2.36. Instead, what are discussed are more difficult to place. One is the power or faculty (*qūwa*) of divination (*al-shuʿūr*) and what Pines renders as "the faculty of courage (*qūwa iqdām*)." Of course, for Aristotle courage is a virtue, not a faculty.[26] Weiss and Butterworth render this Arabic term as "boldness" in EC, which appears to be what Maimonides has in mind. This is the passion or rather one of two passions of which courage is the virtue. According to Aristotle's account in the *Nicomachean Ethics*, courage is a mean with respect to the opposite passions, fear and boldness.[27] Although boldness is not equivalent to anger, Maimonides alludes to the connection between them not only by having identified anger or irascibility as Moses' peculiar vice in EC, chap. 7 but also by the connection between the account in 2.38 and in 2.45, first degree. In 2.38, Maimonides writes of how Moses was that "lone individual, having only his staff, [who] went boldly to (*qadama ʿalā*) the great king in order to save a religious community from the burden of slavery, and had no fear or dread, because it was said to him: *I will be with thee.*" In 2.45, when he describes the "*spirit of the Lord*" he says, "Know that such a force

[26] Cf. EC chap. 4 and Alfarabi, *Selected Aphorisms*, aphor. 8. There the virtue of courage is *shajāʿa*.

[27] See Aristotle EN 3.6, 1115a7–23. For fear (Gr., *phobos*) and boldness or confidence (*tharros*) as opposite passions, see his *Rhetoric* 2.5.

(*qūwa*)[28] did not abandon Moses our Master from the moment he reached a man's estate. It was because of this that he was moved to slay the *Egyptian* and to reprove the one who was in the wrong among (sic!) the two men who struggled. The strength of this force in him shows in the fact that when—after having been filled with fear and having fled—he came to *Midian* as a stranger full of fear and saw some wrong that was done, he could not refrain from putting an end to it and was incapable of patience with regard to it...." Whether the force Maimonides is referring to is what he referred to in 2.38 as *iqdām* or boldness or perhaps what is often translated as "righteous indignation (*nemesis*)" among the Greeks or the very broad Greek term that includes anger among its many meanings, that is, *thumos*, it is intimately connected to what would eventually become Moses' great vice, irascibility.[29]

With all this in mind about Moses, who is after all the most interesting case of a prophet who got an impediment, we turn to 2.39. In this chapter, Maimonides presents a programmatic statement about what he refers to in this chapter as "the Law of *Moses our Master*" and its uniqueness, which helps mightily to explain why he presents such a complicated portrait of Moses. On the one hand, Maimonides seeks to uncover the truth about Moses, which is sometimes not flattering. On the other hand, Maimonides must by all means extoll the uniqueness of Moses. If the giver of the Law is not unique, then why should the "Law of *Moses our Master*" be unique? Although Abraham will be celebrated in 2.45, Maimonides must go

---

[28] Not only is the word Pines renders as "force" here the same as the word rendered as "faculty" in 2.38, but it is also the word Maimonides uses when he writes "all forces are angels" in 2.6. And, of course, this is the same word he uses in 2. Intro, tenth premise: "Everything that is said to be in a body is divided into two classes: either it subsists through the body, as do the accidents, or the body subsists through it, as in the case of natural form (*al-ṣūra al-ṭabīʿa*). Both classes are to be considered as a force (*qūwa*) in the body."

[29] Cf. Aristotle's discussion of *thumos* as one of the components of courage at EN 1116b23–28.

out of his way to underscore the difference between Abraham—a teacher, who instructs merely by means of "speculative proofs (*adilla naẓariyya*)" and "eloquent speeches (*khaṭb ḥasana iḥsānin*)"[30]—and Moses, the philosopher-king who is also prophet and, above all, legislator. This somewhat hyperbolic account of Moses and Abraham is followed closely by some of the most obviously polemical if subtle attacks on Christianity and Islam in the *Guide* and then by a closing attack on so-called Sabians or polytheists. The rhetorical tenor of the whole chapter helps us to understand what we are to make of the last example of hindrance or impediment in the prophetology. It is worth noting that 2.40, whose theme is what make the Law or any law divine—namely, that it aims at intellectual perfection—is explained and framed by near verbatim quotes from Aristotle's *Ethics* and *Politics*. Ultimately, it seems to me that 2.40 is the more serious of the two chapters. Yet, Maimonides invokes the trope of hindrance at a key rhetorical moment in 2.39. Of course, among the most stinging critiques of the Christians against the Law is the suggestion that the Law is something distant and too difficult for man. Consequently, God had to send His son to save man from himself. Maimonides's response to this is the following: "As for the greedy and the vile, the most grievous thing in their opinion is that which hinders (*māniʿ*) their abandoning themselves to debauchery and punishes those who indulge in it. Similarly everyone who is deficient in any respect considers that a hindrance (*māniʿ*) in the way of the vice he prefers because of his moral corruption is a great burden. Accordingly the facility or difficulty of the Law should not be estimated with reference to the passions of all the wicked, vile, morally corrupt men, but should be considered with reference to the man who is perfect among the people." Here we are reminded once again of what only 3.10 is capable of shedding the proper light on.

[30] Cf. the less flattering portrait of Abraham in the similarly numbered 3.29, where he speaks not of his speculative proofs or eloquence but instead of his "arguments and feeble preaching" (3.29, 517).

Hindrance or prevention is strictly a relative matter. Privation as such is relative. Of course, our death, despite or perhaps in part because of its inevitability, seems for each of us to be an evil. Yet from the viewpoint of the whole, our death can hardly be viewed that way.[31] God is incapable of hindrance from any good. About the case of the withholding of prophecy, evidently the Talmud cannot square this with YHVH because it would be contrary to the desert of the individual human being. Philosophy might seem to say the same thing, since for philosophy, as Maimonides puts it, God's act "in its entirety is good, for the good is being." It is less a question, however, of what the desert of the individual is than the desert of the whole.[32]

## Guide *2.32 and the* Letter on Astrology

Although it is tempting to focus solely on the third opinion on prophecy in 2.32 because this chapter is such well worked ground, we are under a special obligation to attend to all three opinions because we must consider not only the matter of impediments but also where this matter fits in the weighing of doubts. In other words, does the use of prevention or impediment or hindrance in 2.32 in the third opinion make it more or less doubtful than the other opinions? Of course, here we need to recall our marching orders from 2.23: the question is less about the number of doubts than the quality of them. If we consider the three opinions in this light, we believe that problems associated with the third opinion will become readily apparent. The result of our inquiries will be that we side with Davidson's (following Abravanel and a host of nineteenth- and twentieth-century scholars, what Kaplan calls the "standard explanation") linking of the three opinions on creation to the three opinions on prophecy, though we do not agree that Maimonides ultimately

[31] See 3.12, 443–444.

[32] Cf. 3.12, 442.

adopts the Platonic opinion.[33] In other words, we will argue for 1:1, 2:3, 3:2, as Harvey encapsulates Davidson's understanding of the relation of creation and prophecy;[34] however, rather than suggesting 2:3 is Maimonides's opinion, we will argue that 3:2 is his position. Perhaps it is not by chance that Maimonides's opinion on prophecy not only takes most open advantage of prevention or impediment from among its uses in the three great themes, but also his approach to prophecy states the opposition between revelation and philosophy more starkly than in the other two themes. It points to the doubts on both side more openly than anywhere else—perhaps the least is to be lost in pointing it out in this connection. For many interpreters, like Kaplan, want to segment Maimonides into a series of distinct "doctrines," perhaps to contain the negative implications of one theme for another.[35]

Leaving aside the creation-prophetology puzzle, let us consider then what the doubts are among the three opinions on prophecy in *Guide* 2.32. The first opinion on prophecy is attributed with disdain to "the multitude among the Pagans (*jumhūr al-jāhiliyya*)" and only thereafter to "some of the common people professing our Law (*baʿaḍ ʿawāmm sharīʿatinā*)." Here, Maimonides rehearses Qur'anic tropes

[33] Review Kaplan, "Maimonides on the Miraculous Element in Prophecy," 251n42; also see W. Z. Harvey, "A Third Approach to Maimonides' Cosmogony-Prophetology Puzzle," 72n7.

[34] One reason we continue to reference Harvey on this is that Davidson for some reason considers the three opinions on creation or cosmogony out of order. He places Plato last rather than second, when Plato's account appears second in both 2.13 and 2.25. Cf. W. Z. Harvey, "A Third Approach to Maimonides' Cosmogony-Prophetology Puzzle," 72 with Davidson, "Maimonides' Secret Position on Creation," 19–20.

[35] The example I have in mind from Kaplan is the way he matches the philosophic view with the "logical requirement" that miracles remain possible, despite their lack of what for lack of a better word we might call their ontological possibility. See Kaplan, "Maimonides on the Miraculous Element in Prophecy," 252.

distinguishing between us and them, not as between Sabians and monotheists, who appear in far more ambiguous lights at various times throughout the *Guide*, but as between the pre-Islamic pagans in contrast to the ignorant multitude of Jews. This sort of language rivals the polemical tone of 2.39,[36] though ultimately the line between us and them is erased. Ignorance is the essential divider. The initial polemical tone has not concealed from nearly every reader of the *Guide* and the Bible that this account reflects the literal meaning of the Bible.[37] In other words, as both Davidson and Harvey admit, the first opinion is the traditional revealed view of prophecy. That Maimonides dismisses it out of hand seems clear enough evidence that he does not accept the opinion, or, to restate it in light of 2.23, he believes the doubts connected with this view are insuperable. We will try to show that this opinion is the only one that qualifies as properly miraculous. The third opinion will fall short of the miraculous in a number of respects. If our exploration of 2.29 through 30 in chapter 1 was not enough, this treatment of the first opinion in 2.32 gives relatively clear indication of what Maimonides's actual view of miracles is.[38]

Since only the first and third opinions make any allusion to the miraculous, we will focus on drawing out the differences between

---

[36] For an indication of the less disdainful treatment of the Sabians, compare 2.39 and its conclusion, which seems to mock the Sabians, with 3.29, 515–516 where Maimonides mocks the counter-marvels of the *Nabatean Agriculture*, precisely because of how out of harmony they are with the Sabians' belief in the eternity of the world.

[37] Cf. the characterization of the most obvious literal interpretation of the Garden of Eden in *Guide* 1.2.

[38] If we had more time, we might also look at Maimonides's *Treatise on Resurrection*. For some indication of how we view that work, the interested reader should see the following: Parens, "Death and Dying, Mortality and Immortality in Moses Maimonides," in *Political Theory on Death and Dying*, 161–70, Erin A. Dolgoy, Kimberly Hurd Hale, and Bruce Peabody, eds. (New York and London: Routledge, 2021).

the doubts attaching to the positive account of the miraculous in the first opinion as opposed to the doubts attaching to the negative account of the miraculous in the third opinion. The main difference is that in the first opinion or account the miraculous is clearly opposed to the nature of existence or being as Maimonides characterizes it starting in 1.71. How he characterizes it became amply evident in our various considerations of 1.73 and 74. The Mutakallimun are opposed to the nature of existence and violate it at every turn. About the third or negative opinion, Maimonides identifies it as the "opinion of our Law and foundation of our doctrine...[which is] identical with the philosophic opinion," except that God can will the prevention or hindrance of prophecy. It is worth noting, however, that even within the second or philosophic opinion the specter of prevention or hindrance is evident. Maimonides remarks that the right nature needs to be actualized. This will happen "provided an obstacle due to temperament or to some external cause does not hinder this (*yaʿaqa... ʿāʾiq*)." Aside from the key issue of God's will, the only other obvious difference in the characterization of what might prevent prophecy from being achieved by the prophet according to the third opinion is that in this one instance Maimonides uses cognates of the root of the other term used interchangeably for preventing or hindering or impeding: *mānīʿ*. By means of careful consideration of the whole passage, we will try to shed a bit more light on a passage that has been almost universally recognized as troublesome.

> For we believe that it may happen that one who is fit for prophecy and prepared for it should not become a prophet, namely, on account of the divine will (*bi-mashīʾa ilāhiyya*). To my mind this is like all the miracles and takes the same course as they. For it is a natural thing that everyone who according to his natural disposition is fit for prophecy and who has been trained in his education and study should become a prophet. He who is prevented (*al-mamnūʿ*) from it is like him who has been prevented (*muniʿa*), like *Jeroboam*, from moving his hand, or, like the *King of Aram's* army going to seek Elisha, from seeing. As for its being

> fundamental with us that the prophet must possess preparation and perfection in the moral and intellectual qualities, it is indubitably the opinion expressed in their dictum: *Prophecy only rests upon a wise, strong, and rich man.* We have explained this in our Commentary on the *Mishnah* and in our great compilation, and we have set forth that the *disciples of the prophets* were always engaged in preparation. As for the fact that one who prepares is sometimes prevented (*qad yumnaʿu*) from becoming a prophet, you may know it from the history of *Baruch, son of Neriah.* For he followed *Jeremiah*, who trained, taught, and prepared him. And he set himself the goal of becoming a prophet, but was prevented (*fi-muniʿa*), as he says: *I am weary with my groaning, and I find no rest.* Thereupon he was told through *Jeremiah*: *Thus shalt thou say unto him: Thus saith the Lord, and so on. And seekest thou great things for thyself? Seek them not.* It is possible to say that this is a clear statement that prophecy is *too great a thing for Baruch.* Similarly it may be said, as we shall explain, that in the passage, *Yea, her prophets find no vision from the Lord*, this was the case because they were in *Exile* (*Galut*). However, we shall find many texts, some of them scriptural and some of them dicta of the *Sages*, all of which maintain this fundamental principle that God turns whom He wills, whenever He wills it, into a prophet – but only someone perfect and superior to the utmost degree. But with regard to one of the ignorant among the common people, this is not possible according to us – I mean that He should turn one of them into a prophet – except as it is possible that He should turn an ass or a frog into a prophet. It is our fundamental principle that there must be training and perfection, whereupon the possibility arises to which the power of the deity becomes attached (361–362).

Kaplan provides useful very extensive commentary on the difficulties surrounding this passage that were remarked on by the medieval commentators such as Ibn Kaspi.[39] Ultimately, we will agree with them that the difficulties likely indicate that Maimonides

[39] Kaplan, "Maimonides on the Miraculous Element in Prophecy," 237 ff.

actually holds to the second opinion. However, despite the striking ambiguities attendant on the passage, let us see whether we can make a bit more sense out of it, specifically by focusing on the matter of prevention or hindrance or obstacle. Even before working through some of the details, I want to remind the reader that earlier in the *Guide* Maimonides uses our pair of terms, *ʿāʾiq* and *māniʿ*, together in the same passages in ways that seem to indicate that they're being used as synonyms.[40] However, Maimonides may be using the different terms separately (*ʿāʾiq* for the second opinion and *māniʿ* for the third opinion) to throw us off the scent of the similarities between the second and third opinions. According to Kaplan, the passage becomes problematic only by the time we turn to the case of *Baruch, son of Neriah*.[41] However, even before that point, the matter is somewhat problematic in the way the entire characterization of prophecy has shoehorned biblical prophecy into a philosophic frame. That was achieved with the deft reference to *Prophecy only rests upon a wise, strong, and rich man.* Although we are compelled to wait until the end of the *Guide* for a fuller account of this passage, it should suffice to say that what the Talmud means by "wise, strong, and rich" is not likely to be exactly what the philosophers mean by naturally perfect and trained and educated for moral and intellectual virtue, if only because the two conceptions of wisdom are so divergent.[42] Leaving that aside, for Kaplan and the medieval commentators the real trouble comes toward the end when the possibility is raised that Baruch is not fit for prophecy. We believe that of even greater interest should be the explanation regarding, on the one hand, Baruch's weariness, and, on the other, the comparable explanation with reference to the *Exile.* Although Kaplan does not explain it here, this is the sort of impediment we saw alluded to in 2.36 and 2.39—and in the second opinion. These

---

[40] See 1.69, 167 and 2.1, 4th speculation, 241.

[41] Kaplan, "Maimonides on the Miraculous Element in Prophecy,"238.

[42] See 3.54, 632–633 and cf. 634–635 with 636.

are impediments resulting not from what Kaplan calls God's "special divine will" but from what might be called natural factors. Special divine will would apparently act only with an eye to the desert of the individual prophet. Kaplan's view and that of many of the commentators is that the withholding of prophecy is an unsuitable desert for a naturally prepared and educated individual aspirant to prophecy, as suggested by the Talmudic refrain regarding desert (3.17, 470).[43]

We hope to show that the traditional focus on the individual prophet is misplaced. By doing so, we intend to show that the proper vantage point from which to judge such withholding is God's goodness more broadly conceived. That is, we recommend considering it in light of the argument in 3.10 that "the true reality of the act of God in its entirety is the good, for the good is being" (440). Ultimately, what happens to Baruch is not about an inappropriate desert of an individual but rather about what can be construed as the natural result of the people Israel going astray. Indeed, a review of all the examples Maimonides provides—*Jeroboam*'s being prevented from moving his hand, the *King of Aram*'s army seeking *Elisha*, as well as *Baruch*—are examples either of those who oppose God (King Jeroboam, who has recently instituted idolatrous worship; or the King of Aram attacking His people and being repelled by Elisha) being punished, merely as a part of a general punishment, or of those attempting to interfere with such a punishment (Baruch is weary and groaning because he is all too well aware of the punishment that is coming). In other words, the prevention has little or nothing to do with the excellence of the particular prophet. In effect, the misunderstanding of the third opinion on prophecy is directly connected with a corollary to 3.10, namely, the observation in 3.12 that what leads human beings like Razi to think evil predominates in human life is a mistaken focus on the individual (441-442).

---

[43] See Kaplan, "Maimonides on the Miraculous Element in Prophecy," 242.

It is here that we need to begin to turn toward the *Letter on Astrology*, lest we misunderstand Maimonides's view of divine punishment of the people Israel. The point of connection is to be found in the one example Maimonides gives in 2.32 that does not reference a single prophetic or prophetically inspired actor, namely, Lamentations 2:9. Her prophets found no vision from the Lord because they were in Exile. This impediment is altogether like that of Moses in 2.36, which we interpreted earlier. Depression, sadness, anger and the like, whether arising temperamentally or resulting from the sort of context Moses confronted in the desert, are all parts of the natural fabric that might impede prophecy. Exile induces sadness, and loss of prophecy results. Leaving aside the endlessly complicated case of Moses, let us consider Maimonides's explanation of the Exile in the *Letter on Astrology*.

> This is why our kingdom was lost and our Temple was destroyed and we were brought to this. For our fathers sinned and are no more because they found many books dealing with these themes of the stargazers, these things being the root of idolatry, as we have made clear in "Laws Concerning Idolatry." They erred and were drawn after them, imagining them to be glorious science and to be of great utility. They did not busy themselves with the art of war or with the conquest of lands, but imagined that those studies would help them....Know, my masters, that every one of those thing concerning judicial astrology that [its adherents] maintain—namely, that something will happen one way and not another, and that the constellation under which one is born will draw him on so that he will be of such and such a kind and so that something will happen to him one way and not another—all those assertions are far from being scientific; they are stupidity. Never did one of those genuinely wise men of the nations busy himself with this matter or write on it. Nor did they...call it a science, other than the Chasdeans, Chaldeans, Canaanites, and Egyptians, for that was their religion in those days. But the wise men of Greece—and they are the philosophers who wrote science and busied themselves with all kinds of

> knowledge—mock and scorn and ridicule those four nations that I have mentioned to you....The wise men of Persia, too, recognized and understood that all that science...is a falsehood and a lie.[44]

The *Letter on Astrology* is addressed to rabbis of Provence who are confused about the status of astrology.[45] The naïve interpretation of this letter is that Maimonides believes that the Exile was the result of a divine special will to punish the people Israel—in much the way that many traditionalist rabbis explain Jewish suffering as divine punishment for this or that failing. Neither what Maimonides argues about miracles, which we touched on in chapter 1, nor what we will inquire into in chapter 7 about divine will can be squared with such a view. Instead, he is providing an object lesson to his inquirers. You fools, Maimonides seems to say, don't you see that *you* have fallen prey to the very cause of the Jewish loss of nationhood? But what sense can we make of his lesson? The Exile was the result of Jewish lack of self-providence. They failed to study war. Why did they fail to study war? Because their belief in the books of astrology had rendered them passive. Of course, Jews did historically succumb to the appeal of idolatry. Is the Exile the punishment of a special divine will for worshipping idols? Or is Maimonides describing the typical source of the loss of human nationhood, namely, mistaken beliefs in powers beyond the human that will take care of the nation? Whether it be the passivity induced by belief in judicial astrology or the passivity induced by a fideistic vision of God, the same basic logic applies: the royal road to ruin for a nation is a failure to understand its own role in its own preservation or salvation. Once again, "the true reality of the act of God in its entirety is the good, for the good is being" (3.10, 440). When we say that the focus on Baruch as an individual is problematic, what we mean is that providence is

---

[44] Ralph Lerner, trans., *Letter on Astrology*, in *Maimonides' Empire of Light* (Chicago: University of Chicago Press, 2000), pp. 178–87, esp. 179–80.

[45] Lerner, *Empire of Light*, 56.

not a matter of special divine will but of the natural order. The proper understanding of the third opinion is that the supposedly negative miraculous withholding is not really a matter of special divine will. Another way of stating the point is that it is not by chance that Maimonides alludes to hindrance or prevention when discussing the second opinion on prophecy. As many have argued by very different means, the difference between the second opinion and the third is little if anything. For stronger conviction that we have come to a proper understanding of what Maimonides is actually arguing in 2.32 about "divine will," we will have to wait to see what our analysis of "will" yields in chapter 7.

# CHAPTER 6

# PROVIDENCE, GENERAL, AND PARTICULAR?

As Leo Strauss explained in his 1937 article on providence, Maimonides discusses general providence in the first part and to a more limited extent in the second part but waits to treat particular providence until the third part of the *Guide*. We suggest that the single greatest act of divine particular providence would be the creation of the world from absolute nonexistence. Strauss also explains, despite the appearance that the *Guide* conforms to the order of works of dialectical theology in treating creation, prophecy, and providence in that order, the account of providence in the third part is actually part of Maimonides's political science or philosophy. At a minimum, he means that the discussion of particular providence does not take place on a purely theoretical basis.[1] We add that the initial impression that the prophetology and account of providence are based on the account of creation is not an adequate understanding of the actual relation of parts of the *Guide*. Although the dispute between creation and eternity may take place at the highest theoretical level, the question remains whether it can ever be resolved on such a basis. Of course, at first glance the *Guide* appears to treat this matter as simply irresolvable, compelling assent to the claims of the Law. Ultimately, we are arguing that even the most basic theoretical placeholder in the *Guide*, namely, the nature of being or existence (*ṭabīʿat al-wujūd*), may not receive theoretical grounding from a demonstrative argument for eternity, but the insupportable character of the

[1] "The Place of the Doctrine of Providence according to Maimonides," 539–541.

deterministic or fideistic alternatives for human life recommend that political philosophy allies itself with such a nature of existence.

Be that as it may, in this chapter, we need to further our argument about impediment and privation with reference to providence. In the first part of this chapter, we will consider the somewhat sparse and indirect uses of impediment or obstacle or veil in the section on particular providence, extending beyond 3.8 through 24 to include 3.25. Although the use of these key privative terms is relatively rare in 3.8 through 24, a moment's reflection reveals that with the theme of providence comes the problem of evil, which Maimonides addresses so eloquently in 3.12. The problem of evil is, of course, the most salient expression of privation in human existence. Ultimately, our interest in impediment or hindrance or obstacle or veil is not due to these specific terms but as markers of privation. From the talk of the morally and intellectually worthy individual wiped out at sea in 3.17 to Maimonides's sudden insight about what prevents overflow near the end of the *Guide* in 3.51, the main issue surrounding providence is why so many who suffer an undeserved bad fate do so. Here, we hardly need explicit references to impediment to see that privation of providence is an inevitable corollary of any inquiry into particular providence. Consequently, in addition to the passages including impediment, we will take a close look at the discussion of the problem of evil that weaves in and out throughout 3.10 through 18. Subsequently, we will also devote detailed attention to the particular case of Job in 3.22 and 23 and conclude our consideration of the textual bases of our inquiry into the privation of providence with the sudden insight (non-prophetic flash) about why the worthy are deprived of providence in 3.51. Finally, we will find a crucial link between providence and creation by drawing important connections between the account of general providence in 1.11 and the account of particularization in 2.19. Although 2.19 appears initially to provide important argumentative support for the highest expression of particular providence, namely, God's particularization of the heavens, that appearance will prove deceiving.

## Impediments and Particular Providence: 3.9–10 and 3.25

So far as we have been able to determine, explicit reference to impediment or hindrance or even veiling occurs in only two chapters within the section clearly devoted to particular providence, 3.8 through 3.24, namely, 3.9 and 3.10. As we saw already in chapter 4, 3.9 presents a distorted account of the role of matter in privation. Indeed, 3.9 identifies matter as "the veil preventing[2] the apprehension of that which is separate from matter as it truly is." Here, Maimonides is continuing the misleading campaign of impugning matter, which as we saw in chapter 4 shares more in common with the biblical view than that of philosophy. What makes 3.10 so extraordinary is its reversal of this misunderstanding of the role of matter. Ultimately, 3.10 shows that not *'adamah* (Heb., dust or earth or matter) but *ʿadam* (Ar., privation) is the culprit. Yet the culprit does not possess the reality or reification that we desire to attribute to evil when seeking revenge.

As Strauss argues or implies both in his 1937 piece on providence and in his division of the *Guide* in the introduction to the Pines edition, 3.25 through 54 is the part of the *Guide* devoted to actions. But as he explains in the "Place of the Doctrine of Providence," Maimonides marks the turn from the theoretical or at least the highest reaches of the Account of the Chariot earlier in part 3 at the end of the biblical Account of the Chariot set forth in 3.1 through 7, when he writes, "If you consider all that we have said in the chapters of this Treatise up to this chapter, the greater part or

[2] Just as Pines resorts to "impediment" to capture what results from "veiling" in 3.51, 625–626, so here he resorts to "prevent" to convey the effect of the veil that Maimonides claims here is matter.

the entirety of the subject in question, except for a few slight details and repetitious speech, whose meaning remains hidden, will become clear to you. Perhaps upon thorough consideration, this too will be revealed, and nothing of this will remain hidden. Do not hope that, after this chapter, you will hear from me even a single word about this subject, be it as an explicit statement or a flashlike allusion....We shall accordingly start upon other subjects from among those that, I hope, I shall explain in this Treatise" (3.7, 430). In "The Place of Providence," Strauss treats this account in 3.7 as marking the dividing line between the theoretical and the practical. It seems more reasonable to view it, as he seems to in his much later outline of the parts of the *Guide* in the introduction to the Pines translation, as marking the division between the account of God and the account of perishable beings.[3] Although 3.25 through 3.54 is surely more concerned with actions than what precedes it, we agree with Strauss in "The Place of Providence" that the account of providence in 3.8 through 24, which concerns particular providence, is part of Maimonides's political science or philosophy.[4] Another way of thinking of the matter, which Strauss argues in his 1937 article, is that the theoretical treatment of providence is the account of general providence that appears in parts 1 and 2, while the account of particular

[3] Strauss marks this break in his introductory outline to the Pines edition on pp. xi-xii as the difference between A' and A", see appendix.

[4] See Strauss, "The Place of the Doctrine of Providence," 538–541. We disagree with the implication of the division of theoretical from practical that the prophetology would be a part of the theoretical part of the *Guide*. Instead, we hold—and suspect that Strauss ultimately came to hold—that the prophetology like the account of particular providence are both part of Maimonides's political philosophy. Ultimately, though, we incline to the view that political philosophy here is being used in the broad sense Strauss intends in *The City and Man* (Chicago: University of Chicago Press, 1964), 20 and in *What Is Political Philosophy?* (Chicago: University of Chicago Press, 1988), 38–40.

providence is part of the practical or political philosophic account in part 3.[5]

We set out on this discussion of ways of dividing the *Guide* because we were acknowledging that several of the references to impediment relevant to particular providence occur not in 3.8 through 24 but in 3.25. If one expected a great drop off in complexity from the dizzying theoretical heights of 3.1 through 7 when turning from 3.24 to 3.25, that is, from the part of the *Guide* concerned with "views" or opinions or beliefs to the part concerning "actions,"[6] the reader will be sorely disappointed. Indeed, 3.25 is one of the more complicated and technically demanding chapters in the *Guide*. Much like 3.12, the chapter on evil, and 3.13, the chapter on the final end or good, this chapter is especially relevant to the inquiry of this book, and I suspect the fact that this discussion takes place in the chapter numbered 25 is not by chance.[7] 3.25 concerns whether any of God's actions can be anything but good. Of course, we know from 3.10 that that cannot be the case. Although the simple answer to the main question is "no,"[8] Maimonides must surely be accomplishing more than answering this simple question. One way of thinking of the matter is that while some chapters in the *Guide* tend to voice either a biblical view, for example, 3.9, or a philosophic view, for example, 3.10, this chapter is extraordinarily synthetic or harmonizing between reason and revelation—not least about our key issue, the issue of obstacles or impediments or hindering.

---

[5] See Strauss, "The Place of the Doctrine of Providence," 539.

[6] See Strauss, introduction, outline in Pines ed., pp. xi and xiii, the distinction between parts A and B in the appendix. Note also that the first word of 3.25 is "the actions (*al-afʿāl*)."

[7] Of course, 12 + 13 = 25.

[8] That this foregone conclusion is the putative question of the chapter becomes apparent when Maimonides writes, "After having explained this, I shall say: A man endowed with intellect is incapable of saying that any action of God is vain, futile, or frivolous" (503).

Almost the first note of the chapter is "obstacle (*ʿāʾiq*). After dividing actions into four classes—futile, frivolous, vain,[9] and good and excellent—Maimonides turns in his second sentence to consider the third bad sort of action, "The action that is called vain is that by which its agent aims at some end (*ghāya*) and that end is not achieved, its achievement being hindered by obstacles (*taʿawwaqa… ʿawāʾiq*)" (502). As we see when we turn to our chapter 7 on creation, the idea that God might perhaps be hindered by obstacles, despite being dispensed with by Maimonides in 1.68, returns again and again through the section on creation if only as part of the argument for eternity. A good reason that Maimonides would address once more the matter of the goodness of God's actions, after addressing them so eloquently in 3.10, is that since then he confronted the shocking position of the Ashʿarite *kalām* which was so precisely and valuably articulated in 3.17 (466–467). Although we saw all *kalām* positions treated together in 1.73–76, and we saw hints of Ashʿarite positions being alluded to in 2.18 in the lead up to Maimonides's own particularization argument; until 3.17, we did not get a clear line in the sand about the ultimate consequences of Ashʿarite fideism. 3.25 then proves to be an opportunity to put as much light between the Law and the Ashʿarite position as possible. After answering the obvious question about whether God's actions can be anything but good, Maimonides proceeds to lay out the agreement between the Law and philosophy on this matter (303–304). The confusion caused by passages such as Isaiah 45:7 that God is He "*who forms the light and creates darkness, who makes peace and creates evil*" about which Maimonides expended valuable interpretive capital is barely a memory. Be that as it may, the Ashʿarite position is that "there are no causes and no effects, but that all His actions correspond to His will so that one should not seek an end (*ghāya*) for

[9] Futile actions lack any end; frivolous actions possess a low end; and vain actions are impeded or fail to achieve their end.

them or say: Why did He do this? as he does what He wills, and this is not consequent upon wisdom—the actions of God are considered by these people as falling under the class of futile or held to be something even inferior to futile actions" (504).[10]

Maimonides follows the critique of the Ashʿarite *kalām* with the observation that everyone recognizes that attributing a frivolous (or low) end to God is impossible. Yet some thought, for example, that God might have created the ape to make human beings laugh. As we know from 3.13, and will see confirmed shortly, such views stem from the misunderstanding that everything might exist for the sake of human beings. Maimonides states in effect such views are due to an ignorance of physics or natural science. The fundamental principle that applies regarding beings that come into and pass out of being is "that the entire purpose (*al-qaṣd kulluhu*) consists in bringing into existence the way you see it everything whose existence is possible" (504). As innocuous as this fundamental principle sounds it means a few things: first, far from "purpose" being somehow uncharacteristic of the philosophic viewpoint, it is essential to it;[11] second, it is also characteristic of that viewpoint that beings achieve their end by achieving their own form, not by serving anything beyond that; which entails, third, as 3.13 makes amply evident, that it makes no sense to ask for an end to the whole beyond the whole itself, any more than it makes sense to ask for the end of a being beyond the fulfillment of its form.

---

[10] We will need to recall this passage when we look at 2.18 shortly and in the next chapter, regarding the counterargument to the suggestion that creation implies that God suffered an impediment preventing Him from actualizing the world. The key argument is that said action was due to will, and it is of the essence of will to will and not to will, without regard to incentives or consequences (2.18, 301). Pines traces this argument to Alghazali's *Incoherence of the Philosophers*. See Translator's Introduction, to his edition of the *Guide*, p. cxxviii.

[11] Cf. 2.19, first half or so.

When Maimonides then turns to address the suggestion that the Ashʿarite position is tantamount to affirming that God's actions are futile ("no end is intended"), he suggests that their inspiration was that "they assert of necessity what everyone asserts who maintains that the world was created in time (*bi-haduth al-ʿālam*): He willed it so, there being no other cause." They then proceed to apply this to "all the particular things (*juz'iyyāt*) in the world." This leads ultimately to the conclusion that everything must lack a purpose. These strange arguments cannot help but cast strange retrospective light on some of the responses to the arguments in favor of eternity made or alluded to in 2.18 and 19.

As we mentioned earlier, perhaps the key ambition of 3.25 is to make it clear that the view of the Law must never be confused with that of the Ashʿarite *kalām*. To that end, Maimonides then considers some texts from the wisdom literature, including Psalms, Job and Ecclesiastes, that seem to suggest that God simply wills what He wills. His response is: "The meaning of these texts and others of the same kind is that the things willed (*yurīda*) by God are necessarily (*ḍarūra*) accomplished, there being no obstacle to hinder (*wa-laissa thumma ʿā'iq yaʿawwaqa*) the carrying out of His volition (*irādatihu*); but that He, may He be exalted, wills (*r.w.d.*) only what is possible, and not everything that is possible, but only that which is required by his wisdom to be such. Similarly no obstacle intervenes[12] between Him, may He be exalted, and the exceedingly excellent action that He wishes to accomplish, and nothing can hinder (*mānıʿ*) it. This is the opinion of all those that adhere to the Law and also the opinion of the philosophers, and it is also our opinion" (505). Aside from the fascinating juxtaposition of will and impediment in 2.14, "another method" (unnumbered Sixth Method, 288) and 2.18, Second Method (300–301), I am not aware of any other places in the *Guide*

---

[12] This reference to "this obstacle intervenes" is interpolated by Pines on the basis of the phrase "there being no obstacle to hinder" in the first independent clause of the previous sentence.

than this passage in 3.25 where Maimonides so relates and juxtaposes hindrance or obstacle or impediment and will. Here, the results are surprisingly different. In 2.14 and 2.18, the reply to the eternalist critique of creation by the philosophers that God could not be impeded or hindered or incentivized was that God wills the world into being after absolute nonexistence, simply because will must either will or not will (2.18, 301). Here (3.25), in contrast, no impediment can exist because God's nature is such that He cannot be impeded, but His will is anything but merely willing. This will wills with a purpose—indeed, only an excellent one, determined by His wisdom. Indeed, will appears here to be completely subservient to wisdom or intellect. Most surprisingly of all, Maimonides concludes that "this is the opinion of all those that adhere to the Law and also the opinion of the philosophers, and it is also our opinion." The consensus is extraordinary. It may not be by chance that the following sentences proffered by Maimonides comes closer than any other I'm aware of to affirming "eternal creation": "For while we believe that the world has been produced in time (*al-ʿālam ḥādith*), none of our scholars and none of our men of knowledge believe that this came about through the will and nothing else. For they say that His wisdom, may He be exalted—the apprehension of which is beyond us—obligatorily necessitated the existence of this world as a whole at the moment (*ʿinda mā*) when it came into existence, and that the selfsame immutable wisdom necessitated nonexistence before (*qablu*) the world came into existence." Although this comes close to "eternal creation," it still falls short of it because of the way it speaks of time—that is, as if there were time before creation, which as we have seen is, according to Maimonides's Aristotelian way of framing time, a nonsensical way of speaking.[13] It could reasonably be objected that these reflections on the use of impediment in 3.25 fall more naturally within the ambit of our discussion on

[13] See our discussion of *Guide* 2.13 in chapter 3.

creation. We discuss it here because it gives us such a useful frame for considering more carefully the discussion of evil and particular providence in 3.10 through 18.

## The Problem of Evil as Privation: 3.10 through 18

Although we reference 3.10 in our title for this section, we will begin in earnest with the unusually short 3.11. After all, we have already touched on 3.10 several times. Still, we linger for a few more moments on 3.10 to bring out its relevance for the chapters that follow. Chapters ten and eleven may be the most Platonic chapters in the whole *Guide*. We make this claim because, despite Maimonides's well known preference for Aristotle over Plato, two things which are intimately bound together appear in these two chapters: we refer to the claim that God is the cause only of good in 3.10, and the claim that the cause of human conflict, which proves to be a major source of evil in human life, is ignorance in 3.11. These two themes are so intimately bound up with one another and so Platonic in character—even if in some ways the former claim is echoed by many others—that we need to take a few moments to consider how these two notions are connected, and what they have to do with particular providence.

Although it is not uncommon for great thinkers from Plato to Aristotle to Augustine to Maimonides to Averroes to Thomas Aquinas to affirm that God is the cause only of good and in turn that evil is merely the privation of good or of being; pairing this with the claim that the cause of conflict among human beings is ignorance not only adds depth to the other claim but also confirms what we had already suspected—namely, that Maimonides is in far greater harmony with Plato and Aristotle than he is with Augustine and Aquinas on will. We had inferred as much based on the way that Maimonides uses terms such as will or volition and choice. That is, he does not attribute to will as strong a sense of freedom as does the Christian tradition with its talk of "freedom of the will." Indeed, he uses will as the key term opposed to intellect in a manner that is reminiscent of the way Plato and Aristotle oppose "desire" to reason or intellect.[14]

Let us consider what 3.10 and 3.11 mean for the inquiry into particular providence, especially as it relates to evil as privation. Although 3.11 may stand out for its Platonic character, a look backwards reveals how well this fits with the initial impetus of the *Guide*. The claim that human strife as a central evil of human life is rooted in ignorance reinforces the primacy of intellectual virtue in Maimonides's account. In contrast, the Christian understanding of free will tends to make a moral matter of all strife. What we have referred to before as his breathtaking denigration of morality in comparison with Judaism's overwhelming focus on action was from 1.2 already pointing us toward where we have currently arrived. Ignorance is something like what we would today call a "silent killer." You don't even recognize it if you're not aware of it.

As we turn toward 3.12 and Maimonides's explicit inquiry into evil, the singular locus of privation in relation to providence, we will gain further insight into the importance of knowledge in Maimonides's account of particular providence. The rhetorical tone of 3.12 seems calculated to convey one key insight: do not imagine that the whole exists for your individual sake. This is among the principal errors of and one of the greatest sources of unnecessary suffering in human life. This is one my favorite chapters in the *Guide*. Of course, its argument is not unique to Maimonides. It is at least as old as Plato and is among the most widely shared of all views among

---

[14] Consider various translations of *mashi'a* and related terms such as *irāda*. See *Maimonides and Spinoza*, chap. 4, "Freedom and Determinism." That Maimonides has a weaker sense of "will" fits well with the fact that strong libertarian doctrines of freedom seem to go hand in glove with a doctrine of original sin. Of course, that doctrine in turn requires a notion of God (as the Son) as the key to human salvation from such sin. In contrast, in Judaism we rely on the Law as the means by which we are to rectify ourselves.

philosophers.[15] There are three species of evil in human life: those stemming from coming into being and passing away, those resulting from strife between human beings, and those we inflict on ourselves. These three occur with increasing prevalence. The first are evils only from the viewpoint of the individual. From the perspective of the whole, it is inevitable that we will all die and that some will suffer from diseases; however, all this occurs, as Aristotle puts it, as "otherwise than for the most part" or as accidental.[16] We have already met with the second species of evil in 3.11. Although conflict sometimes seems prevalent, it is never what is for the most part. When we turn finally to evils suffered by individuals, these are, it appears, without exception self-inflicted. This is how strongly and insistently Maimonides stands by his claim in 3.10 about being and good.

One might assume that Maimonides would go on to argue that human beings need simply to get a hold of themselves. After all, haven't we seen Maimonides affirm often or at least in *Eight Chapters*, chap. 8 that the Law and philosophy agree that our actions are up to us? We see here much of the nuance about freedom one sees in Aristotle's *Nicomachean Ethics* book 3, chapters 1 through 5. The matter is a bit more complicated than the compressed account in EC would allow. As Aristotle concludes his discussion, the law must say that our actions are up to us so long as they are voluntary (a low physical bar equally applicable to animals and children as well as adults), but the lawgiver must admit that our habits are up to us only

---

[15] To name just a few, see Plato's *Laws* 3.687c–d. Obviously, Stoicism takes great inspiration from this insight. Jean-Jacques Rousseau has his Savoyard Vicar convey this insight by way of a dialogue between "The Inspired Man" and "The Reasoner" in *Émile*, Allan Bloom, trans., (New York: Basic Books, 1979), pp. 300–302. For Maimonides's framing of 3.12 with the case of Abu Bakr al-Razi, see my *Maimonides and Spinoza*, 116–17.

[16] On that which is "otherwise than for the most part," see Aristotle *Met.* 6.2. This helps explain why Aristotle refers to destruction of something living as "accidental," despite what I refer to as its inevitability. See *Met.* 8.5, 1045a2.

in the beginning.[17] Maimonides acknowledges here in 3.12 the sort of thing that might have inspired Pines's declaration that Maimonides is deterministic (only if one accepts current definitions of human freedom),[18] namely, that since the soul is "a corporeal faculty (*qūwa*)" it is "consequent upon the temperament of the body." At the same time, Maimonides disdains those who succumb to the demands of desire, which he describes as "infinite" (445). He describes our frustration when comparing ourselves with others that we lack the luxuries they have. And then turns to the example of someone who takes to sea to provide luxuries, perhaps the first allusion to the case of death at sea in the *Guide*,[19] who then complains when he is stricken by misfortunes. Of course, there are few insights as universally shared by philosophers as well as revealed traditions as that which warns against succumbing to the siren song of desire. But philosophy and some interpretations of the Law part ways over what is to blame for such excess, desire as privation or matter-flesh. What attends the blaming of the flesh, as we saw in 3.8, was a drift toward asceticism. Though one might think that whether matter or privation is to blame matters little, herein lies the difference. As Maimonides explains in EC, asceticism is a confusion of a mere means with the end: the means of inclining to an extreme to rein in one's desires with an aspiration to root out desire as an end. Furthermore, despite the slight bow to the determination of natural temperament, Maimonides does indeed part ways with fideism as well as astral determinism, as he implies by mocking those who complain when their excesses get the better of them.

---

[17] EN 1114b30–35,

[18] *Guide*, Translator's Introduction, xcv, n63.

[19] Cf. with *Guide* 3.17, 465–66, 472. And see Joel Kraemer on Maimonides's loss of his beloved brother, David, at sea in *Maimonides: The Life and World of One of Civilization's Greatest Minds* (New York: Doubleday, 2008), 244–53. I do not share Kraemer's view that Maimonides's views on providence changed, or that they changed due to the depth of the loss of his brother.

Let us turn now to 3.13. We will turn here only briefly both because of the great complexity of the chapter and because I have already published many of my relevant thoughts elsewhere.[20] Here, though, we are most interested in the way that 3.13 continues to humble human being. If, in 3.12, the byword was that human beings view experience as evil because they overstate their own importance as individuals, here, in 3.13, that theme is followed through on with the elevation of the heavenly bodies or rather of the separate intellects that are responsible for their movements over human beings. That such an elevation is characteristic of the philosophic view is evident not only because philosophy comes into being first as inquiry into the whole, including cosmology, but also because the Bible tends to elevate human being. The first indications of that are, of course, already present in the opening pages of the Bible: in God's demotion of the heavenly bodies by denying they are the cause of light[21] and by the affinity between human being and God—since the former is the image and likeness of the latter. In 3.13, Maimonides underscores that human beings, though most splendid among sublunar beings, is not as sublime as the intellects of the heavenly bodies (455). The elevation of the heavenly bodies runs contrary to many interpretations of Genesis, which insist that man exists to worship God and that is the point of it all (450–452). Maimonides's elevation of the heavenly bodies or their intellects in 3.13 prepares the further humbling of human being in 3.14.

In 3.14, Maimonides reaches the rhetorical peak of the humbling of human beings, which will then be followed by one of the most hyperbolic chapters of the *Guide*, namely, 3.15, the most important chapter for proponents of the skeptical reading of Maimonides. But let us not get ahead of ourselves or fail to see 3.15 in its

---

[20] *Maimonides and Spinoza*, 153–161.

[21] See my citation of Strauss's "Jerusalem and Athens," in *Studies in Platonic Political Philosophy* (Chicago: University of Chicago Press, 1983) in *Maimonides and Spinoza*, 158n49.

rhetorical context. In *Guide* 3.14, Maimonides echoes the intonations of the "starry skies above," which he invokes near the opening of the *Mishneh Torah*.[22] Here, Maimonides uses the immensity of the universe and the greatness of the heavens to humble human beings, who as we've seen since 3.12 are so prone to elevate themselves as individuals. He writes, for example, "If the whole of the earth would not constitute even the smallest part of the sphere of the fixed stars, what is the relation of the human species to all these created things, and how can one of us imagine that they exist for his sake and because of him and that they are instruments for his benefit" (457). Maimonides also goes on to note that though it is absurd from the philosophic viewpoint to think that the heavenly beings concern themselves with individual human beings, it is permissible to think that they are concerned with human individuals insofar as the latter are members of a species of earthly beings. Ultimately, it would make no sense to make the nobler (heavenly intellects) be responsible for the baser (human intellects). Here Maimonides foreshadows views he will propound in 3.17 through 18, though not without interposing the smokescreen of 3.15 and 16. Note that before concluding the chapter, Maimonides acknowledges that the Talmudic rabbis seem to lack detailed knowledge of or to possess distorted notions regarding the heavens. Why he does this here is not immediately obvious—though he does thereby confirm his dependence on the philosophers for such knowledge.

I refer to 3.15 and 16 as part of a smokescreen because everything he argued about privation, evil, and providence in 3.10 through 14 depends on arguments contradicted in 3.15 and 16. The latter two chapters appear to call into question everything Maimonides built up so carefully in 1.71 through 76 about the "nature of existence" and about the dependability of intellect as opposed to

[22] *Mishneh Torah*, "Laws Concerning the Foundations of the Law," chapter 2, §2.

imagination. Furthermore, little could prepare the reader for the vehemence with which he rails against the philosophers about their views regarding divine knowledge as it relates to providence, attacking Alexander's account, only to turn around in 3.17 through 18 to side with the philosophers about providence, ultimately. The rhetorical tone of both chapters fifteen and sixteen are out of the ordinary.

Despite opening 3.15 with a declaration that the impossible has a stable nature, Maimonides proceeds to consider the bare minimum on which all schools agree, namely, that the principle of non-contradiction cannot be violated. Then however he considers other matters that would seem to undermine his original claim that everyone agrees that the impossible has a stable nature.[23] He considers the views of some Mutakallimun and then of the adherents of creation from absolute nonexistence. Only after this additional inventory does he launch into a short diatribe questioning the very concept of nature as well as the dependability of the intellect. If the second part of chapter fifteen is to be taken on its face, then skepticism would seem to know few if any limits.[24]

When Maimonides then turns to 3.16, he opens with some of his most polemical remarks about philosophy and philosophers. We will not repeat here what we already quoted from the opening of 3.16 back in chapter 3, though we will note that the arguments provided here are, as Maimonides notes, derived from one of the two Hellenistic commentators on Aristotle whom he and many others

---

[23] On this, compare Strauss's encapsulation of 3.15 in his outline (see appendix) in the Pines edition: "The nature of the impossible or the meaning of omnipotence."

[24] See Stern, *Matter and Form of Maimonides' "Guide,"* 241–242. It is not by chance that our book argues that the emphasis on matter is misplaced. What Maimonides argues about privation provides greater support for the philosophic understanding of the "nature of existence" and the dependability of intellect than Stern seems willing to grant.

consider truest to and most insightful about Aristotle, namely, Alexander of Aphrodisias. We have seen Maimonides elaborate on arguments provided by Alexander in connection with the causes of disagreement (1.31) and the question of what to consider when weighing doubts (2.23). Pines does not exaggerate when he suggests that the coherence of Maimonides's account of Aristotle derives in no small part from his reliance on Alexander as a guide.[25] Suffice it to say that the comments with which Maimonides opens 3.16 about the philosophers may be the harshest in the *Guide*. Maimonides uses religious language that the philosophers have here "stumbled" without the possibility of "absolution (*iqāla*)" together with the language of "disgrace" thematized in chapter 3.[26] A key feature of the chapter that adds to its polemical tone is his liberal use of personal pronouns, from his repeated use of the first person singular in Pines's first paragraph to ample use of "us" and "them" language in his third paragraph.

Despite the opening rhetorical attack on the philosophers, Pines's second paragraph of 3.16 opens with an explanation of what motivated the philosophic views he attacks. In brief, they were motivated by the prevalence of suffering among the "excellent (*al-fuḍalā'*)" and the prospering of the "wicked (*al-sharīrīn*)"—the classic problem of evil. Yet the problem was already addressed very directly from the side of human individuals in 3.12 with the response that evil is considered a problem only by those who fail to understand its nature as privation and above all who fail to understand how privation relates to the individual as opposed to the species. Seen in light of 3.12, 3.16's exploration of God's knowledge of or ignorance of particulars appears quite differently from the polemical tone with which Maimonides defends the revealed view that God

[25] Pines, Translator's Introduction, pp. lxiv ff. Also see Pines's index for other Maimonidean references to Alexander.

[26] As in 3.17, Pines renders *al-shanīʿa* as "incongruous" rather than "disgraceful." See Lane for the religious overtones of *iqāla*.

knows every particular. Here, we also take a leaf out of 3.14: though it may make sense that the heavenly intellects know about individuals through their species, it makes little sense that they should stoop to the level of concern with each individual human being (457-458). Given the superiority of God to the heavenly intellects, it doesn't take much to infer the implications of this for divine omniscience. It is worth noting that even after describing the disagreement between the revealed view and the philosophic view, Maimonides concludes the long third paragraph in Pines's translation by noting: on the one hand, there were philosophers before Aristotle who agreed with the former view that "God knows everything and that nothing secret is at all hidden from Him." Who these thinkers might be is completely unclear—unless Maimonides means something other than what he appears to mean by the vague locution about God's knowing everything. This adds to the polemical air, especially because he concludes by noting that Alexander sided with the philosophers because "good men are attained by evils."

As we turn from 3.16 to 3.17, we will shift our focus somewhat. Even the sort of rhetorical analysis we have just engaged in with respect to 3.16 would be too long and cumbersome for 3.17 for our current purposes, due to its complexity and length. As we have already noted, obstacle or impediment isn't a feature of 3.17 and 18; however, that is because the problem of evil is the most obvious expression of privation in relation to providence. Consequently, Maimonides has no need to add explicit reference to impediment or obstacle or hindrance to highlight the fact that the problem of evil is the impediment of divine particular providence. Here, we will focus on two features of 3.17.[27] Of course, we will strive to add evidence

[27] Two articles on Maimonides on particular providence have become classics: Alvin J. Reines, "Maimonides' Concepts of Providence and Theodicy," *Hebrew Union College Annual* 43 (1972): 169–206 and Charles M. Raffel, "Providence as Consequent upon the Intellect: Maimonides' Theory of Providence," *AJS Review* 12 (1987) 1: 25–71. Raffel is right in wondering whether Reines's conceptual analysis is sufficient. Raffel's piece is one of the longest

to our inquiry into Maimonides's view about and arguments regarding privation as it relates to providence, or the problem of evil, but we will also see whether our claim is plausible that, despite the apparent plethora of opinions on providence in 3.17, they boil down to the opposition between philosophy and Law or reason and revelation. If we can continue to show that much as there aren't really more than two positions on creation and prophecy, so there aren't more than that number regarding providence, then we will be in a better position to question the claims of scholars like Stern and W. Z. Harvey that Maimonides does not recognize tension between reason and revelation.[28] Among other things, if there really are so many differing opinions, then the weighing of doubts underscored in 2.23 is not only much more difficult but it also is lost from sight—as it seems to have been by Maimonides scholars.

The way that Maimonides enumerates the positions on providence in 3.17 intentionally emphasizes, even overstates, the number of positions. We will attempt to show that despite the appearance of upwards of eight positions, they are essentially reducible to two. He begins with Epicurus, giving him greater play than he had for cosmogony in 2.13 (284–85) or for prophecy in 2.32 (360). Much as he dismissed Epicurus in 2.13 because his arguments

---

journal articles I have ever seen. The length was warranted here. A bit like Kaplan's piece, Raffel's gives pointers to the whole scholarly landscape touching more lightly on the medievals, esp. Ibn Caspi or Kaspi, up through Reines and Norbert Samuelson. For a more extensive treatment of the medieval commentary tradition on Maimonides on providence, the interested reader should consult Dov Schwartz, "The Debate over the Maimonidean Theory of Providence in Thirteenth-Century Jewish Philosophy," *Jewish Studies Quarterly* 2 (1995) 2: 185–96. Jason Kalman, "Job the Patient/Maimonides the Physician: A Case Study in the Unity of Maimonides' Thought," *AJS Review* 32 (2008) 1: 117–140, gives a comprehensive treatment of providence in Maimonides's works beyond the *Guide*, which is useful even if one doesn't accept his Foucauldian premises.

[28] Cf. W. Z. Harvey, "A Third Approach to Maimonides' Cosmogony-Prophetology Puzzle," 74n14; and Stern, *Matter and Form of Maimonides' "Guide,"* 14–15.

demonstrating God's existence, unity, and incorporeality on the assumption of eternity should suffice to repudiate his view, so here he dismisses Epicurus because he relies on atoms and chance (even worse in some respects than the Mutakallimun) and because "Aristotle has demonstrated that this opinion is inadmissible (*istiḥāla*)."[29]

We will leave Aristotle's opinion to one side for now, given that his is the position that all the others oppose.

In effect, then, we intend to argue that all the rest of the opinions are reducible to the revealed position, much as we insinuated about the philosophic positions. The core revealed opinion is in a sense either the third (Ashʿarite) opinion or the fourth (Muʿtazilite) opinion, depending on whether one approaches them genetically or eidetically.[30] Ultimately, the Muʿtazilite opinion is the reasonable point at which the believer in revelation starts. There is one God, He is just. As the omnipotent creator of the world, He is capable of knowing and caring for every particular. Precisely because He is just, human beings have choice. The difficulty comes in accounting for the suffering of the innocent. The Ashʿarite opinion is the unreasonable point at which the believer in revelation will end if

[29] Part of our purpose in mentioning Epicurus here is to note that, despite appearances to the contrary, as Strauss has remarked about the Platonic-Aristotelian Alfarabi, "He has infinitely more in common with a philosophic materialist than with any non-philosophic believer however well intentioned." Leo Strauss, "Farabi's *Plato*," in *Louis Ginzberg*, Jubilee volume, Marx, Lieberman, Spiegel, and Zeitlin, eds. (New York: American Academy for Jewish Research, 1945), 392. In other words, aside from the capacity of human beings to provide for themselves (3.17, 465), what Maimonides remarks about Aristotle's view could be said equally about Epicurus: "There is no difference between the fall of the leaf and the fall of the stone, on the one hand, or the drowning of the excellent and superior man that were on board the ship, on the other" (3.17, 466).

[30] We have already remarked on and explored the reducibility of the many positions, especially of the Muʿtazilite and Ashʿarite, to one in *Maimonides and Spinoza*, 118–124. So far as possible I will avoid repetition here, though some may be inevitable. I will also dwell less on the details of Maimonides's text itself.

consistent regarding God's omnipotence and omniscience. If God really does know every particular, then the suffering of every being requires recompense. The length of absurdity to which this leads is the Muʿtazilite querying of the creator regarding the suffering of animals (3.17, 468).

When Maimonides turns to the fifth opinion, that is, "the opinion of our Law," he then subdivides them into that of Moses, the Sages, the latter-day Gaonim, and finally Maimonides's own opinion. Despite the appearance of four positions contained within the fifth position, there are contained here once again the two basic positions: the philosophic and the revealed. The account of the positions of Moses, the Sages, and the latter-day Gaonim are merely the genetic presentation, this time given in real time. That is, in the account of the Ashʿarite (third position) and Muʿtazilite (fourth position) he presented these two schools of *kalām* in the reverse of the historical order. The earlier (Muʿtazilite) school is frequently described as rationalist. It was, in the sense that it put more faith in the capacity of reason to uncover moral truths. Thus, this school is the proponent of the rational law teaching.[31] The later (Ashʿarite) is openly anti-rationalist and fideist. Like Alfarabi in his *Enumeration of the Sciences*, in 3.17 Maimonides presents these two Islamic schools of *kalām* from the less rationalist to the more—in the spirit that history moves from the less to the more rational, from the less reflective to the more. Yet the historical fact is that the teaching of the less consistent Muʿtazilites led inevitably—once logic was applied more thoroughly (and in this sense the Ashʿarites are more rational[!])—to the more. When he turns to Jewish *kalām* and presents it in the actual historical order, it follows a pattern closer to

[31] See Parens and Macfarland, *Medieval Political Philosophy: A Sourcebook*, 2nd edition (Ithaca, NY; Cornell University Press, 2011), 149n7, citing Alexander Altmann, "Saadya's Conception of the Law," *Bulletin of the John Rylands Library* 28 (1944) 2: 320–39 and Leo Strauss, "The Law of Reason in the *Kuzari*," in *Persecution and the Art of Writing*, 11, 97, 99.

that of actual Muslim history.[32] And ultimately Maimonides's objective is to appeal to the origins in Moses and appear to call his reader back to the origins, noting as he does near the beginning of his own account that "I am not relying on the conclusion to which demonstration has led me, but upon what has clearly appeared as the intention of the book of God and of the books of our prophets." In other words, Maimonides opens by supporting views that sound Muʿtazilite, in part because they are in harmony with those of Moses. For example, "For I for one believe that in this lowly world—I mean that which is beneath the sphere of the moon—divine providence watches only over the individuals belonging to the human species and that in this species alone all the circumstances of the individuals and the good and evil that befall them are consequent upon the deserts…" (471). It is not surprising that the earlier school of *kalām* would be closer to the original teaching of whatever scripture. Much like the Muʿtazilites though, the Sages went on to worry about undeserved suffering of particular human beings, raising questions about the "*sufferings of love.*" It is not by chance that both the Sages and the Muʿtazilites have stumbled across the problem of evil or of the privation of particular providence. Their responses are identical: if one suffers undeservedly here, then one will surely be rewarded in the next life, that is, "in order that his reward should be greater (*līʿaẓam jazā'ūhu*)."[33]

Although it may appear initially that Maimonides is taking the side of the Muʿtazilite *kalām*,[34] the subtle indicators he gives that

[32] For Maimonides's historical survey of the movement from the Sages to the latter-day Gaonim, see especially Pines ed. 470 (almost a quarter down the page) through 471, top paragraph.

[33] Cf. 3.17, 468 with 471.

[34] On Maimonides's approach to providence as a critique of the Muʿtazilite *kalām* as appropriated by Saadya Gaon, see Lenn Goodman, "Maimonides' Reponses to Sáadya Gaon's Theodicy and Their Islamic Background," in *Studies in Islamic and Judaic Traditon II*, William Brinner and Stephen Ricks, eds. (Atlanta, GA: Scholars' Press, 1989), p. 3, cited in Jason Kalman, "Job

this *kalām* will lead, when made more consistent, to the Ashʿarite *kalām* imply that he cannot ultimately take this position. After all, this position, he claims, is merely his affirmation of the intention of revelation (471). Based on his approaches to both creation and prophecy, not to mention his methods of proving God's existence, unity, and incorporeality, it is clear that Maimonides will not follow the guidance of revelation without inquiry. In addition, desert can be interpreted in a variety of ways, as will become more apparent not only as we proceed through the rest of 3.17 and into 3.18 but perhaps especially in relation to the case of Job as treated in 3.22 and 23. After he affirms the scriptural claim that God upholds the desert of each human individual (471), he turns to link providence to the same mechanism as appeared in prophecy, namely, "divine overflow (*al-fayḍ al-ilāhiyya*)." Here, something quite odd occurs. Rather than turn immediately to talk about the desert or merit of given individuals, Maimonides links overflow to the species, that is, the human species. It appears that here[35] just as in 2. 6, 12, and 36 overflow is not, as we might now say, individual specific. Now, it is true that over the next two pages of 3.17, he inventories scriptural passages, all to try to show that the Bible only envisions reward and punishment of the individual desert of the human species—as opposed to other animals. Yet how that desert is to be determined is left till the last moment—and in a manner that connects back to the initial reference to "divine overflow." Before settling on what determines to whom divine (that is, intellectual) overflow occurs, Maimonides raises the question, why does God watch over human individuals? Which almost immediately turns into the question, why did God give intellect to man? This question seems intended to make the reader think of Maimonides's rehearsal earlier in this chapter of the second opinion on particular providence, that is, Aristotle's account

the Patient/Maimonides the Physician: A Case Study in the Unity of Maimonides' Thought," 124n27.

[35] See 471-472.

of God's peculiar providence to the human species. Although Aristotle's God, of course, does not concern himself with human individuals, he did give to human beings the peculiar gift of intellect, which enables human beings to be self-provident.[36] Maimonides allows this question about why God gave intellect to man to lead down a rabbit hole referencing God's will or His wisdom or nature, depending on who answers the question. Of course, we had thought that it was Maimonides who was answering our questions! Still, he pauses to affirm that he does not think that anything is hidden from God (appearing to mean that God sees or knows every particular). Yet he places before his abrupt and far from self-explanatory answer to the question we already posed ourselves before he interposed his series of questions, namely, to whom does the divine intellect overflow? "But I believe that providence is consequent upon the intellect (*al-ʿināya tābiʿa li-l-ʿaql*) and attached to it." Although this extremely terse conclusion is not clearly explained in 3.17—above all, not making it clear whose intellect overflow is consequent upon, that of the giver (a trivial meaning if it were the case, since it goes without saying) or the receiver—Maimonides is almost completely clear about what he means in 3.18. He states there, as if completing an interrupted sentence: "providence is, as I have mentioned, consequent upon the intellect. Accordingly, divine providence does not watch in an equal manner over all the individuals of the species [despite the apparent indifference of its flow!], but providence is graded as their human perfection is graded" (475). Not surprisingly, he

[36] Given how studiously Maimonides avoids reference either to "practical intellect" or "prudence," it is worth comparing this passage (3.17, 465), especially its reference to "govern[ing], think]ing], and reflect[ing]" with the other passages in which he clearly references this form of intellect (namely, 1.53, 121; 1.72, 190–91). Also see my discussion of this in *Maimonides and Spinoza*, 169–71 and Steven Harvey, "Alfarabi, Averroes, and the Medieval Islamic Understanding of Phrónesis," in *Phronesis—die Tugend der Geisteswissenschaften*, Gyburg Radke-Uhlmann, ed. (Heidelberg: Universitätsverlag, 2012), 177–94.

turns immediately to reference the example of the difference in rank of the prophecies of different prophets—thus, confirming that in a sense prophecy is merely one expression of divine providence. In case it was lost on the reader that Maimonides's argument has now become indistinguishable from that of Aristotle,[37] he adds the following reference to Alfarabi, which confirms that Aristotle, Alfarabi, and Maimonides or Maimonides's interpretation of the Law are on the same page: "The [biblical] texts that occur with regard to this notion are so numerous that they cannot be counted; I refer to the notion of providence watching over human individuals according to the measure of their perfection and excellence. The philosophers too mention this notion. Abū Naṣr [al-Fārābī] says in his Commentary on Aristotle's 'Nicomachean [Ethics]': Those who have the capacity of making their souls pass from one moral quality to another are those of whom Plato has said that God's providence watches over them to a higher degree." From 3.12 to 3.18, Maimonides affirms time and again the need to see one's own experience in light of the good of the species. The philosophic insight that God or nature concerns itself with the good of the species rather than the individual is the key theoretical insight needed if one is going to engage in imitation of the God who must appear to be angry to the simple and foolish while in fact transcending every passion?[38] Nearly the final note of the chapter is that through the preceding account in which Maimonides has shifted from what sounded like the Muʿtazilite position to the Aristotelian position, "the fundamental principles of Law will become safe for you and conformable to you to speculative philosophic opinions" (476). We have, I believe, shown that despite the plethora of apparent positions, there really are only two: the philosophic and the revealed positions.

---

[37] Cf. Alvin Reines, "Maimonides' Concepts of Providence and Theodicy," 185n68.

[38] Cf. 3.32, 528–29 and 1.54, 126–27 with 1.36, 82.

## The Primacy of Intellectual Virtue in Maimonides's Job: 3.22, 23, and 51

We have at various times in the previous section affirmed a movement from Maimonides's echoing of the Muʿtazilite *kalām* emphasis on the Law's concern with the moral desert of human beings to his echoing of Aristotle's argument that providence is "consequent upon the intellect." That movement in what Maimonides characterizes as "my own belief…as the intention of the book of God and of the books of our prophets" is echoed by a meaningful ordering if not as movement in his account of the Book of Job in 3.22 through 23. In many interpretations of Maimonides's teaching in 3.17 as well as in the chapters on Job, however, this ambiguity is not presented as a movement. For example, Raffel has written of the opposition between the "we-account" or "our-account" (what I've been identifying with the Muʿtazilite *kalām*) and the "I-account" (the at least quasi-Aristotelian account) in Maimonides's presentation of his own opinion on providence in 3.17.[39] That there is movement in Maimonides's own opinion, however, echoes in a striking way the ordering or movement from one position to another in the Book of Job. Martin Yaffe recapitulates what Maimonides himself posits without clarification or elaboration (3.23, 494) as the series of opinions of Eliphaz,

[39] Charles M. Raffel, "Providence as Consequent upon the Intellect," 37 and 43–51. Raffel settled on pursuing "dual criteria" from philosophy and Law as of p. 36, when he indicated the need to follow Herbert Davidson's lead in running counter to the purportedly influence-tracing approach of Strauss and Pines. See pp. 27–28. Ultimately, Raffel will speak of "stages" in Maimonides's account in 3.17 and 18, though he does not view Maimonides as moving from one position to another (the Muʿtazilite to the Aristotelian) so much as going through a process that appears aimed at reconciling conflicting elements that appear in different stages. Ultimately, Raffel doesn't seem to find Maimonides's account 'conclusive or compelling' (71).

Bildad, and Zophar in his interpretation of the Book of Job.[40] What I have so far identified with the Muʿtazilite *kalām*, that is, the emphasis on just deserts, Maimonides identifies with Eliphaz (493), and Yaffe following Maimonides links to the Torah. In turn, the position of Bildad emphasizes that the innocent must not suffer here unless "to make great your reward" (493). In other words, he detects in this view a consequence of the first view, assuming that God is just. Yaffe following Maimonides in 3.23 attributes this view to the Muʿtazilite *kalām*, though it should be underscored that both the first and second views were expressed by both the Muʿtazilite *kalām* and the Law of Moses.[41] When finally Maimonides turns to the view of Zophar, he states, "everything follows from the will alone; no reason whatsoever should be sought for His actions" (494). Maimonides and Yaffe attribute the view of Zophar to the Ashʿarite *kalām*. The most striking fact about all this is that the Bible itself, even if it does not thematically link these three positions at least presents them in the order Yaffe encapsulates as Torah, Muʿtazilite, and Ashʿarite.[42] By presenting these three positions on providence in the biblical order, he hints at the movement from the earlier to the later historical positions (that is, from Muʿtazilite to Ashʿarite), which he suppressed at least initially back in 3.17. Perhaps most surprising of all is the implication that the Bible itself or at least the Book of Job includes within its ambit the potentiality to devolve into the Ashʿarite opinion—a possibility that Maimonides tries to deflect elsewhere in the *Guide*.[43]

---

[40] Martin D. Yaffe, "Providence in Medieval Aristotelianism: Moses Maimonides and Thomas Aquinas on the Book of Job," *Hebrew Studies* 20/21 (1979/1980): 62–74, esp. 68–70.

[41] Review 3.17, 467–68.

[42] See Maimonides's key citations for Eliphaz (Job 4:18–19, cited in Pines ed., 493n21); Bildad (Job 8:6–7, cited in Pines ed., 493n22), and Zophar (Job 11:5–7, cited in Pines ed., 494n25).

[43] For deflection, see 1.71, 177, and consider the way that Maimonides shows that the Muʿtazilite *kalām* cannot help but undercut human freedom to

More important than the inadequate views of Eliphaz, Bildad, and Zophar are, of course, those of Job and Elihu. For our purposes here, it will suffice to dwell on Job and his transformation. These issues will lead us seamlessly to 3.51. Raffel rightly points to the importance of Samuel Ibn Tibbon's letter to Maimonides, if only as a means of bringing out some of the threads that challenge most readers. According to Raffel, Ibn Tibbon has three dimensions to his account of Maimonides on providence especially as it culminates in 3.51: (a) miraculous intervention, (b) physical immunity through divination, and (c) intellectual immunity.[44] It is hardly surprising that, so far as we know, Maimonides never replied to Ibn Tibbon's letter. It is unclear what could have induced Ibn Tibbon to adopt such a literal reading of Maimonides's citation of Psalm 91 in 3.51.[45] The impetus for this whole line of argument comes from Maimonides's argument in 3.22 that Job went from a moment in his story when he suffered greatly to a moment when he ceased suffering or from a part of the story in which he loses all to a moment when he is given anew. But Maimonides presents this simply as follows: "The most marvelous and extraordinary thing about this [moment in his] story is the fact that knowledge is not attributed in it to *Job*. He is not said to be a *wise* or a *comprehending* or an *intelligent man*. Only moral virtue and righteousness in action are ascribed to him. For if he had been *wise*, his situation would not have been obscure for him, as will become clear" (3.22, 487). The change in Job or in his

---

the extent they acknowledge the belief they share with the Ashʿarites that God is truly omniscient (3.17, 468–69). For acknowledgment of the danger of devolving into the worse but more consistent Ashʿarite position, see Maimonides's treatment of the reasons for the commandments in 3.31. Fideists view the search for reasons to be anathema to God's rule.

[44] Raffel, "Providence as Consequent upon the Intellect," 34.

[45] Cf. Raffel, "Providence as Consequent upon the Intellect," 33–34 with *Guide* 3.51, 627n44, citing Psalm 91:7–8. Maimonides's quote is "*A thousand may fall at thy side, and ten thousand at thy right hand; it shall not come nigh thee. Only with thine eyes shalt thou behold, and see the recompense of the wicked.*"

situation leads to pointed questions about what accounts for the change. Maimonides is not interested in his changed conditions but only in his response to them. For whatever reason, even Ibn Tibbon seems not to have been sufficiently attuned to this. The suggestion that the change in Job could be tantamount to an actual physical immunity seems to have missed the way in which Maimonides treats what the Torah expresses in physical terms in almost purely internal terms.

In both Reines and Raffel, the effort to clarify this matter leads to contradictions or at least tensions within their arguments. Reines argues within a few pages: on the one hand, the talk of no evil touching a human being is not meant to suggest that one whose intellect has been perfected can be physically immune from, say, an earthquake but only that one is what Raffel would call "intellectually immune";[46] on the other hand, what Job suffered early on was the just desert of a merely moral man![47] Here, Reines seems to ascribe to Maimonides a punitive spirit that isn't to be found. Raffel attempts to gain purchase on these interpretive challenges by drawing a clear distinction between the providence consequent on practical as opposed to theoretical intellect.[48] Although Raffel is correct in trying to gain greater clarity about what Maimonides means in claiming that "providence is consequent upon the intellect," and although it is true that the practical intellect is directly involved in moral action and thinking, it seems to us that the focus on kinds of intellect misses the focus of Maimonides's argument much as claiming that Job's early suffering is just recompense for being merely moral. Maimonides provides the necessary clarification in 3.23. There it becomes clear that what changed was not Job's situation but his opinions: "However, the latter [that is, Job] said all that he did say as

---

[46] Reines, "Maimonides' Concepts of Providence and Theodicy," 191n89.

[47] Reines, "Maimonides' Concepts of Providence and Theodicy," 195.

[48] Raffel, "Providence as Consequent upon the Intellect," 63.

long as he had no true knowledge and knew the deity only because of his acceptance of authority (*taqlīdan*), just as the multitude adhering to a Law know it. But when he knew God with a certain knowledge, he admitted that true happiness, which is the knowledge of the deity, is guaranteed to all who know Him and that a human being cannot be troubled in it by any of all the misfortunes in question." The problem, then, is not as Raffel seems to suggest that at an earlier stage Job was merely the recipient of overflow to his practical intellect but at a later stage received overflow to his theoretical intellect.[49] Indeed, there is little reason to suspect that Maimonides means to distinguish these different activities of the same intellect in quite such rigid ways. This focus misses the more important point: that Maimonides is once again reiterating his shocking inversion in the relation of morality and contemplation. He does not mean to insinuate that being merely moral entails being deserving of punishment. Rather, he means to emphasize that knowledge of God provides a change in perspective. The key to that change in perspective seems to be a combination of opinions conveyed in *Guide* 3.10 through 12, which derive from a more fitting understanding of God. In 3.10, God is the cause only of good. What privations we suffer are either due to us, or to the ignorance of ourselves or other human beings, or to features of the cosmos that are required for the coming into being and passing away of individuals for the sake of the species. This change in perspective is decisive. If one wants to

[49] Cf. Raffel, "Providence as Consequent upon the Intellect," 63 with Reines's very extensive discussion of the "acquired intellect" ("Maimonides' Concepts of Providence and Theodicy," 189–203). Reines's discussion leaves one with the mistaken impression that Maimonides teaches a great deal about the acquired intellect. Reines's discussion gives almost no citations to the *Guide* because what little Maimonides says (cf. 1.72, 193) is not of much use in piecing together his elaborate account. Also cf. Maimonides's very light allusions to the separate intellects and perhaps to what he refers to as the hylic and acquired intellects in 1.72 in *Eight Chapters*, chap. 1 (Weiss and Butteworth ed., 64nn12–13).

call this "intellectual immunity," one wouldn't be far off. However, what this does not mean is that contemplating God provides one with a physical shield from physical suffering. Or to put this in terms of Raffel's recounting of Samuel Ibn Tibbon's division into (a) miraculous intervention, (b) physical immunity through divination, and (c) intellectual immunity; any talk of "physical immunity through divination" is tantamount to a "miraculous intervention." Ibn Tibbon appears to have read Maimonides's references to Psalm 91 literally when he should have read them figuratively. Maimonides sees in Job the exemplification of a change in perspective brought about through theoretical knowledge. Yet such theoretical knowledge does not have merely intellectual consequences; it has moral consequences. This becomes apparent when we turn to 3.51.

After having set forth the palace image and having denigrated one more time the acceptance of opinions based merely on the authority of others, in 3.51, Maimonides of course outlines a new kind of worship, intellectual worship, which he equates with the Talmudic conception of "*worship of the heart*." This transformation of the Talmudic conception of God is evident at least as early as the *Mishneh Torah*. Of course, in the introduction, Maimonides argues that his code together with the Written Law is sufficient to grasp all that is contained in both the Written (Torah) and Oral (Talmud) Law. With that seismic claim, he then turns in "H. Talmud Torah" to argue that Talmud can be divided into its parts. The ultimate result is that Talmud proper comes to be understood as the Account of the Beginning and the Account of the Chariot or *Pardes*.[50] Maimonides places the Account of the Beginning, which he redefines in the *Guide* as physics, and the Account of the Chariot, which he redefines in the *Guide* as metaphysics, as the very heart and soul of Talmud. It is in this spirit that we must come to understand the "*worship of the heart*" of *Guide* 3.51. No matter how emotional

[50] *Mishneh Torah*, "Laws concerning the Study of the Torah," 1.10-12.

Maimonides's account in 3.51 might seem to get, one must always remember that the love of God is only as strong as the knowledge of Him.[51]

When Maimonides goes on to describe the process whereby one prepares to achieve the fitting kind of love of God through inquiry, he sets forth a process that echoes the one he described in H. Talmud Torah: one that grabs larger and larger chunks of time for inquiry. The process he describes is one of turning inward certainly (3.51, 622–23); however, more than anything it encapsulates what it means to live for one's community externally while living for knowledge internally. In brief, this is a revisiting of the trope made famous by some of Maimonides's philosophic teachers, the weed or solitary.[52] One of the limitations of the pieces by Reines and Raffel is that they both fail to capture that Maimonides intends his vision of perfection as an extraordinary balancing act with parts that cannot be placed in easy harmony. This does not mean that Maimonides's account of particular providence falls short, as Halbertal states more flatfootedly than either Reines or Raffel.[53] Rather, this brings us back to the frame of this book as a whole. The tension between

---

[51] See 3.51, 627 and *Mishneh Torah*, "Laws concerning Repentance," 10.6.

[52] See Alfarabi, *Political Regime*, Ibn Bajja, *Governance of the* Solitary, and Ibn Tufayl, *Hayy the Son of Yaqzan* all in Parens and Macfarland, eds. *Medieval Political Philosophy: A Sourcebook*. In the *Political Regime*, see esp. pp. 53–55. Also see Parens, *Leo Strauss and the Recovery of Medieval Political Philosophy*, chap. 3; Michael S. Kochin, "Weeds: Cultivating the Imagination in Medieval Arabic Political Philosophy," *Journal of the History of Ideas* 60 (1999) 3: 399–416; and Peter S. Groff, "Cultivating Weeds: The Place of Solitude in the Political Philosophies of Ibn Bājja and Nietzsche," *Philosophy East and West* 70 (2020) 3: 699–739.

[53] Moshe Halbertal, *Maimonides: Life and Thought*, trans. J. Linsider (Princeton: Princeton University Press, 2014), p. 332, as cited in Robyn Ashworth-Steen, "How Satisfactory Is Maimonides' Solution to the Problem of Evil," *European Judaism: A Journal for the New Europe* 50 (2017) 1: 113–122, esp. 114n7.

philosophy and Law, between contemplation and morality, between the human individual and the city is real—captured first by Socrates in the *Republic* in the philosopher-king conceit. Maimonides captures this reality in an exquisite fashion not only in the account he gives of the two different lives anyone devoted to this sort of inquiry must live in 3.51, but also by having indicated so clearly the presence of this tension in *Guide* 1.34 (75) and 3.34 (534).

The almost inexhaustible richness of 3.51 has diverted us from moving as quickly as we should have to the next step in his argument there. Seen against the backdrop of the tension between the external and internal faces of human perfection Maimonides describes, we must try to determine what the sudden insight about the "impediment" or "veil" add to our previous forays into privation. To begin with, it is worth noting that there are not that many occasions in the *Guide* when Maimonides dramatizes a sudden insight. The other such occasion is in the introduction to part 3, just before presenting the mystifying recapitulation of the biblical Account of the Chariot (3.1–7). There, Maimonides states, when characterizing the necessity that compelled him to reveal the truths that he reveals in the *Guide*, he merely "followed conjecture and supposition; no divine revelation (*waḥy*) has come to me to teach me that the intention in the matter in question was such and such, nor did I receive what I believe in these matters from a teacher." However, just a few lines later he claims, "Now rightly guided reflection and divine aid (*al-maʿūna al-ilāhiyya*) have moved me to a position, which I shall describe." He goes on to describe that position as one in which he has been enabled to give an account of *Ezekiel*'s Account of the Chariot which appears merely to repeat his account in a different language. Back in 3.51, Maimonides does not even claim "divine aid." Here, he says, "A most extraordinary speculation (*naẓar gharīb jiddan*) has occurred to me just now (*wa-qad*) through which doubts may be dispelled and divine secrets (*asrār ilāhiyya*) revealed." Yet he does claim to touch on divine secrets. By now we have grown more than a little suspicious about what it would mean for Maimonides to claim that overflow occurs suddenly and to specific people. Leaving that aside, as we have mentioned before, he goes on to argue that when a human being with the proper intellectual nature and preparation fails to receive divine particular providence, it is due to the recipient. The way he puts it is:

> Thus providence always watches over an individual endowed with perfect apprehension, whose intellect never ceases from being occupied with God. On the other hand, an individual endowed with perfect apprehension, whose thought for a certain time is emptied of God; providence withdraws from him during the time when he is occupied with something else....Hence it seems to me that all prophets or excellent and perfect men whom one of the evils of this world befell, had this evil happen to them during such a time of distraction, the greatness of the calamity being proportionate to the duration of the period of distraction or to the vileness of the matter with which he was occupied. If this is so, the great doubt that induced the philosophers to deny divine providence watches over all human individuals ...is dispelled....For the thing that necessarily brings about providence and deliverance from the sea of chance consists in the intellectual overflow. Yet an impediment may prevent (*wa-qad inḥajaba*) for some time its reaching the excellent and good man in question, or again it was not obtained at all by such and such imperfect and wicked man, and therefore the chance occurrences that befell happened to him.

Given what we have argued previously—that providence takes a kind of precedence among the greatest themes of the *Guide*, creation, prophecy, and providence, because there is a sense in which creation and prophecy can be viewed as expressions of providence—Maimonides's explicit extension of this account to prophecy, when he casually refers to "all prophets or excellent and perfect men" not only confirms that but also leads us to think that what is argued here about "impediment" or "veil" should be thought to inform the account given in 2.32. Perhaps the talk of God's will preventing prophecy in 2.32 cannot be taken literally. At a bare minimum, this passage makes it amply evident that the only impediment to divine overflow is self-imposed. To restate this in the terms of particular providence, such providence is guaranteed to anyone with the right nature and preparation. That it is called "particular" is due only to the receiver. Maimonides's account of impediment or obstacle or hindrance, that is, privation, in relation to providence gives no indication that God acts with particular providence on behalf of any individual human being, despite the Muʿtazilite moments Maimonides permitted to color his account in 3.17. This last installment on privation casts a strange and powerful light back on the rest of the *Guide*. It will certainly help us to look at creation in a new light.

## Providence: General and Particular?

We began this chapter with observations drawn from Strauss about the difference between the discussions of general providence in *Guide* parts 1 and 2 and the discussion of particular providence in part 3, especially 3.8 through 24. As we neared the end of part 3 in the section immediately preceding this one, we came to see an important expression of Strauss's observation that the account of particular providence is a part of political science or philosophy. Maimonides's description of the tension between the internal search for God and the external concern with one's community is the very heart and soul of political philosophy. One could wonder whether our characterization of the *Guide* as a whole as engaging in political philosophy is warranted when we consider the theoretical reaches touched on in parts 1 and 2, among them an inquiry into general providence. But part 1, much like a Platonic dialogue, is saturated with human concerns from its very beginning. Not only do the lexicographical chapters touch on the secrets of the Law with reference to the Bible, indicating at every turn that whatever discussion of general providence takes place there has significance for how one is to interpret the Bible, but also the very first chapter indicates that

Maimonides's approach to words apparently indicating God's corporeality in fact have great significance for how we are to think of being a human being. That being made in the image and likeness of God means possessing an intellect is not only a theoretical claim but also a claim with almost incalculable political philosophic consequences.

Even Maimonides's discussions of general providence in part 1 reverberate very loudly not only theoretically but also practically or politically throughout the rest of the *Guide*. In particular, I have in mind Maimonides's discussion of God's providence with respect to the heavenly bodies in 1.11. In this chapter, we ran across a claim about providence that ties the discussion in 3.8 through 24 back to 1.11, namely, Maimonides's claim in 3.14 that it would be too much to imagine that the separate intellects ruling the heavenly bodies would stoop to concern themselves with individual human beings (457–58). Maimonides writes, "If we claimed that the final end of the spheres consists in the governance of, for instance, a human, individual or of several individuals (*shakhṣ insān āw ʿidda āshkhāṣ*) this would be impossible according to philosophic speculation. However inasmuch as we think that their final end consists in the governance of the human species, there is no absurdity in thinking that the final end of these great individual bodies is the existence of the individuals of the various species, the number of which individuals cannot—according to their doctrine—ever have an end." Now, it is undeniable that 3.14 along with 3.15 are attempting to at least appear to establish distance between Maimonides and the philosophers. We will not revisit here our reasons for thinking that this is part of a "smokescreen"; however, when we turn back to 1.11, we see strange echoes of this observation about the separate intellects as linked to the species rather than individuals. Of course, for the philosophers, whatever can be argued about the separate intellects can be argued *a fortiori* of God.

1.11 is the first of a series of three chapters (1.11 through 13) with a striking echo in 1.22 through 24.[54] These two sets of three chapters all deal with general providence, and the later set concern in particular the privation of providence. We will touch on the second set in our next chapter because in that second set Maimonides takes up not only the privation of general providence, which is chance, but also "will." For now, we must limit ourselves to 1.11. As Strauss suggests, part 1, chapters 1 through 49, which he dubs the lexicographical chapters because most of them treat a particular biblical term, a "chapter heading,"[55] contain terms that seem to portray God as corporeal. 1.11 is among those concerning place and change of place.[56] The chapter heading of 1.11 is "sitting (*yeshivah*)." Its first meaning is the literal meaning "being seated." Its second and figurative meaning "denote[s] all steady, stable, and changeless states." Of course, when the Bible speaks of God as sitting, Maimonides wants us to interpret this figuratively to mean that God is unchanging, which he makes clear when he quotes Malachi 3:7. Not only is God unchanging but any relation God has to anything other than Himself—which as he insinuates here he will go on to explain in 1.50 through 70 is really no relation at all—must not change. This unchangingness occurs most frequently "with reference to heaven, as [it] is changeless and without diversity; I mean to say that the individuals in it do not change, as do the individuals constituted by the terrestrial things which are subject to generation and corruption." God is said to be sitting also in relation to the terrestrial species

[54] I thank Brother Amadeus Cundiff for taking the time to sort through Strauss's elaborate comments on the lexicographical chapters to produce a chart that helped to confirm the peculiarities surrounding these chapters. Those elaborate comments appear at Strauss, "How to Begin to Study *The Guide of the Perplexed*," (Pines ed.), xxv and xxx.

[55] Strauss, "How to Begin to Study *The Guide of the Perplexed*," (Pines ed.), xxv.

[56] Strauss, "How to Begin to Study *The Guide of the Perplexed*," (Pines ed.), xi. See appendix.

because "these species are permanent, well ordered, endowed with a stable existence, such as is the existence of the individuals of heaven." When Maimonides reaches the penultimate sentence of the chapter, he states as straightforwardly as he ever does that God's only relation to the terrestrial beings is to the species (1.11, 38).

What interests us for the next chapter is that Maimonides makes it clear that God's relation to heavenly bodies and intellects is not a relation to or with individuals. These individuals have the status of a species.[57] Given what we know from our chapter 4,[58] the "particularization" of the planets and of the stars at play in *Guide* 2.19 would seem to concern an odd sort of "individual." Here, individuality appears to stem not from the matter but from the form. And as such it appears to be characteristic of a species. What the exact relation of "will" can be to such an individual is not an easy question to answer. With these problems still open, we conclude this chapter.

---

[57] Cf. Thomas Aquinas, *De ente et essentia*, chap. 4.

[58] We refer here to our discussion in chapter 4 of the dialogue between the philosopher and the Mutakallim in Maimonides's long discussion of 1.73, 10th premise about the different senses in which matter and form particularize.

## CHAPTER 7

# CREATION, IMPEDIMENT OR WILL?

In the two preceding chapters, we have inquired into impediment or privation as it relates to prophecy and then providence. In chapter 5, our inquiry into the obstacle to prophecy, will or volition at least initially seemed to play a prominent role. In chapter 6, our inquiry into the prevention of particular providence or the problem of evil, will did not seem to play a significant role. In other words, the only evidence of a role for will was that the human being of excellent nature and preparation, who was apparently indistinguishable from the prophet, could be impeded from providence by his own inattention to God. Whether that inattention was due to will or reason or simple distraction is not something Maimonides ever addresses.

When we turn to the issue of creation or the dispute between creation and eternity, will seems to play a prominent role. Indeed, will appears cheek by jowl with impediment, which has led us to the title of the current chapter. What from the perspective of philosophy could only be attributed to impediment, revelation appears to attribute to will. As Maimonides notes in 2.18, in a passage Pines has reasonably linked to Alghazali, "the true reality of...will [is] to will and not to will." While an impediment requires an impeding cause, will is as it were *sui generis*—apparently willing without incentives or impediments. Such an explanation of creation we might expect from Alghazali; however, given the intensity of Maimonides's critique of the Mutakallimun in 1.73 through 76 (and elsewhere in the *Guide* such as 3.17), one is left a bit startled when Maimonides appears to speak of God's will as acting *sans* incentive or purpose. This does not square with what we have already seen in 3.25, leaping ahead of Maimonides, nor will it square even with 2.19, where Maimonides will argue at first as if will is rightly or 'naturally' connected to "purpose," while necessity is not.

To address creation as it relates to will and impediment, we will begin where we left off in our last chapter with an inquiry into the two series of three chapters related to general providence in part one: 1.11 through 13 and 1.22 through 24. We begin there because, as we already noted in the last chapter, 1.22 through 24 link the privation of general providence to divine will. If we are to understand Maimonides's claim that God's will particularizes the order or disorder of the heavenly bodies in 2.19, we must first understand the observations Maimonides has to offer in part one about God as will, as the alternative to God as intellect. Of course, he says on more than one occasion that these faculties, which we know from our own experience, cannot mean the same thing in the case of God—indeed, they must ultimately be indistinguishable. Nevertheless, from the beginning of the *Guide* when he interprets Genesis's talk of man being made in the image and likeness of God, Maimonides attaches our likeness to intellect, not to will. When he turns eventually in part one to Hebrew correlates to the philosophic notions of intellect with which he begins, the key terms in 1.39 through 42 are no clearer for human being than they are for God. Yet Maimonides's explanation of the meaning of key lexicographical terms from the Bible concerning human and divine "psychology" gives rise to an oscillation between intellect and will, which will inform our inquiry into the divine will. Our consideration of 1.39 through 42 will lead us to a consideration of Maimonides's disagreements with Onqelos and Jonthan ben Uziel regarding God's will in 1.66 and 3.2, respectively. Those disagreements will help frame the way we read 2.18 through 21.

In the second part of this chapter, we will turn to impediments and the necessary existence argument in 2.intro and 2.1. Of course, the necessary existence argument is traced to Avicenna, but it has such a long itinerary after Avicenna and so much is done with it by various authors that it is often treated as a great watershed in the history of debates about creation and eternity. Some Maimonidean scholars treat Maimonides this way too. However, important evidence exists in *Guide* 2.intro and 2.1 that Maimonides views this argument as little more than a variation on an Aristotelian theme. Our reading of 2.1 in particular will go against the grain of recent readings that treat it as preparation for 2.19. Furthermore, as noted earlier, some scholars in recent decades have come to argue that Maimonides does not maintain creation proper but some form of "eternal creation." We want to look with care at his necessary existence argument to see whether he really intends to make room for eternal creation. To us, it seems that eternal creation is little more than a way of avoiding the weighing of doubts that Maimonides exhorts us to engage in in 2.23. Most importantly, we do not agree that eternal creation is capable of underwriting things like God's having given the Law to a particular people at a particular time and place. For that, one would seem to require a sense of will that makes creation proper (or creation "after" absolute nonexistence) possible.

In the third part of this chapter, we will pick up from the comparison of God and the Active Intellect in 1.68 to follow out the theme of impediments as it touches on both God and the AI through to 2.14. In 2.4 and 2.12, Maimonides positions the Active Intellect not only to play an important role in prophecy and by implication providence but also to serve as a lesser being with notable similarities to God, which will shine indirect light on God. Although Maimonides posited that God could not be impeded as early as 1.68, either He acts to impede others (2.32) or He somehow appears to suffer impediment when it comes to creating the world. Not until 2.14, Sixth Method will Maimonides make it clear why God must not be thought to suffer impediment.

In the fourth part, we will turn finally to the most important series of chapters in the *Guide* for determining Maimonides's argument regarding impediments to or will in God, 2.18 through 21.

The key terms in which he poses this problem are will, necessity, and purpose. Of course, the will of YHVH must never be confused with the necessity of the Prime Unmoved Mover. By means of convolutions regarding purpose, Maimonides brings the reader to wonder whether the God who particularizes in 2.19 really could be a creator, as he has led the reader to believe He is.

## THE PRIVATION OF GENERAL PROVIDENCE AND WILL

We touched on *Guide* 1.11 and its relation to 2.19 near the end of the previous chapter. There, we observed that in 1.11 Maimonides underscores God's unchangeableness and the consequence that He does not concern Himself with individuals other than the heavenly bodies, those individuals being peculiar and indeed akin to the species of the beings we know that come into being and pass away. This seems to imply that when he goes on in 2.19 to argue that God particularizes the heavenly bodies that He isn't really exercising particular providence in a way that we would recognize. This cannot but raise doubts about the claim that his having proven particularization proves in turn that such a being would be capable of creating the world. The reader will not be surprised to hear that 1.12 and 13 yield more of the same. Indeed, what makes these chapters strange is that they reaffirm the same basic observation, whether sitting, rising, or standing is attributed to God, in each case, though they might have different figurative meanings for other beings, they always mean the same thing with respect to God, namely, that God is stable. Despite the fact that at least in the case of "rising," God would seem to be moving, even in this case it must always be interpreted to refer to God's stability or unchanging relation to what is. The reference to general providence is confirmed then not only in 1.11 but throughout these chapters.

Although there are plenty of other chapters among the lexicographical chapters that indicate motion of a body,[1] 1.22, 23, and 24 possess similarities to 1.11, 12, and 13 that are remarkable and which point us to the crucial additional insights Maimonides intends to add to those already mentioned in relation to 1.11 through 13.[2] In these two series of three, the first item is an opposite or contrary of the second item and the third and second items are highly similar.[3] If 1.11 through 13 encapsulate the stability or unchangingness of general providence, 1.22 through 24 thematize the privation of general providence. Although it will not be until 1.25 that Maimonides will make God's Indwelling or *Shekhinah* or at least the verbal form of this especially corporealizing figure in post-biblical Judaism the chapter heading, this series of chapters, 1.22 through 24, as it were paves the way for this chapter on the divine presence.[4] When the Torah refers to God's Indwelling, according to Maimonides in 1.25, "it is used in the sense of the permanence of His Indwelling—I mean His created light—in a place, or the permanence

[1] For those closest by, see 1.15 (to stand erect), 1.18 (to approach, to touch, to come near), 1.21 (to pass). Others include 1.19 (to fill)—cf. 1.25 (to dwell, which references the *Shekhinah*)—1.21 (to pass, which is unique in its connection to the most anthropomorphic passage in the Bible, the one in which God appears to pass by Moses), and 1.30 (to eat, which is unique in its proximity to an activity of a being who comes into being and passes away, though it is moderated by the intermediation of fire).

[2] On these two series of three, see the last section in the previous chapter.

[3] Sitting (1.11) is apparently opposite to rising (1.12); rising (1.12) and standing (1.13) are sufficiently alike that they are sometimes used as synonyms. Similarly, to come (1.22) is a contrary to going out (1.23), as Maimonides himself mentions (1.23, 52); going out is at least for the most part synonymous with going (1.24).

[4] The Arabic equivalent of the Hebrew *Shekhinah* (namely, *sakīna*) has appeared previously at least in 1.10, 19, 21, and 22. For Maimonides's conscious effort to avoid making the Hebrew word, *Shekhinah,* into a chapter heading, see Strauss, "How to Begin to Study *The Guide of the Perplexed*," (Pines ed.), xxxi–ii.

of providence with regard to a certain matter" (55). Of course, given Maimonides's mission to de-corporealize the Bible, it is not surprising that he treats God's Indwelling as something He creates to symbolize His presence.

Be that as it may, 1.22 through 24 reference God's providence by reference to His Indwelling (Ar., *sakīna*) in 1.22. However, already in chapter twenty-two the Hebrew verb for "come" (*bo'*), unlike sitting, rising, or standing, is linked to the privation of providence. The way that Maimonides puts it is the following: "This term is also used figuratively to denote the coming about of something that is not at all corporeal....It is, in consequence, applied figuratively even to certain privations" (51–2). It is worth mentioning that the biblical proof texts for this privative usage are from the Book of Job. Beyond that, chapter twenty-two does not go much further than to connect "to come" with the "descent of His decree" or "His Indwelling." In contrast, chapter twenty-three on "going out," refers literally to a body going out but figuratively to the going out of a whole series of incorporeal things such as words, deeds, laws, and somewhat ambiguously "light," which again anticipates the created light of the Indwelling ahead in 1.25. But more importantly, again "decree," that is, God's decree is subject to a "going out" in a strange setting that cannot but bring to mind the coming into being of the world:

> His decree, which at present is hidden from us, will become manifest. I refer to the coming into being of something after its not having existed, for everything that comes into being from God, may He be exalted, is due to His decree. Thus: *By the word of the Lord were the Heavens made, and all the host of them by the breath of His mouth [Ps. 33:6].* In this verse God's acts are likened to those that proceed from kings, whose instrument in giving effect to their will (*irāda*) is speech. However, God, may He be exalted, does not require an instrument by means of which He could act, for His acts are accomplished exclusively by means of His will (*irāda*) alone; neither is there any speech at all, as shall

> be made clear. Inasmuch as the term *going out*, as we have made clear, was figuratively applied to the manifestation of an act of God—for Scripture says: *For, behold, the Lord goeth out of His place*—the term *returning* [*shibah*] is figuratively applied to the cessation of such an act likewise brought about in virtue of God's will. It says accordingly, *I will go and return to My place*, the signification of which is that the *Indwelling* [al-*shekhinah*] that had been among us is removed. This removal is followed by a privation of providence (*ʿadam al-ʿināya*), as far as we are concerned... For a privation of providence leaves one abandoned and a target to all that may happen and come about, so that his ill and weal come about according to chance. How terrible is this threat!

The faint train of notions that started in chapter twenty-two are now in full tilt. Previously, when discussing God's general providence, Maimonides had no recourse whatsoever to the notion of will. Here, "will (*irāda*)" comes into play, on the one hand, because of coming into being and, on the other hand, because of a "privation of providence (*ʿadam al-ʿināya*)." As we will see shortly, privation or impediment and will come to be inextricably bound up with one another. What from the viewpoint of eternity or nature must be understood as an impediment to something potential becoming actualized is readily understood as simply dependent on will from the viewpoint of creation. As we know from 2.23, the question is what are the doubts on each side? Although will might be thought to dissolve every challenge, it is dogged by the problem of purpose. It almost goes without saying that Maimonides cannot accept the easy way out of the fideist: God's will is God's will.

1.24 follows out the path that "going out" followed. It is little wonder that Maimonides started with "going out (Heb., *yeṣi'ah*)" rather than "going (Heb., *halikhah*)." Despite the greater simplicity of the English translation of the latter term, it is inherently less figurative, given how directly it is connected to the motion of living things. Its second meaning and first figurative meaning still refers to bodies if to ones that are subtler than living ones. Its third meaning follows roughly the same path with the going of "voice" if not "speech." It is used of God's voice in what is surely one of the most corporeal moments of the Bible in the opening of Genesis. Leaving aside that corporeal association, Maimonides subdivides or complicates the third meaning with "going" referring to "the spread of a thing or the withdrawal of providence." The sudden shift to the privation of providence was prepared by the previous chapter. Although Maimonides will add a fourth meaning ("living a good life"—alluding to the very basis of why Jewish law is referred to as *halakhah*, namely, following God's ways), we are interested in the abruptness of Maimonides's turn to the withdrawal or as we prefer to refer to it, the privation of providence. This privation is referred to, then, with one of the most powerful and troubling figures of the Bible: *the hiding of the face*. This in turn is accompanied by one of the most powerful impressions left by the biblical God, namely, His anger. The privation of providence, which was captured in the previous chapter as being left to chance, is here presented as being subject to God's anger or, to use the more colorful English expression, His wrath. It almost goes without saying that Maimonides is at great pains to insist, on the one hand, that all Jews must believe that God does not have a body, and, on the other, that he does not require that all believe the inevitable inference from that fact, namely, that God cannot possess passions.[5] When the reader combines the

[5] It is in 1.35 that Maimonides makes clear that all Jews must believe that God is incorporeal. The inference that God cannot have passions will be made most explicit in 1.36. Although in 1.35 Maimonides seems to suggest that all should be taught that God is not "subject to affections," that is part of a series of claims that he says must be "explained to everyone according to his capacity and ought to be inculcated in virtue of traditional authority (*taqlīd*)" (81). Given that Maimonides knows that fear of God's anger must continue to be used to shame those who do not know any better, this all seems to square well with the way he set forth the 13 roots of belief that all Jews should adhere to in *Commentary on the Mishnah*, Sanhedrin, "Pereq Ḥeleq,"chap. 10, 3rd root or principle.

insights of chapter twenty-four with those of chapter twenty-three, the result is that God's anger is linked to being left to chance. The privation of general providence is far from the apparent particular providence, even though it be negative, of God's anger. When combined with chapter twenty-two, will appears to be merely the other side of the coin of chance. This is hardly what a reader would expect, and it seems to anticipate some of what we will discover about will even when we turn to Maimonides's most intensive use of will in the *Guide*, namely, 2.19.

This early treatment of will is then built on and brought into some tension with subsequent discussions of intellect and will. Of course, God's will is one thing, and human will quite another. Nevertheless, before turning to some of Maimonides's comments on God's will in 1.50 through 70, we need to look at Maimonides's exploration of biblical views of both human and divine will in 1.39 through 42. That 1.1 presents an account of both human being and God more reminiscent of reason than of revelation has been mentioned previously. This series of four chapters near the end of the thirties of part one show up as at least somewhat at odds with 1.1. These chapters offer what I have referred to earlier as a biblical rather than a philosophic anthropology.

The series is "*heart* (Heb., *lev*)" (1.39), "*air* (Heb., *ruaḥ*)" (1.40), "soul (*nefesh*)" (1.41), and "living (*ḥay*)" (1.42). In the first two of these three chapters, the ones on heart and air (or more commonly "spirit"), both of these are meant at times to refer to either God's intellect or will or both figuratively. In the remaining two chapters on "soul" and "living," Maimonides claims that, with respect to God at least, the former references will and the latter knowledge, if not exactly intellect. Of the four terms, the first, "heart," is the most prominent in scripture as referring to the human principle. Maimonides lists five meanings for heart: (1) "the principle of life of every being," (2) "the middle of everything," (3) human "thought (*al-fikra*)," (3a) human "opinion," (4) God's "will (*al-irāda*)" and "providence (*ʿināya*)," and (5) "intellect (*al-ʿaql*)." The most striking fact is that even in the case of God, let alone human beings, the Bible does not have one word for these two powers or faculties, will and intellect, which philosophers are at such pains to distinguish. Ultimately, this is only emphasized by Maimonides's noticeable ambiguity about how the word is used with reference to God: "It is in this sense—I mean that indicative of intellect—that the term is applied figuratively to God in all the passages in question, save certain exceptional ones where it is sometimes used to indicate the will" (89). It is unclear whether the term is used to refer to both in some and only intellect in others or to intellect in most and will in just a few exceptional cases. This must make us wonder whether Maimonides ever needed to emphasize his denial of attributes quite so much if the Bible doesn't use any of these terms with precision.

Our curiosity about the implications for the discussion of attributes reaches an early peak in 1.53. There Maimonides insists that God's willing a multiplicity of actions implies nothing about whether God has attributes or is simple. The will, simple though it may be thought to be, is capable of producing a multiplicity of effects or performing a multiplicity of actions.[6] To make his point, he compares the multiplicity of effects achieved by what Aristotle might call a non-rational potency, namely, fire.[7] Oddly, this example makes

[6] The strange way Maimonides puts it is: "Though an agent is one, diverse acts may proceed from him, even if he does not possess will and all the more if he acts through will."

[7] Cf. Aristotle, *Met.* 9.2, where Aristotle discusses "heat" rather than fire. Aristotle's point is to contrast a non-rational potency with a rational one. It is the rational one that can have good as opposed to bad effects. In contrast, heat always does nothing but heat. Interestingly, while Maimonides emphasizes the multiplicity of actions of fire, he goes on to state that fire "performs all these actions by virtue of one quality, namely, heat." This tweak of an

one associate will more with a non-rational potency than a rational one. I cannot prove that Maimonides knew of the Aristotelian passage. However, this line of thinking has especially strange resonances when one looks ahead from the vantage point of 1.53 to God's willing the impediment of prophecy or providence.[8] At the same time, Maimonides's inability to point to a Hebrew term pinpointing will in contrast to intellect makes one wonder how different what Maimonides writes in 1.53 would be if it were to reference intellect rather than will. As we recall from our earlier inquiries into overflow (*fayḍ*) from God or the Active Intellect, both are described as overflowing superabundantly but also without discernment or preference toward all things. Maimonides's characterization of God as will in 1.53 seems as if it could just as well be used to characterize intellect. This in turn makes what Maimonides argues in the rest of 1.53 about how power, knowledge, living, and will are not distinct attributes in God start to make even more sense. Yet one wonders whether they coincide with intellect or knowledge more than will.

Let us return from our digression on 1.53 to the series of four chapters: 1.39 through 42. With respect to *ruaḥ* (1.40), translated by Pines as "air," Maimonides identifies six meanings: (1) the element, (2) blowing wind, (3) animal spirit, (4) "the thing that remains of man after death," (5) divine intellectual overflow, and (6) "purpose and will (*al-gharaḍ wa-l-irāda*)" or purpose and "governance

---

Aristotelian observation might be compared with the similar tweaks to the passage from EN regarding the sense of touch (see note 34 in chap. 2) as well as the passage from *De anima* regarding the difference between the senses and the intellect, which supports the notion that the intellect is immaterial and immortal (see note 33 in chap. 2).

[8] As in the previous two chapters, comparing 2.32 with 3.51—though in 3.51 it would appear that God never withholds providence from those who are worthy, in the final analysis.

(*al-tadbīr*)."[9] Much as he did about "heart," Maimonides is at the peak of his ambiguity with respect to God. He writes, "In all cases in which the term *air* is applied to God, it is used in the fifth sense; in some of them also in the last sense, which is that of will, as we have explained." Here (1.40) Maimonides is less ambiguous than he was in the previous chapter, that is, it is clear that where will is the meaning of *ruaḥ*, it is both will and intellect. Strikingly, in the case of both heart and *ruaḥ*, the main sense is intellect. One wonders whether this is more Maimonides's sense of the intent of the Bible or perhaps it is his intention to pull the Bible in that direction.

In 1.41, "soul (*nefesh*)" has five meanings: (1) "animal soul common to every sentient being," (2) blood, (3) "rational soul," (4) "the thing that remains after death," and (5) the will. Maimonides attributes to the Bible rare precision in the use of this word. According to him, when used with reference to God it only refers to the will. Yet Maimonides makes trouble for this straightforward interpretation. He cites, "*And His soul was grieved in the misery of Israel*" (I Sam. 2.35). According to Maimonides, Jonathan ben Uziel decided not to translate it because he supposed that it was attributing an animal soul to God. Maimonides tries to make sense of the passage by reading into it an entire drama of the people Israel serving God improperly, subsequently repenting, and God's "refraining from letting their misery and wretchedness continue." As he goes on to note, this is "strange"—presumably because it appears to attribute change to God or because it insinuates that God punishes by causing evil. Evidently, here we are far from either the stability of sitting, rising, or

[9] When Maimonides references "governance" for the second time in this passage, he says, "as we shall explain in the chapters that deal with governance." Pines usefully infers that Maimonides is here referring to *Guide* 3.2. See Pines ed. p. 90, note 21. As we will see shortly, we will need to touch on Maimonides's extremely elusive Account of the Chariot interpretation in 3.1–7 to round out our discussion on intellect and will in 1.39–42.

standing or the constant overflow of God in part two—not to mention God's causing only good in 3.10.

In 1.42, "living (*ḥay*)" has three meanings, two of which are subdivided: (1) "a being that grows and is sentient," (2) "recovery from a very severe illness," (2a) and living, which are respectively opposed to death and severe illness, (3) the acquisition of knowledge, (3a) correct versus false opinion. It is noteworthy that in this case "living" does not refer to God but only to how for human beings "*good* is *life*" and "*evil* is *death*." This is made all the more striking by the fact that in 1.53 Maimonides will acknowledge, as he does thereafter,[10] that "living" is often attributed to God. It would appear then that just as we thought we were on the verge of finding a term that refers to God unambiguously as intellect that that meaning falls through. It would seem that God is either confused with living beings, which pass away, or that living when attributed to God means little more than good in the manner of living rather than dying. To sum up, although Maimonides interprets the Bible as intending intellect more than will with these key terms, will seems to prevent any clarity about God as intellect. Our sense that Maimonides has suspicions about will as it relates to God will only grow as we proceed in this chapter.

Before we are able to turn to part two of the *Guide*, we must follow out a thread that appeared briefly earlier in this book and which will lead us briefly to part three of the *Guide*, specifically to 3.1 through 7 on the *Ma'aseh Merkavah*, namely, the strange disagreement between Maimonides and Onqelos about God's will and the crucial passage from Exodus 32: "and the tables were the work of God" in 1.66. This chapter seems to be the first occasion on which Maimonides indicates any disagreement he might have with the Hellenizing Aramaic translators of the Bible, Onqelos the Proselyte and Jonathan ben Uziel. Although Maimonides leans heavily on

[10] See 1.56 through 58.

Onqelos and Jonathan because they both uphold the teaching he intends for the widest audience, namely, they are almost unfailingly anti-corporeal in their translations of the Bible, he has subtle disagreements with each of them. At first his disagreements appear not to be linked at all; however, closer examination will reveal a subtle thread concerning God's will.

The reader will recall that we touched on *Guide* 1.66 in our first chapter because it set the stage for Maimonides's discussion of what we have referred to as the Half-and-Half Teaching. I described the chapters leading up to and including 1.67 as the "first half" of the Half-and-Half Teaching, that is, the creation half. Maimonides takes issue in 1.66 with Onqelos's translation choices regarding the following verse: "When [the Lord] finished speaking with [Moses] on Mount Sinai, He gave Moses the two tablets of the Covenant, stone tablets inscribed with the finger of God."[11] As I acknowledged earlier, rather than fully de-corporealize this passage by replacing "finger" with "will," Onqelos merely translates, according to Maimonides, *written with a finger belonging to the Lord.* Interestingly, Maimonides goes on to explain that Onqelos "intends to signify by this that the finger is a created instrument that has cut into the tables through the will of God. I do not know what has led him to make this interpretation" (1.66, 161). Maimonides goes on to wonder whether "the existence of the writing on the tables is any stranger than the existence of the stars in the sphere?" Well, frankly, it is. As I argued earlier, what appears to lead Onqelos to stumble here in his quest to decorporealize is the difference between written conventions and natural or superlunary beings like the heavenly bodies. Perhaps the thing that gives Onqelos pause is that God's will in relation to written conventions is working at a particular time and place, while the creation of the heavenly bodies is either created or

[11] This is a slightly modified version of the translation of Exod. 32:18 in the *Jewish Study Bible* (Oxford: Oxford University Press and the Jewish Publication Society, 1985, 1999, 2004), 183.

eternal but no matter how one looks at it somehow transcending the earthly realm. Much as Maimonides argued for speaking of the Indwelling of God as a "created light" (1.25), so it would appear Onqelos inclined toward a created finger as the cause of the writing on the tablets.[12] The next time a disagreement occurs with one of Maimonides's Hellenizing Aramaic translators, in his interpretation of the *Ma'aseh Merkavah*, 3.1–7, will provide us with additional clues about what Maimonides is trying to explain regarding the animus of the Hellenizing translators with respect to God and will.

Although, in 3.2, Maimonides takes only very subtle issue with Jonathan ben Uziel's approach to *ruaḥ*,[13] the issue he will take will shed light on Maimonides's disagreement with the Aramaic translators. Maimonides writes,

> For he says concerning the *living creatures: Whither the air [ruaḥ] will be [yihyeh] they will go; they turned not when they went. Ruaḥ* here does not mean wind, but purpose (*gharaḍ*), as we have made clear when speaking of the equivocality of *ruaḥ*. He says accordingly that the *living creature* runs in the direction in which it is the divine purpose that the *living creature* runs. *Jonathan ben Uziel*, peace be on him, has already interpreted this too in a similar way, saying: *They went wherever the will was that they should go, and they did not turn when going.* Now inasmuch as his saying reads, *Whither the air will be they will go*, and consequently its outer meaning signifies that sometimes God will wish in the future that the *living creature* should go in a certain direction and then it would take that direction and sometimes again He will wish that it should go in another direction different from the

---

[12] Of course, Onqelos's appearing to attribute the finger to God Himself is surprising, given his typically de-corporealizing approach to God.

[13] We will not concern ourselves with the more profound disagreement voiced in 3.4 (424) about the *ofannim* and *ḥayyot*. For a recent treatment of this disagreement, see Howard Kreisel, "From Esotericism to Science: The Account of the Chariot in Maimonidean Philosophy till the End of the Thirteenth Century" in *Judaism as Philosophy* (New York: Academic Studies Press, 2015), 209–269, esp. 241n82.

> first and it would go accordingly; he goes back to the passage and explains this obscure point, letting us know that that is not so and that *yihyeh* [*will be*] has here the meaning of *hayah* [*has been*], as is often the case in Hebrew. Thus the direction in which God wished the *living creature* to go had been determined; the *living creature* takes the direction that God has wished it to take; and the will is constant regarding this direction.

This is not an easy passage. Let us begin with the simplest divergence between Maimonides and Jonathan: how to interpret the meaning of *ruaḥ* in this passage. Maimonides refers the reader back to 1.40 in the second quoted sentence. There we saw that *ruaḥ* had six meanings. The sixth was "purpose and will (*al-gharaḍ wa-l-irāda*)." As our discussion of 2.18 through 21 will make amply evident, purpose and will are far from synonymous. Although Maimonides will argue initially as if purpose and will are together in opposition to necessity, over the course of those chapters they will be drawn into opposition. We have already seen warrant to think that there might be a problem here. After all, when in 2.18 Maimonides alludes to the Ghazalian view of will, he avers: "the true reality of… will [is] to will and not to will," that is, without purpose or incentive. Seen against the backdrop of the earlier contention in 2.18 through 21 over will and purpose, the earlier equivalence in 1.40 of will and purpose, then appears in a very strange light indeed in 3.2. Despite 1.40, it would appear that when Maimonides writes about "purpose" one suspects that he has one thing in mind, and when Jonathan references "will" here he has quite another. After all, one of the most ancient reasons for thinking the gods were associated with the heavenly bodies was the very wandering of those bodies. Of course, we need look no further than 2.19 to realize that the great challenge of Maimonides much like that of every other philosopher is to argue that whatever will one attributes to God it must be compatible with purpose. Although we cannot prove this here, we suspect that Jonathan thinks of God's will as less purposeful or freer than does Maimonides. Despite the apparent convergence over will and purpose in 3.2, it seems to us that Maimonides is indicating very subtly that the Aramaic translators though they were fully on board with the de-corporealizing project, that he may diverge with them over the constancy of God's will. Although de-corporealizing is certainly an effect of philosophy, that does not mean that these translators considered the "nature of existence" to be their North Star as Maimonides seems to.

## Impediments, the Necessary Existence Argument, and Eternal Creation

The introduction and first chapter of part two provide indispensable framing for our eventual consideration of 2.18 through 21. In particular, we are interested in 2.intro, 18th premise and 2.1, 4th speculation. We focus on these moments because impediment plays a role here that will pave the way for its role in 2.18 through 21. The main focus of scholars in 2.intro and 2.1 is on Maimonides's use less of Aristotle's argument for God's existence from motion, or the so-called physical proof, than the necessary existence argument.

Josef Stern has developed a provocative argument about Maimonides's use of the necessary existence argument drawn from Avicenna. Although Stern's primary focus is on 1.71 and 2.2, the stage is set for the second argument of 2.2 in 2.intro and 2.1. Stern joins his argument in the first of his two central chapters: "Maimonidean Skepticism I."[14] We are less interested in the details of his argument than in his conclusions. He concludes that the argument for God's existence from creation and the argument for God's existence from eternity briefly outlined in 1.71 (181) and 2.2 (252) refer to the same God, noting that W. Z. Harvey and Joel L. Kraemer do not agree that the God is the same in both cases.[15] Now, since chapter 1 we

---

[14] See Stern, *Matter and Form of Maimonides' "Guide,"* 151–159.

[15] Stern, *Matter and Form of Maimonides' "Guide,"* 154n35 cites W. Z. Harvey, "Maimonides' First Commandment, Physics, and Doubt," in *Hazon Nahum: Studies in Jewish Law, Thought, and History: Presented to Dr. Norman*

have been arguing, as do Kraemer and Harvey, that the God of eternity and the God of creation must be different. Certainly, Maimonides gives different accounts in 1.50 through 70. Nevertheless, Stern is correct that the necessary existence argument is intended to encompass both accounts of God. It is so simple an argument that it is able to do that. That is both why Avicenna invented it, and why Maimonides employs it. That is different from saying that the Necessary Existent means the same thing in both contexts.

The effects of Stern's argument that the Necessary Existent can be both creator and eternal cause of an eternal world, however, are strikingly similar to the effects of the arguments of W. Z. Harvey and Howard Kreisel, mentioned in chapter 1, that Maimonides ultimately overcomes the opposition between eternity and creation by insinuating or implying or perhaps stating between the lines an eternal creation argument.[16] This similarity is in some ways expected and in others not. Given that all three of these authors[17] maintain the Twerskian view that there really is not any tension between

---

*Lamm on the Occasion of His Seventieth Birthday*, J. Elman and J. S. Gurock, eds., (New York: Yeshiva University Press, 1997), 153 and Joel Kraemer, "How (Not) to Read *The Guide of the Perplexed*," *Jerusalem Studies in Arabic and Islam* 32 (2006): 350–403, esp. pp. 365–67. (Stern mixes up his two citations, which is of course easy to do with the author-date system.) Also Stern cites Joel Kraemer, *Maimonides: The Life and World of One of Civilization's Greatest Minds* (New York: Doubleday Press, 2008). The remaining page number he gives (p. 17) though attached to the wrong author-date is no use here. He seems to mean, instead, pp. 327–28.

[16] W. Z. Harvey, "A Third Approach to Maimonides' Cosmogony-Prophetology Puzzle," originally in HTR 74 (1981): 287–301; reprinted in *Maimonides: A Collection of Critical Essays*, Joseph Buijs, ed. (Notre Dame, IN: University of Notre Dame Press, 1990), 71–88, esp. p. 79n54 and Howard Kreisel, "Maimonides on the Eternity of the World," in *Judaism as Philosophy: Studies in Maimonides and the Medieval Jewish Philosophers of Provence* (New York: Academic Studies Press, 2015), 40–69, esp. p. 63. See chapter 1, note 22.

[17] W.Z. Harvey, Howard Kreisel, and Josef Stern

philosophy and Law, these effects are not surprising. However, one would think that as a proponent of skepticism Stern would feel more strongly the tension between eternity and creation in making these claims about the Necessary Existent. At the same time that he argues the two arguments from the opposing assumptions of eternity and creation presuppose the same God, Stern also argues that the Necessary Existent, as Maimonides envisions him is an "Abrahamic particularizer."[18] In other words, Stern seems to hold that the arguments provided in 2.intro and 2.1, especially those regarding the Necessary Existent are in fact preparing the argument for creation in 2.19. It is more typical to suppose that the arguments in 2.intro and 2.1 rest on the assumption of eternity, as promised at the end of 1.71 (183–84). Stern is able to make such a claim about the Necessary Existent as the "Abrahamic particularizer" because he views 2.2 as providing a distinct argument from that of the philosophers. We have difficulty seeing how the rough sketch in 2.2, which is not substantively different from the one argued in 1.71, offers an argument as distinctive as Stern claims.

Be that as it may, as we now take a closer look at Maimonides's arguments about impediments as they arise in his development of the necessary existence argument in 2.intro and 2.1, we will try to show that at least according to Maimonides's lights the necessary existence argument so vaunted by Avicenna is not so novel as it first seems. Indeed, we will try to show that Aristotle himself has the necessary existence argument in seed, *pace* Avicenna. Unfortunately, one more digression must be taken before turning to impediments. Stern considers Maimonides's move at the end of 2.4 (258–59) to distinguish the Necessary Existent from the Prime Unmoved Mover to be a watershed that makes possible his argument that the God of eternity and of creation are the same God.[19] We see the matter

[18] Stern, *Matter and Form*, 156–7.
[19] Stern, *Matter and Form*, 155–56.

differently. Although we agree that Maimonides's combination of the argument from motion with the necessary existence argument in 2.intro and 2.1 facilitates a distinction between the highest mover and God as Necessary Existent in 2.4, we do not share the view that Maimonides's approach to the Necessary Existent is meant to establish one account of God as common to eternity and creation, though he does intend a rhetorical accommodation between the two accounts of God. Rather, Maimonides combines the necessary existence argument and the argument from motion in this way as part of rendering Aristotle's arguments compatible with the monotheistic setting. That is, he distinguishes the Necessary Existent from the highest mover to draw a clearer line between God and the separate intellects than Aristotle does between the Prime Unmoved Mover and the subordinate unmoved movers. In other words, this subordination of the highest cause of motion to the Necessary Existent will contribute to another important argument Maimonides sets forth in 2.1, namely, the proof that God is one. Although it is true that Aristotle is the thinker who got the Western tradition to take sufficiently seriously what it means to be one or as we render his key term "simple,"[20] the similarity of the PUM and the other unmoved movers is great enough to need modification in a monotheistic setting. After all, 2.4 is part of Maimonides's argument about the angels or separate intellects.[21] We cannot agree with Stern that Maimonides intends to engage in a serious dispute with the philosophers about the separate intellects.[22] We do not argue this because we hold that

---

[20] "Simple (*haplos*)." Cf. *Guide* 1.57, 132, 3rd para. with *Met.* 4.5, 4th meaning of "necessary," esp. 1015b12.

[21] See Strauss, outline in "How to Begin to Study *The Guide of the Perplexed*," in Pines ed., p. xii. See appendix.

[22] Stern, *Matter and Form*, chap. 7, pp. 250–305, esp. the three discrepancies between 1.72 and the account of the separate intellects in 2.3 through 12 (pp. 273–289). Cf. Maimonides's remark in 1.72, 193, which plays such a central role in debunking the separate intellects for Stern, "However, the case of the intellects of the heavens, that of the existence of the separate intellects,

Maimonides remains committed to Aristotle's account of the motions of the heavenly bodies. On the contrary, we accept that all the challenges to providing a causal explanation for the apparent disorder of the motions of the planets and the placement of the stars would lead Maimonides to hold the accounts of separate intellects quite lightly. Nevertheless, we would explain Maimonides's silence about the separate intellects in 1.72 as deriving from the fact that Maimonides wants to place them—if they exist—in their proper subordination to God. For that reason, he waits until he lays the ground that he needs for taking up the separate intellects until after he has proven God's existence, unity, and incorporeality. Following Avicenna, he takes advantage of the necessary existence argument to underscore the difference between God and all other eternal beings.

Leaving these complications aside, we intend here to look with some care at the arguments Maimonides makes about impediments in connection with God as Necessary Existent. Once again, our intention is to provide needed argumentative context for Maimonides's arguments about God and impediments in 2.18 through 21. The 18th premise in 2.intro is the first in a series of premises (the 18th through at least the 24th premises) needed for the necessary existence argument proffered in the 3rd and 4th speculations in 2.1.[23] It

---

and that of the representation of the acquired intellect, which is also separate, are open to speculation and research. The proofs with regard to them are well hidden though correct; many doubts arise with regard to them; the critic may well find in them objects for his criticism and the caviller objects for his cavilling." When one puts comments like this together with Maimonides's heavy reliance on the separate intellects to humble human being in 3.13 and 14, one suspects that Maimonides's critique of the separate intellects is perhaps less severe than Stern suggests.

[23] That all these premises serve the necessary existence argument is evident from the way they all discuss the relation between essence and existence and about the composition not only of matter and form (as in the twenty-second premise) but also the composition of "notions" as in the twenty-first premise. Note also, for example, how in the nineteenth premise, Maimonides

is worth noting how deeply integrated with the other premises it is, so that the 25th and 26th premises , so essential to the "physical proof," seem to be of-a-piece with the 18th through the 24th. We do not agree with those who argue that Maimonides is here establishing a significant departure from Aristotle, despite what we've already noted about his demotion of PUM and other movers or as he calls them separate intellects.

Here is the 18th premise: "Everything that passes from potentiality to actuality has something other than itself that causes it to pass, and this cause is of necessity outside that thing. For if that cause were that thing and there were no obstacle to prevent this passage (*wa-lam yakun thumma māniʿ*), the thing would not have been for a certain time in potential but would have always been in actu. If, however, the cause of the passage from potentiality to actuality subsisted in the thing, and if there was at the same time an obstacle (*māniʿ*) to it, which was subsequently removed, there is no doubt that the factor that put an end to the obstacle (*al-māniʿ*) is the one that caused that potentiality to pass into actuality. Understand this." These lines will resonate as we consider Maimonides's many arguments confronting the possibility of creation. If God created the world whether it be *after* nonexistence (that is, ex nihilo) or *from* nonexistence (that is, as the beginning of time, though not eternally),[24] one cannot avoid thinking that God would have been impeded from acting. What is perhaps most striking about this premise as essential for the necessary existence argument is that all the talk of obstacles here is counterfactual. Evidently, the only way to think of God as the necessary existent Who causes beings that exist potentially to actually come into being is to think of God as being

---

refers to being "possible with regard to existence" in much the same way as in the eighteenth premise he refers to being "in potential" and especially of the "passage from potentiality to actuality."

[24] Review *Guide* 2.17, 296.

impeded. This is a counterfactual because, of course, as we know from 1.68, God cannot be impeded.

Perhaps what is most noteworthy about the eighteenth premise is that it is a version of the Aristotelian argument that actuality has preponderance over (or as he puts it is "prior" to) potentiality.[25] Indeed, the opposition between the necessary existent and possible existents is little more than a recasting of this most basic opposition, *pace* Avicenna's claims to novelty, as we will show shortly. One of the reasons that we doubt the sense in overstating the novelty of Avicenna's necessary existence argument is that Aristotle states something akin to this argument when, in *Metaphysics* 12.6, just two chapters before the proof of God's existence from motion, he reminds the reader of how universal the view is that actuality is preponderant over potency. Unlike the Mutakallimun, who, as we know from chapter 1, do not recognize this preponderance, all the philosophers appear to agree on this, even materialists like Leucippus and Democritus.[26]

The 4th speculation in 2.1 makes evident that the 3rd and 4th speculations are of a piece—and seems to bear out our suggestion that the necessary existence argument is merely a variation on the theme of potency and act.[27] To simplify, let us state this as a proportion—act : potency :: necessary : possible. The cause that makes the being capable of moving from potency to actuality is described as follows by Maimonides:

> Now everything that passes from potentiality into actuality has something outside itself that causes it to pass, as has been mentioned in the eighteenth premise. It is also clear that this something, which in one particular case causes to pass from potentiality to actuality, had been a cause of this passage in potentia and

[25] For further insight into Aristotle's use of the claim that actuality is prior to potentiality, see *Met.* 9.8.

[26] *Met.* 12.6, 1072a5–10.

[27] Cf. 5th and 6th Methods in 1.74 of "proving" a creator or creation.

> then only became a cause in actu. Now the reason for its having been in potentia might lie either in an obstacle (*li-mâniʿ*) subsisting in its own right or in a relation—which has been absent before—between it and the thing it is to cause to pass from potentiality to actuality. When this relation is realized, it actually causes the thing to pass from potentiality to actuality. Now these two explanations necessarily require something that causes to pass from potentiality to actuality or a factor that puts an end to a hindrance (*ʿā'iq*). And the same thing must necessarily be said of the second something that causes to pass from potentiality to actuality or of the second factor that puts an end to a hindrance (*al-ʿā'iq*). And this series of causes or factors cannot continue to infinity. There is no doubt that, in the last resort, one must come to something that causes the passage from potentiality to actuality, that is perpetually existent in one and the same state, and in which there is no potentiality at all. I mean to say that in it, in its essence, there is nothing in potential. For if there were possibility in its essence (*fī dhātihi imkān*), the thing in question would at some time become nonexistent, as has been mentioned in the twenty-third premise.

Maimonides precedes shortly thereafter to appeal even to the 16th premise, reaching back into the premises from the first to the seventeenth all of which are needed for the so-called physical proof.

Although we acknowledge that nowhere in the 4th speculation does Maimonides use explicitly the language of necessary existence,[28] he does indeed build his whole argument on the 18th premise. The reason that he does not have recourse to necessary existence is that actuality is doing all the work of necessity there. Somewhat strikingly, the 3rd speculation relies heavily on the 19th premise. Consequently, we see Maimonides reaching back and forth, as it were, to the earlier premise for the later speculation and to the later premise for the earlier speculation. It seems obvious to us that the 18th

[28] Though his somewhat strange use of "possibility (*imkān*)" toward the end of the block quote above, see Pines ed., 249n15, may be alluding to this connection.

premise marks the change in direction in premises away from the argument from motion to the argument from necessary existence.

One way to think of the relation of the 3rd and 4th speculations is that the third is much more elaborate because in it Maimonides seeks to uncover the Aristotelian roots of Avicenna's necessary existence argument. In the 3rd speculation, Maimonides shifts from an argument drawn directly from *Met.* 12.6 and 9.8 to the highly Avicennian talk of necessary existence nearly half-way through the proof. Maimonides signals the Aristotelian provenance of the third speculation as a whole, *pace* Avicenna, when he writes: "A third philosophic speculation about this subject is taken over from Aristotle's argumentation, even though he sets if forth with a view to another purpose." Interestingly, at least the version of the argument in *Met.* 9.8 (1050b10–25), which this is drawn from, serves in part to prove that the world cannot pass out of being. True, this was not originally argued to prove that God exists. However, the claim that for all the beings that pass out of being or are possible of existence there must be a cause that is necessary of existence is really just a recasting of the priority of actuality to potency.

Leaving all this aside, although Maimonides does not mention it in the 3rd speculation, his talk of prevention, obstacle, and hindrance in the 4th speculation is quite curious in view of that earlier pronouncement in 1.68 that God cannot be impeded. As I said, the argument is a counterfactual argument, which is not one of the kinds of argument that Aristotle tended to favor.[29] Despite the simplicity of the 4th speculation, it contains the marrow of the necessary existence argument. What it does not contain is all the niceties of the distinctions that Maimonides is enabled to draw between the purely necessary existent and lesser beings by the argument of the third speculation. The distinctions multiply as Maimonides scurries to

[29] Of course, contemporary philosophy with its focus on modal arguments is shot through with counterfactual arguments.

make good on the fact that there are any distinctions at all between God as purely necessary or actual and the separate intellects which though they are eternal are not purely actual or necessary.[30]

## Impediments to God or Active Intellect?

We do not intend to linger long over this question because we already know the answer, based on previous perusals of 1.68 and 2.18 that neither God nor the Active Intellect (AI) can be impeded. Yet Maimonides's manner of broaching these questions will reveal something about how we are to think about his reliance on privation in general and impediment in particular—that is, impediments of or obstacles to being and action.

Although 2.4 and 2.12 do not contain any references to the impediment of the Active Intellect (AI), they do provide important context for our consideration of impediment of both God and the AI, that is, context on the AI. In 2.4, the Active Intellect makes, aside from its purely negative role in 1.68, to my knowledge, its first appearance in the *Guide*. 2.4 recapitulates the essential teaching of Aristotle's account of the motions of the heavenly bodies by means of the soul and intellect of these bodies in *Met.* 12.7. Although Maimonides will not thematize the issue of "overflow (*f.y.ḍ*)" until 2.12, he does write here of how good overflows from these spheres causing motion out of love (256). "Later philosophers" came up with different numbers of spheres, here ten separate intellects culminating in

---

[30] See the account of the distinction between a being necessary with respect to its essence and a being necessary with respect to its cause in 2.1, 4th speculation on p. 248 of the Pines ed. Of course, the former is God and the latter characterizes the separate intellects. And cf. this with Seymour Feldman's account of the disputes among Avicenna, Averroes, and Crescas (with Maimonides effectively in the camp of Avicenna) and of what Averroes condemns as the mixing of the necessary and the possible (Seymour Feldman, "The Theory of Eternal Creation in Hasdai Crescas and Some of His Predecessors," *Viator* 11 [1980]: 289–320, esp. 302, 307, and 310–11). We will return to Feldman below.

the Active Intellect (257). And here, in keeping with his predecessors reaching back through Avicenna and Alfarabi to Themistius and Alexander of Aphrodisias and ultimately to Aristotle, Maimonides links the AI to the movement of the human intellect from potency to act, setting the stage for 2.32 and its account of prophecy.[31] Maimonides concludes 2.4 with his account of the distinction between God as Necessary Existent and the highest mover, thus placing the PUM in rank closer to the AI than to God. He also promises to explain in what respects this account does and does not fit with "our Law."

In 2.12, Maimonides offers his most extended reflection on the parabolic or allegorical significance of "overflow." Why he chooses to discuss this here (esp. pp. 278–280) at the very end of his discussion of the angels or intellects is not immediately apparent. Of course, this chapter immediately precedes the inception of the account of creation versus eternity. Strangely, this chapter concerns not only overflow but obstacles to it or at least obstacles to the action of any agent on any patient. In other words, this chapter is characterized by its unexpected vagueness and generality. It begins in this vague way, far from clearly limited to the sublunar: "It is clear that everything produced in time (*ḥ.d.th*) has of necessity an efficient cause that causes it to be produced after not having been existent." It continues with a discussion reminiscent of the 9th and 10th premises in 2.intro. Quickly, the question arises: why an effect is produced or created at one time and not another? "Now of necessity there can be no doubt that the impossibility that the act produced in time could come about before it was produced is due either to the absence of a certain relation between the agent and the object of action—if the agent is a body—or to the absence of the requisite preparation of matter—if the agent is not a body. All these

[31] Without mentioning the AI, Maimonides did anticipate this process in 1.72 (193) with its reference to the Acquired Intellect and its relation to the separate intellects.

preliminary remarks are in accordance with what in natural speculation is established as an obligatory doctrine, without any attention being given at present to the question of the eternity of the world or its being produced in time (*ḥ.d.th*). For that is not the subject of the present chapter." This appears to be one of those times when Maimonides protests too much, apparently limiting the reach of his reflections to "natural speculation," evidently with an eye to drawing his reader's attention to the very topic he dismisses. After all, what immediately follows and leads into the discussion of how "overflow" is merely a parabolic way of speaking about how that which is immaterial could affect what is material is an account of the action of the most immaterial of material things, fire, and how it acts at a distance. It is little exaggeration to say that Maimonides is preparing the uninformed reader to make the leap from trying to think about causality among natural things to think about causality of the beings that transcend the sphere of the moon. That leap will only be possible with parabolic talk about overflow. More importantly for us here and now is the way in which the penultimate sentence of the second paragraph in Pines's edition makes it clear that immaterial beings, at least the immaterial intellects Maimonides considers in the context of "overflow," cannot be impeded. This should make us wonder why Maimonides relies so heavily on talk of obstacles or impediments or hindrances to the AI but especially to God as Creator.

Before turning finally to 2.18, we must stop briefly in 2.14 again. As we saw in chapter 3, Maimonides entertains arguments in 2.14 against creation, offered by defenders of eternity. There we saw that proponents of eternity criticize creation because it seems to imply that God was impeded from creating the world before the time that He created it. There we were slightly more concerned with issues connected to time and 2.13. Here, we are more concerned with the very notion that God could be impeded. One need only entertain the idea to see that it sits well with neither eternity nor creation. In the case of eternity, it would seem to imply that God is not purely actual; in the case of creation, it would derogate from God's unlimited power. At least part of the answer of the dialectical theologians to such philosophic talk of impediment is to deny that God could be impeded any more than he could be incentivized. Unless we retreat to some notion that willing means to will or not to will without incentive or purpose or impediment (2.18, 301), it appears that we can make little sense of creation.

## The Itinerary of Will in Guide 2. 18 through 21

Yet such cannot be Maimonides's own view of creation because, according to 2.19, God is supposed to be vindicated as the Creator by his particularization argument because the cosmos requires a being whose will has a purpose. In other words, in 2.18 and 2.19, Maimonides presents two radically different accounts of will: in the former case as without a purpose and in the latter as with a purpose. As it happens, 2.18 is also the high point in the *Guide* for Maimonides's account of impediment in connection with eternity and creation. Although we cannot say yet exactly how purpose and impediments are connected, we recall that the odd form Maimonides's particularization argument takes in 2.19 is that it is precisely the dis-order in the motions of the planets and placement of the stars that indicates divine creative will. That dis-order is opposed to necessity is obvious, but that dis-order is the marker of a purposive will seems more than strange. A careful reading of this sequence of chapters, 2.18 through 21, will reveal striking contradictions between various claims about purpose: at times purpose is connected to will and at times to necessity. After we reveal Maimonides's contradictions regarding purpose, it will be much clearer what he is actually arguing regarding impediments and dis-order. At this point, it is also worth recalling one of the conclusions from our inquiry into general providence in part one of the *Guide*. As 1.11 teaches and the subsequent series (1.11 through 13 and 1.22 through 24) indicate, God's providence for the heavenly bodies though they might be called individuals is ultimately really to be understood as a form of general providence. This would seem to imply that either the dis-order of the planets is a marker of their merely being left to chance (1.23, 53) or of a particularization of form (rather than matter), whose purpose we do not yet understand (1.73, 10th premise, 208). Given Maimonides's evident preference for an account privileging either divine intellect or divine will rather than Epicurean neglect, the latter option seems to be the more plausible. We have gotten ahead of ourselves.

Maimonides begins his inquiry into these methods used to defend eternity, which he will try to poke holes in with a discussion of the Active Intellect, in a manner reminiscent of how he foreshadowed his thoughts about creation and eternity in 2.12 before beginning the discussion of creation and eternity. Here he starts not with God but with the Active Intellect (AI). The possibility that the Active Intellect (AI) should be impeded is discussed by Alfarabi in his "Letter on the Intellect." Farabi arrives quickly at a conclusion contrary to the one Maimonides declared in 1.68: not only God but also the AI cannot be impeded. The only impediment or "obstacle (*ʿā'iq*)" must be in the matter of the recipient (2.18, 300). Here, Maimonides makes clever use of the lack of impediments to the AI in order to try to resist the implication that since neither God nor the Active Intellect can be impeded, the world must have been eternal. Instead, Maimonides seems to argue that one should not infer from the fact that the AI's action takes place at one time and not another that the AI has moved from potentiality to actuality. Similarly, no such inference should be drawn about God. Although this may address the fact that eternally existing beings ought not be thought of as changing from potentiality to actuality, still it does not help much with the question whether the world is to be thought of as having come to be from absolute nonexistence (2.17, 296).

Perhaps because Maimonides's response to this "First Method" has not gotten to the bottom of the challenge posed by impediments, in the "Second Method" he moves to a more or less direct confrontation between "impediments (*mawāniʿ*)" and "will (*irāda*)" (2.18, 300–301). Given our focus on will and impediment and the sheer density of the references to impediment, we will quote this passage in full.

> The second method is the one in which eternity is shown to be necessary because there do not subsist for Him, may He be exalted, any incentives, supervening accidents, and impediments (*wa-l-mawāniʿ*). It is difficult to resolve this doubt, and the solution is subtle. Hear it.
>
> Know that every agent endowed with will (*irāda*), who performs his acts for the sake of something, must of necessity act at a certain time and not act at another time because of impediments (*mawāniʿ*) or supervening accidents. To take an example: a man, for instance, may wish to have a house but does not build it because of impediments (*al-mawāniʿ*)—if the building materials are not at hand or if they, though being at hand, have not been prepared for receiving the form because of the absence of tools. Sometimes, too, both the materials and the tools are at hand, but the man does not build because he does not wish to build since he can dispense with a shelter. If, however, accidents like heat or cold supervene, he is compelled to seek a shelter, whereupon he will wish to build. It has thus become clear that supervening accidents may change the will (*al-irāda*) and that impediments (*wa-l-mawāniʿ*) may oppose the will (*al-irāda*) in such a way that it is not executed. All this, however, only occurs when acts are in service of something that is external to the essence of the will (*dhāt al-irāda*). If, however, that act has no purpose (*ghāya*) whatever except to be consequent upon will, that will has no need of incentives. And the one who wills is not obliged, even if there are no impediments, to act always. For there is no external end for the sake of which he acts and that would render it necessary to act whenever there are no impediments (*mawāniʿ*) preventing the attainment of the end (*al-ghāya*). For in the case envisaged, the act is consequent upon the will alone.
>
> Somebody might object: All this is correct, but does not the supposition that one wishes at one time and does not wish at

> another time imply in itself a change? We shall reply to him: No, for the true reality and the quiddity of will (*ḥaqīqat al-irāda wa-māhiyyatihā*) means: to will and not to will. If the will in question belongs to a material being, so that some external end is sought thereby, then the will is subject to change because of impediments (*al-mawāniʿ*) and supervening accidents. But as for a being separate from matter, its will, which does not exist in any respect for the sake of some other thing, is not subject to change. The fact that it may wish one thing now and another thing tomorrow does not constitute a change in its essence.

Much like the movement from potency to actuality, Maimonides resists the notion that creation can be refuted by drawing comparisons between God and beings who can be impeded—but here he focuses on the will of the being that putatively can be impeded. That God creates the world at some time or creates the world and thereby creates time should not be thought to indicate that God was previously impeded from creating and then was freed of said impediment. Rather, because God's will cannot be impeded and cannot be influenced by any external incentive or supervening accident, God must be thought to have a will that can will anything, that is, "wish one thing now and another thing tomorrow." Notice that Maimonides does not attempt to argue that God transcends time and has a will that acts outside of time. After all, when philosophers and theologians make such arguments, they fail to acknowledge that to claim that God can act in history or engage in particular providence must mean that God, despite transcending time, is somehow capable of entering into time. More importantly, we see Maimonides here adopting an argument that one might expect to hear more from an Ashʿarite Mutakallim than Maimonides. As I have mentioned before, Pines links to Alghazali the claim that it is of the nature of will to will or not will. However, Pines does so immediately after referring the reader to a passage from 3.22, which talks of the will as particularizing and purposing things.[32] Although Pines seems to think these claims are in harmony, we have reason to highlight the issue we've already telegraphed. The will as characterized in 2.18 is not oriented toward any purpose. Its willing or not willing is precisely characterized by its lack of reference to any end or purpose. The will as characterized as early as 2.19 but also at times in 2.22 is emphatically oriented toward purposes. The challenge posed by purposes or ends here is that they would predetermine the trajectory of the will.

Whether the problem we are referring to is due to some incoherence in the writings of Alghazali is not our concern here. Rather, our concern is to bring out both the differences between what is argued in 2.18 and 2.19 and then to track the surprising amount of movement in Maimonides's apparent target position over the course of 2.19 through 21. The source of that movement derives from the movement of purpose from association with will to association with necessity. After all, Aristotelian necessity is characterized above all by the orientation of all natural beings to a given end. More about this shortly.

Here, we will glance at two different readings of at least parts of 2.19 through 21, which suggest that other scholars have either detected the mobility we've referred to or have misinterpreted Maimonides precisely because his position is so slippery. What I have characterized as Maimonides's slipperiness or mobility regarding the place of purpose in his account of the opposition between necessity and will, W. Z. Harvey alludes to when he writes, "Maimonides claims that as opposed to Aristotle who had held that all things exist by divine necessity, he holds that they exist by divine *purpose*. However, he completely neutralizes this claim when he subsequently pronounces that the word 'purpose' is used equivocally when applied to

[32] Cf. Pines, Translator's Introduction, p. cxxviii with p. cxxvii.

the purposes of men and of God."[33] In contrast, Seymour Feldman takes an approach to Maimonides's argument in these chapters that is less attentive to its fluidity. Feldman lumps Maimonides together with Alghazali in opposition not so much to Aristotle as to an odd caricature of Aristotle. Indeed, Feldman suggests that Maimonides's Aristotelian necessity smacks more of Spinoza than Aristotle.[34] Although he does not make this explicit, we suspect that Feldman argues this because of the strangeness of Maimonides's initial detachment of purpose or teleology from Maimonides's account of Aristotle. Although Harvey's reading of the relevant texts is subtler than Feldman's and he is better attuned to Maimonides's intent in these chapters, still Harvey has already by this point accepted the convergence of Moses Narbonne and Abulafia on "eternal creation" in a spirit anticipating Hasdai Crescas as Maimonides's ultimate aim.[35] Feldman's sense that Maimonides intends to oppose the position of creation to that of eternity seems far closer to the overall intent of the *Guide*, despite the haziness of 2.19 through 21. The following will have to suffice as an account of our view with considerable debt to the clarity Feldman's historical analysis made

[33] W. Z. Harvey, "A Third Approach to the Cosmogony-Prophetology Puzzle," 77. At the end of the first of these two sentences, Harvey cites pages from 2.19 and 2.21. And the paragraph in which they occur Harvey concludes that Maimonides has mixed up his position with Aristotle's to the point that their overall views on necessity and will become indistinguishable (p. 78). I agree with that; however, it seems to me that it is primarily the fluidity Maimonides attaches to purpose that accounts for this blurring into indistinguishability.

[34] Seymour Feldman, "The Theory of Eternal Creation in Hasdai Crescas and Some of His Predecessors," *Viator* 11 (1980): 289–320, esp. 294n16. Feldman cites 2.20 and 2.25 as the basis for his claim that Maimonides's Aristotle here looks more like a modern than Aristotle.

[35] W. Z. Harvey, "A Third Approach to the Cosmogony-Prophetology Puzzle," 76.

possible.[36] On the one hand, the modus operandi of Alfarabi and Avicenna was to redefine creation such that it could be absorbed into a Neoplatonic frame. To my mind, this is one philosophic tack one can take. I have described this in an article I published on Alfarabi's *Harmonization.*[37] On the other hand, rather than conceal one's allegiance to eternity by denuding creation of any real content, one can argue as Maimonides does. He allows the radical character of the opposition between creation and eternity to flare up. He does not attempt to finesse the opposition by reconceptualizing being in such a way that even philosophy seems to require that God possess knowledge of every individual. As indispensable as it would be for bolstering the authority of the Law, Maimonides does not rest easy on the same side as Alghazali, as Feldman insinuates. Maimonides's *Guide* comes closer to a work containing arguments as opposed as those of Alghazali and that of Averroes without the hard push from each side to decide in favor of one or the other. It is as dialectical as both Alghazali's *Incoherence of the Philosophers* and Averroes's *Incoherence of the Incoherence,* but with greater generosity to each side than either of those more polemical works are able to provide.

In 2.19, Maimonides moves over the course of this most important chapter in defense of creation from the view that "purpose" is linked to will in opposition to necessity to at least hint at acknowledging that purpose may in fact be characteristic of necessity. Quick comparison of the opening where the opposition linking purpose to

[36] We can hardly do justice to the sophistication of Feldman's analysis of the varying positions on "eternal creation" here.

[37] See Parens, "Alfarabi's Harmonization: Authentic and Exoteric," *ISHRAQ*, Islamic philosophy yearbook, (Moscow: Institute of Philosophy of the Russian Academy of Sciences and the Iranian Institute of Philosophy, 2022), 301–320. Usually, I would not go along with Feldman in attributing a version of "eternal creation" to Alfarabi and Avicenna. Feldman does an excellent job, though, of articulating the differences and similarities among Alfarabi and Avicenna, Thomas and Bonaventure, Averroes, and Crescas in their various approaches to what can very broadly be called "eternal creation."

will (2.19, 303) with some of Maimonides's statements later in the chapter (2.19, 310–311) reveal a drift toward such hints. It is the following passage near the end of 2.19 that suggests such a drift. Maimonides is reviewing how the dis-order or what he calls "differences" (309) in the paths of the planets (306–309) and the distribution of the stars (310) suggests that there must be a cause, possessed of will, who can purpose (*qaṣd*) these differences. He writes,

> What is the cause for this having been purposed? What is known may be epitomized as follows: All this has been produced for an object that we do not know and is not an aimless and fortuitous act. In fact you know that the veins and nerves of any individual dog or ass have not happened fortuitously, nor are their measures fortuitous. Neither is it by chance that one vein is thick and another thin, that one nerve has many ramifications and another is not thus ramified, that one descends straight down and another is bent. All is as it is with a view to useful effects whose necessity (*ḍarūriyya*) is known. How then can one who uses his intellect imagine that the positions, measures, and numbers of the stars and motions of their various spheres are without an object or fortuituous? There is no doubt that all of these things are necessary (*ḍarūrī*) according to the purpose of one who purposes (*qaṣd al-qāṣid*). On the other hand, the supposition that all these things have been ordered in virtue of necessity (*al-lazūm*) and not in virtue of a purpose (*qaṣd*) is very remote indeed. To my mind there is no proof stronger than the one founded upon the differences between the motions of the spheres and upon the fact that the stars are fixed in the spheres. For this reason you will find that all the prophets used the stars and spheres as proofs for the deity existing necessarily.

We are not suggesting that Maimonides sets aside all ambiguity and speaks directly to the reader here. It is undeniable that the preferred term for "necessity" in reference to the manner of God's relation to the world in this chapter is various cognates based on the root *l.z.m.* And in the quoted passage that term is used. Yet it is worth noting that in the first appearance in this passage of the other term often used to refer to one of the modes of being "necessity," *ḍarūra*, does seem to speak of the purposes of natural things as being necessary. Among the most important things this passage does is to note for the reader the connection between "purpose (*qaṣd*)" and "end (*ghāya*)." Although to my knowledge "end (*ghāya*)" is not used in this chapter, it has been used essentially as the equivalent to purpose in other chapters of the *Guide*. To begin with, we already ran across an allusion to this link in 3.25 in a chapter devoted to showing that none of God's actions are fortuitous, which of course is central in our current passage. There in 3.25 the suggestion that God's actions are never fortuitous is connected directly to the notion that all of God's actions aim at some "end (*ghāya*)." At the time, it was clear that this view was not peculiar to the Bible; rather it was central to the philosophers—and thus presumably compatible with necessity. Yet the connection to "purpose (*qaṣd*)" in 3.25 was a weak one. In the earlier and related chapter on the end of individuals (that is, their form) and the problem of the end of the whole (3.13), there is a passage that links end and purpose with strong reverberations with 2.19: "Know that the existence of this final end (*al-ghāya*) in natural things has of necessity led the philosophers to a belief in a principle other than nature; namely, the one that Aristotle calls the intellectual or divine principle, that being the one that makes one thing for the sake of another. Know too that to the mind of an equitable man, one of the strongest proofs for the production of the world in time (*ḥadath al-ʿālam*) is the fact, demonstrated with reference to natural beings, that every one of these has a certain final end (*ghāya*), some of them existing for the sake of others; for this is a proof of purpose on the part of a being possessing purpose (*dalīlan ʿalay qaṣd qāṣid*). And purpose can only be conceived with reference to the production in time of something so produced. I shall return to the subject of this chapter, namely, to the discussion of the final end." Although Maimonides places markers around this passage identifying it as a digression, and although he seems to suggest that talk of purpose only befits "production in time" or creation *ex nihilo*, it is quite clear here that end and purpose have essentially the same meaning.

Indeed, this passage enables us to recast what is at stake in 2.19 through 21. What appears at first in 2.19 as dis-order in the motions of the planets and the placement of the stars is, based on 3.25 and 3.13, in fact nothing more than an end or purpose the wisdom of which is hidden from us. There are two different views one can take of such a situation: either one can defer to God saying that His wisdom is mysterious or one can suspect that one merely has not arrived at an understanding of the underlying causal explanation. Maimonides's argument in 2.19 gives cover to the former argument; however, at the same time it points to the latter argument. We have already explained why we hold that the latter argument makes more sense in connection with 1.11. None of the talk of the particularization of the motions of the planets or their "differences" (309–310) suggests that God purposes an individual as an individual. Rather God particularizes the form of a being, who, given the uniformity of heavenly matter, is like a species (1.11, 38). This purposing hardly signifies the particular providence of YHVH.

Previously, we suggested that Maimonides cultivates trust in the idea of God's will as that which purposes the apparent disorderliness in the motions of the planets. However, whether God is understood under the guise of necessity or the guise of will, it would appear God's purpose must be wise, according to Maimonides. Evidently then it is not quite true that it is the nature of God's will to will or not will. Rather it is the nature of God's will always to will the good. Privation, impediment, or disorder shows up then either merely as an indication of our own lack of insight or as a part of God's general providence.

In 2.20, Maimonides goes so far as to attribute some notion of "will" even to Aristotle's account of necessity, but even in this regard Aristotle is presented as opposed to purpose and particularization. Maimonides frames this approach to "will" in Aristotle by noting that Aristotle opposes the natural order to chance. The superlunary motions "remain always in certain states," while sublunar things, the things on earth, occur either "always or for the most part." Aristotle is presented here as opposing those who claim the heavens came to be somehow spontaneously or by chance. Nothing, not even the sublunar is due to chance but to causes.[38] Maimonides takes the opportunity to address the question whether Aristotle thinks of the order of the whole as purposed. Here is what he writes, "But it is not clear to me that Aristotle believes that, because these beings have not come into being spontaneously, it follows necessarily that they have come into being in virtue of the purpose of one who purposed and the will of one who willed. For to me a combination between existing in virtue of necessity and being produced in time in virtue of a purpose and a will—a combination uniting these two—comes near to a combination of two opposites."

That Aristotle's account has little room for will seems apparent. Yet the slippage introduced by "purpose" undermines Maimonides's purported desire to hold these positions apart. He turns next to opposing Aristotle's view of the divine cause to that of the Creator by arguing that the philosopher's God thinks of the whole deriving from God as the intellectually apprehended being derives from the mind of God as intellect, reminding us strongly of 1.68. He then proceeds to undermine completely the claim that will cannot be involved—one of the reasons W. Z. Harvey cites for inclining toward the view that Maimonides adopts eternal creation or at least muddles will and necessity utterly: "For this First Cause—though it is according to him an intellect of the highest and most perfect rank of being so that he says that it wills (*murīd*) what is necessarily (*l.z.m.*) derived from it and rejoices and takes pleasure in it – cannot will anything contrary to this " (2.20, 314). This passage in Maimonides

[38] This account of chance in the sublunar realm should be contrasted with the opposing impression left by 3.17.

reminds one strongly of Aristotle's account of the "necessary (*anangkiaos*)" in its divine sense in *Metaphysics* 5.5. Unlike lower senses of the necessary, it is the opposite of that which is compelled. It is here that Aristotle identifies the highest sense of the necessary with the simple (*haplos*) and denies that as such they could be compelled in any way.[39] After acknowledging this moment of the merging of will and necessity, Maimonides uses the first-person singular again to claim to be confused. He claims to be uncertain whether the "latter-day men" to whom he will dedicate the next chapter understood Aristotle as equating necessity and will or they disagreed with him when they merged the two. That Aristotle uses analogical language suggesting there is not tension between necessity and will is undeniable. Yet as he tells us, his account of the gods is the same as the ancient teaching, so long as one removes all the anthropomorphism from it.[40]

In 2.21, "latter-day philosophers" are presented as arguing that being the Agent or Maker (*fāʿil*), purposing, and willing are all characteristic of God as well as being "the one who chooses freely (*mukhtār*)," and particularizes. By the middle of this chapter, Maimonides draws the Ghazalian distinction between the cause from which "this diversity (*dhālika al-ikhtilāf*)" proceeds necessarily[41] and "the agent (*fāʿil*) " who particularizes; however, toward the beginning of our inquiry, we saw Maimonides argue that there is no difference between a maker or agent and the philosopher's account of cause (1.69). In so many words, Maimonides here rejects the mode of defending philosophy and the Laws that his predecessors

[39] 1015b12-16.

[40] See *Met.* 12.8, end.

[41] It is worth noting that Pines renders *lazama* (necessitate) and cognates as "necessarily proceeded" and "proceed" in this and the following chapter.

defended by developing one or another compromise position that might be labelled "eternal creation."[42]

It would not be too much of an exaggeration to say that despite Maimonides's great esteem not only for Avicenna but especially for Alfarabi that he has chosen a different way of handling the conflict between philosophy and Law than his predecessors. Here is how he characterizes the way they have equated "necessity" with "purpose": "It has already become clear to you, who are engaged in the study of this my Treatise, that these people have altered the term 'necessity,' but have let its meaning remain. Perhaps they intended to choose a more beautiful expression or to get rid of one that is shocking.... But this is not the meaning of purpose, as we propose to conceive it" (2.21, 315). Rather than adjudicate the dispute between philosophy and Law or eternity and creation through harmonizations of the sort adopted by Alfarabi and Avicenna or even that of Averroes, Maimonides cultivates the sort of dispute one witnesses between Alghazali and Averroes: this dispute is encapsulated in the phrase we adopted early on to express the essential meaning of 2.23, namely, the "weighing of doubts."

Through the remainder of 2.21, Maimonides sets forth an account of the Aristotelian view of "necessity" by which "he merely means to signify causality," not temporal procession. Maimonides's parting shot at Aristotelian necessity or procession only has effect if one thinks of the whole as deriving from God or being produced by God. To put this differently, the problem with necessity only occurs so long as one thinks of God as the efficient cause. It is unclear how this criticism could apply to a necessary being who acts as a final cause, prior not temporally but causally to all beings that partake of potency (or possibility) in its pure actuality (or necessity). If this is what Maimonides meant in 1.69 in equating Maker with cause, then

[42] Again, see Seymour Feldman, "The Theory of Eternal Creation in Hasdai Crescas and Some of His Predecessors," *Viator* 11 (1980): 289–320.

he was wrong. In any event, the critique of procession blends more or less seamlessly into Maimonides's argument in 2.22 that Aristotle was correct about everything up to the sphere of the moon. It is not by chance that 2.22 is followed by 2.23 close to where we began our inquiry. As our crucial methodological chapter, 2.23 reminds us that, despite Maimonides's consistent inveighing against Aristotle, what we should consider is not how many times Maimonides claims to disagree with Aristotle but what are the doubts on each side between creation and eternity, between the vulgar view of prophecy and the philosophic view, and between the biblical view of providence and the philosophic view.

# CONCLUSION

As we look back over the chapters of this book, a number of features that were not apparent in the beginning appear salient in retrospect. Despite Maimonides's avowed preference for Aristotle vis-à-vis Plato, we are struck by the ways in which our interpretation has uncovered unexpected Platonic threads and insights in the *Guide*. Now, the "dialogical" character of the *Guide* and, in that respect, its similarity to Plato's dialogues has often been remarked on. Here we are referring not to that Platonic feature of the *Guide* nor are we referring to the surprising connection between ignorance and evil in 3.11. Rather, we have in mind how what might be called the plot—or at least one important plot—of the *Guide* has unfolded and the most important arguments have stood out. Strauss first identified in *The City and Man* and then made explicit in the title of his last book, *The Argument and the Action of Plato's "Laws,"*[1] the surprising insight that the action (or plot) of Plato's dialogues works differently and is often in tension with the arguments. Strauss's student, Seth Benardete, expanded on this idea with his contrast between the genetic and eidetic dimensions of the dialogues.[2] Of course, the action is genetic, and the arguments are eidetic. Strangely, though, in the *Guide* the more genetic aspect concerns the limits of knowledge, and

---

[1] Leo Strauss, *The Argument and the Action of Plato's "Laws,"* (Chicago: University of Chicago Press, 1975).

[2] See, for example, Seth Benardete, *Socrates' Second Sailing: On Plato's "Republic,"* (Chicago: University of Chicago Press, 1989), pp. 1–5; *Plato's "Laws": The Discovery of Being*, (Chicago: University of Chicago Press, 2000), esp. chapter 1, "The Eidetic and the Genetic," and there esp. pp. 18–24; *The Argument of the Action: Essays on Greek Poetry and Philosophy* (Chicago: University of Chicago Press, 2000), pp. 282–83.

the more eidetic part the three great themes.[3] In other words, the status of knowledge itself plays a more genetic or, as Benardete sometimes puts it, mythical role in the *Guide*, rather than the eidetic role we might have expected. Here is what we have in mind: Part 1 of this book, concerned with the limits of knowledge, reveals the genetic unfolding of Maimonides's discussions of the limits of knowledge: step 1 is the Talmudic prohibitions of inquiry into what is above, below, in front, and in back; step 2 is Maimonides's transformation of those prohibitions into limits of knowledge; step 3 is the realization of the vagueness of those limits or the opening up of the space of doubts; and step 4 is the weighing of the doubts recommended by *Guide* 2.23. We could probably add additional steps to this series such as the invocation of the authority of the Law and the disgrace it is meant to elicit and the invocation of the authority of Aristotle and the disgrace before it. There is something quite different about this unfolding or "plot" of Maimonides's account of the limits of knowledge, as compared with the more fixed character of the pairs of doubts on each side of creation, prophecy, and providence. The link between the genetic and eidetic or part 1 and part 2 here is what we have called obstacle or privation. Perhaps it is to be expected that this, at first, innocuous connection should act so differently in each of these dimensions of the *Guide*. That privation should link the two parts yet act differently in each is less surprising to those of us who have wondered at the odd ambiguity in the very concept of privation in, as it were, its original home, Aristotle's

---

[3] This comparison with Plato is not meant to be rigid or airtight. Other hints of problems with it: In the three great themes, some will want to argue that it is significant that creation appears first and is surely temporally first. Our response is that we continue to stick by our argument that particular providence is a prior genus to creation. Another apparent problem is that prophecy is an action. The reader may then wonder why this action doesn't appear as part of the genetic account, which has about it a sort of plot, as do actions. We can only suggest that this connection is a superficial one.

physics.[4] In the action of the *Guide,* privation serves to capture the very substance of the inquiry as it were. Limits of knowledge, where they truly exist, cannot be gotten beyond. The very drama of the *Guide* is the task of pushing those limits well beyond where Maimonides on a first reading seems to insinuate that they exist. In contrast, privation appears to be something but proves not to be anything at all in the second part. Ultimately, it is nonsensical to suggest that God would prevent prophecy; the problem of evil is hardly a problem; and privation exists only in relation to creation, not in relation to the eternal, that is, everything above the sphere of the moon.

Leaving aside this wholly unexpected connection to Plato, let us turn back in a more orderly way to the parts and chapters of this book. Let us look back to chapter 1 on the Half-and-Half Teaching, starting with the very surface of the *Guide.* As we mentioned in a footnote in chapter 1, this teaching does not literally consist of one half the creation account and the other half the Aristotelian eternalist account. Putting it in a literal-minded way, the six days of creation are not equivalent to the indefinite period after God's resting from creating. At the same time, the "half-and-half" figure captures somewhat the outsized role of creation evident in its tendency to "swallow" the other half. In other words, the reader is led to imagine that the Creator or YHVH could create a world according to Aristotle's specifications, at least beneath the "sphere of the moon," since he is capable of creating whatever he decides to create. Yet it is undeniable that being the Creator of heaven and earth is meant to secure the possibility that God might not always follow his "custom," that is, to make possible not only all the miracles but perhaps

[4] See Ronna Burger's question to Seth Benardete as to whether he thought of privation's relation to matter and form as a key example of what he came to speak of as the "indeterminate dyad," in Seth Benardete, *Encounters and Reflections: Conversations with Seth Benardete*, Ronna Burger and Michael Davis, eds. (Chicago: University of Chicago Press, 2002), 148.

especially those miracles that are emblematic of his special relationship to the people Israel, including above all his giving the Law by way of the prophet Moses. Given all that, we should resist our temptation to thoughtlessly assume that the Creator God is truly compatible with what Maimonides claims is Aristotle's correctness about everything up to the sphere of the moon (2.22 and 24). Chapter 1 begins to reveal what the rest of the book will also contribute to revealing, namely, that the two accounts of God as YHVH and as the Prime Unmoved Mover (PUM, or something just above that) are not as compatible as the first impression left by 1.50 through 70 might lead one to believe. Although there are some respects in which one can apply a negative theology to both YHVH and the PUM, the extent of that negative theology is quite different. YHVH is beyond not only discursive but also intuitive human knowledge; the PUM can at least be intuited. This subtle but key difference is emblematic of the many facets and difficulties associated with the account of the limits of knowledge.

One of the greatest sources of confusion in the secondary literature about the limits of knowledge, which we discussed in chapter 2, is the false inference that one can rely on the negative theology in the sense applicable to YHVH to rule out any knowledge about God or perhaps about anything but the objects of our immediate sense experience on earth—as if Maimonides weren't even open to the possibility that God is the PUM rather than YHVH and as if Maimonides had set down clear in-principle limits on human knowledge of the kind laid down by Kant. Indeed, Maimonides intentionally tempts the interpreter of the *Guide* to maximize what is unknowable for human beings. After all, discouraging further inquiry by most readers is very much a part of Maimonides's defense of the Law. Just how far he is willing to go in that is evident from his remarks in the introduction to part 1 about how he is willing to satisfy the one in a thousand even if he must fail to satisfy the ignoramuses, which are then only confirmed by the many things he says along the way about how the path being laid out in the *Guide* is suitable only for the solitary (1.34, 3.34, and 3.51). Leaving aside the defense of the Law, chapter 2 is most concerned with the limits of knowledge and their vagueness as crucial to the defense of philosophy. While the skeptics, with real grounds in the text since it is so highly ambiguous, come to take for granted that the limits are clear; the dogmatists tend to forget the talk of limits of knowledge, if only because they see evidence of human knowledge above the sphere of the moon dispersed throughout the *Guide*. As we said already in the conclusion above, there really are steps in Maimonides's inquiry into the limits of knowledge: the Talmudic prohibition of inquiry into the highest matters, the transformation of the prohibition into limits of knowledge, the realization of the vagueness of the limits or the appearance of the space of doubts, and the weighing of doubts, based on *Guide* 2.23. Once we moved in chapter 2 beyond the initial discussion of the limits of knowledge in 1.31 through 34 as well as the negative theology of 1.50 through 70 into parts 2 and 3, we were able to make our initial inquiry into the purportedly undecidable dispute between creation and eternity. Of course, Maimonides does not approach this problem head on. As we learn even from a cursory reading of 2.19, he argues for creation by arguing that only a God capable of particularizing the heavens could be responsible for the apparent disorder of the motions of the planets and the uneven distribution of the bodies in the so-called sphere of the fixed stars. Rather than taking Maimonides's words in that hotly contested passage from 2.24 (covered in such detail by Davidson, W. Z. Harvey, and Kraemer—and then in *Aleph* 8) as determinative or decisive, like Tzvi Langermann, we wondered whether Maimonides really intended to rule out the possibility that someone else after him might make sense of the apparent disorder of the heavens. Nevertheless, Maimonides's argument in 2.19 for a particularizer serves at least on its face to defend creation and thereby the Law. The vagueness of the limit of the sphere of the moon will appear again and again in the arguments about prophecy and particular providence. What he argues about these elevated themes certainly insinuates more knowledge of God than would appear to be fitting if all human knowledge stops at the sphere of the moon.

In chapter 3, we turned to consider the interplay between the space of doubts beyond the supposed limit at the sphere of the moon and Maimonides's subtle discussion of "authority" in the *Guide*. Because the limits are vague, a space of doubt about what human beings can know opens up above the sphere of the moon especially in connection with the problem set out in the previous chapter in Maimonides's defense of creation. Maimonides does not attempt to prove directly that God is a Creator, indeed, he does not even attempt to prove directly that the world is created (for reasons alluded to in 1.71); rather, he merely attempts to show that the apparent disorder of the motions of the heavens would seem to require something more than an Aristotelian PUM. The PUM is adequate for a world that follows an order in accordance with that God's necessity; however, heavenly disorder seems to require a more hands-on God. Our willingness to accept this rather elaborate argument for the Creator depends on the recognition that neither God's essence as necessary or as characterized by will nor whether the world is created or eternal can be demonstrated directly. These dilemmas, about which there seem to be no simple demonstrations, are the purported reasons why we should side with the Law. Aristotelian eternity undermines the Law in its foundation (2.25). Of course, the pivot to Law is not itself an argument. Rather, we agree to side with the Law because it or the scripture in which it appears possesses unprecedented authority. This Maimonides pointed at earlier in the *Guide* when he reviewed Alexander of Aphrodisias's causes of disagreement, to which Maimonides appends the fact of the unprecedented authority of monotheistic scriptures (1.31). Although authority is essential for the maintenance of law, it has little place in the pursuit of the truth. Chapter 3 explored Maimonides's multifaceted inquiry into the subtle interplay between authority and the disgrace one feels before authorities of different kinds, most notably, the Law and Aristotle. Although authority and disgrace interfere with the proper weighing of doubts, Maimonides allows these two things to serve that purpose. Indeed, in the very chapter where he lays down the right approach to the weighing of doubts (2.23), he appeals to the authority of the Law to disgrace at least some in his audience into accepting the view of the Law. Once again, this is a part of his defense of the Law or Judaism.

With chapter 4, we pivoted to the second part of our book and, first, to the problem of privation. As we have noted so often before, privation proved central to the weighing of doubts in our inquiries into creation, prophecy, and providence. But even before we turned to these high themes, we began with the more obvious role of privation in relation to morality. For decades, scholars have suggested that Maimonides seems to have changed his views on morality from his *Commentary on the Mishnah*, in particular his *Eight Chapters* and its apparent advocacy of the mean in the spirit of Aristotle, to his *Guide*, with its apparent asceticism. This mistaken talk of development derives from inattention to the fact that Maimonides sometimes speaks in the voice of the Law and sometimes in that of philosophy in the *Guide*. As brilliant as Josef Stern's *Matter and Form* is, it relies too heavily on the initial impression that the asceticism of *Guide* 3.8 represents Maimonides's final view. In fact, 3.8, or at least parts of it, represents only his recapitulation of the asceticism of the Bible. The Bible points the finger at flesh or dust or matter. In doing so, it misses the admittedly mysterious role of privation in human life. In 3.10, though, Maimonides does not directly undo the effect of 3.8; rather, he shifts attention from an animus toward matter toward privation. This argument between Law and philosophy or between matter and privation reminds the attentive reader of similar confusions by the Mutakallimun, who seemed unable to grasp just how prevalent privation is in human experience—thinking that the only thing that truly "is" privation is the void, that is, absolute privation. Lacking the subtlety to grasp relative privations such as death as the privation of life, the Mutakallimun were blinded to the true nature of God. They, like the occasional passage in the Bible, seemed to think that God could sully His "hands" with things like evil. Of course, privation plays an important role not only in the moral realm and in the grand scheme of things—that God can be the cause only of good—but also throughout Maimonides's account of the three great themes: creation, prophecy, and providence. Getting privation right proves to be essential to getting the whole of experience right.

In chapter 5, we began not with creation but with prophecy. Our rationale was that prophecy is the one of these great themes in which the role of privation, that is, prevention of prophecy by God's will, was the most obvious. Ultimately, we would have preferred to be able to begin with particular providence, but Maimonides decided to be slightly subtler and less direct in his treatment of providence than of prophecy. This is not surprising: Although prophecy plays a central role in the genesis of Law, it is only a specific case of providence—and as such less central than providence. That is, being as forthright about the role of privation in providence as he was about it in prophecy might have been riskier. Although we continue to maintain that both creation and prophecy are manifestations of God's particular providence—and therefore particular providence has a kind of eidetic primacy in the *Guide*—Maimonides allows the importance and centrality of particular providence to be overlooked by positioning it in its typical place in dialectical theology, namely, at the end. Of course, the order of dialectical theology is genetic like that of the Mishnah: According to the genetic point of view, one begins with creation, follows it by the Law that is given for human life, and follows that in turn by an account of particular providence because judgment of a human life must come at the end.

Since Maimonides draws an explicit connection between the three positions on creation and the three positions on prophecy, we thought it best to consider the contention about which positions line up with which among Kaplan, Davidson, and W. Z. Harvey. Attention to these scholars' assessments of Maimonides's three positions revealed their shared problematic assumption that the Platonic position on creation vs. eternity was compatible with all the miracles. Above all, Plato's approach, both as Maimonides understands it and in itself, is compatible only with miracles that fail to include the most important ones—such as that God could give the Law to a particular people at a particular time and place, namely, particular providence as understood by the Bible. This misunderstanding of Plato has made it too easy for a generation of scholars to suppose that there really is no conflict between creation and eternity or, for that matter, philosophy and Law. Among other things, this has led to complacent acceptance that Maimonides must anticipate the synthesizing conception of "eternal creation" so prevalent among not only Christian but also Jewish thinkers after Maimonides. Of course, the problems with attributing "eternal creation" were taken up not only in chapter 1 but also in chapter 7. Returning here to chapter 5, our focus on prophecy led us into the challenge of interpreting 2.32. Although privation is most evident in this account of prophecy, in comparison to the relevant chapters on creation and providence, what Maimonides ultimately means in suggesting that God could will to prevent prophecy in someone worthy by nature and education of receiving it has left commentators and scholars stumped for centuries. We should perhaps not be surprised that, given the greater eidetic importance of the account of particular providence, that we were not able to gain true clarity about Maimonides's argument about the third position on prophecy until we understood his teaching on particular providence in 3.51. Yet even before that in 2.32, surrounding chapters such as 2.36, and in his *Letter on Astrology* Maimonides gives indications that what appears like God's will might well be due to some humbler sort of cause preventing prophecy. This is one of our first clues that what Maimonides means by God's will is far from obvious. This will return to us as a problem, once again, in chapter 7.

But before then in chapter 6, we contended with particular providence, including the important light it casts back on prophecy. It is in chapter 6 that we look most closely at Strauss's argument that the prophetology (2.32–48) and particular providence (3.8–24) sections are part of Maimonides's political philosophy or science. Among other things, what this means is that these two sections contain more of Maimonides's defense of philosophy than the earlier and purportedly more theoretical section on creation vs. eternity (2.13–31), which contains more of what Strauss refers to as Maimonides's "enlightened *kalām*" or defense of the Law. Once again, we maintain that despite the greater theoretical elevation of the section on creation vs. eternity—including the much-vaunted announcement of the "true perplexity" in 2.24—that it is in the political philosophical sections that Maimonides is most able to get purchase on the dispute between philosophy and Law. Much like Socrates's claim that he risked being blinded by trying to look directly at the Good, so Maimonides indicates that creation vs. eternity (if not the "true perplexity") cannot be resolved through demonstration or even directly through dialectic. What is at stake in the conflict between creation and eternity is not something merely theoretical, it is, to use all-too-recent language something far more "existential" than that. Even if the theoretical is higher, our only albeit indirect means of access to such questions may well be by way of the more existential avenue of political philosophy. What this means in chapter 6 is that the role and place of privation in particular providence is as close to the surface as any argument Maimonides makes about privation in connection with the three great themes. If 3.17 through 18 and 3.22 through 23 were not clear enough that particular providence is consequent on the intellect of the receiver, then

3.51 states in no uncertain terms that God's particular providence to human beings hangs wholly on the receptiveness of the human intellect since divine overflow is universally effusive. This resolution of the problem of evil means, as we mentioned above in this conclusion, that this so-called problem evaporates. We do not mean by this that nothing is evil; however, we do mean with Maimonides that evil is purely relative (3.10).

When at last we turn to creation vs. eternity in chapter 7, we are returned to the thick of Maimonides's account of obstacle or impediment or prevention. We begin with providence, though. If chapter 6 left us suspicious that particular providence evaporates into general providence, then chapter 7 must contend more directly with general providence. Indeed, what *Guide* part 1 has to say about general providence provides indispensable if unexpected preparation for the proper understanding of surely one of the most important theoretical, even if dialectical, arguments of the *Guide*, namely, 2.19's argument that God is the particularizer of the dis-order of some of the motions of the planets and placement of the stars. The key difficulty centers on what it means to call a planet a particular. One thing is certain: they are not particulars in the way that earthly members of species are. What this really means for the argument about particularization requires chapter 7 to be explained. Here, it must suffice to say that in 2.19 Maimonides hardly proves about God's will what he appears at first to be trying to prove. After all, according to his explicit statements, for God to will properly He must aim at some purpose—in open contradiction of the previous chapter (2.18) in the *Guide*. Yet willing the dis-order of the planets hardly appears to indicate God's wisdom. Evidently, God can only will their order. Could it really be the case that the wisdom of God's ordering of the planets must be eternally beyond us? We at least doubt that Maimonides would have been so surprised by the elegant solution of Newton, based on centuries of intervening advances on the problem of planetary physics. Leaving aside the supposedly "true perplexity," we remain convinced that the problem of philosophy and Law is a better point of entry than the purportedly true perplexity to not only the existential but also to the deepest theoretical insights accessible to philosophy.

# APPENDIX

## Leo Strauss's Outline of the *Guide of the Perplexed*[1]

### A. Views (I 1–III 24)

A'. Views regarding God and the angels (I 1–III 7)

I. Biblical terms applied to God (I 1–70)

א. Terms suggesting the corporeality of God (and the angels) (I 1–49)

1. The two most important passages of the Torah that seem to suggest that God is corporeal (I 1–7)
2. Terms designating place, change of place, the organs of human locomotion, etc. (I 8–28)
3. Terms designating wrath and consuming (or taking food) that if applied to divine things refer to idolatry on the one hand and to human knowledge on the other (I 29–36)
4. Terms designating parts and actions of animals (I 37–49)

ב. Terms suggesting multiplicity in God (I 50–70)

5. Given that God is absolutely one and incomparable, what is the meaning of the terms applied to God in nonfigurative speech (I 50-60)
6. The names of God and the utterances of God (I 61–67)
7. The apparent multiplicity in God consequent upon His knowledge, His causality, and His governance (I 68–70)

II. Demonstrations of the existence, unity, and incorporeality of God (I 71–II 31))

---

[1] From Leo Strauss's Outline of the *Guide of the Perplexed,* Pines translation (Chicago: University of Chicago Press, 1963), pp. xi-xiii.

1. Introductory (I 71–73)
2. Refutation of the Kalām demonstrations (I 74–76)
3. The philosophic demonstrations (II 1)
4. Maimonides' demonstrations (II 2)
5. The angels (II 3–12)
6. Creation of the world, i.e., defense of the belief in creation of nothing against the philosophers (II 13–24)
7. Creation and the Law (II 25–31)

III. Prophecy (II 32–48)

1. Natural endowment and training[:] the prerequisites of prophecy (II 32–34)
2. The difference between the prophecy of Moses and that of the other prophets (II 35)
3. The essence of prophecy (II 36–38)
4. The legislative prophecy (of Moses) and the Law (II 39–40)
5. Legal study of prophecy of the prophets other than Moses (II 41–44)
6. The degrees of prophecy (II 45)
7. How to understand the divine actions and works and the divinely commanded actions and works as presented by the prophets (II 46–48)

IV. The account of the Chariot (III 1–7)

A''. Views regarding bodily beings that come into being and perish, and in particular man (III 8–54)

V. Providence (III 8–24)

1. State of the problem: matter is the ground of all evils and yet matter is created by the absolutely good God (III 8–14)
2. The nature of the impossible or the meaning of omnipotence (III 15)

3. The philosophic arguments against omniscience (III 16)
4. The views regarding providence (III 17–18)
5. Jewish views on omniscience and Maimonides' discourse on the subject (III 19–21)
6. The book of Job as the authoritative treatment of providence (III 22–23)
7. The teaching of the Torah on omniscience (III 24)

### B. Actions (III 25–54)

VI. The actions commanded by God and done by God (III 25–50)

1. The rationality of God's actions in general and of His legislation in particular (III 25–26)
2. The manifestly rational part of the commandments of the Torah (III 27–28)
3. The rationale of the apparently irrational parts of the commandments of the Torah (III 29–33)
4. The inevitable limits to the rationality of the commandments of the Torah (III 34)
5. Division of the commandments into classes and explanation of the usefulness of each class (III 35)
6. Explanation of all or almost all commandments (III 36–49)
7. The narrative in the Torah (III 50)

VII. Man's perfection and God's providence (III 51–54)

1. True knowledge of God Himself is the prerequisite of providence (III 51–52)
2. True knowledge of what constitutes the human individual himself is the prerequisite of knowledge of the workings of providence (III 53–54)

# BIBLIOGRAPHY


Alexander of Aphrodisias. *The De Anima of Alexander of Aphrodisias: A Translation and Commentary*, translated by Athanasios Fotinis. Lanham, MD: University Press of America, 1979, 1980. Greek edition, *Alexandri Aphrodisiensis praeter commentaria scripta minora: de anima liber cum mantissa*, edited by I. Bruns. Berlin, n.p., 1887.

Altmann, Alexander. "Maimonides on the Intellect and the Scope of Metaphysics." In *Von der mittelalterlichen zur modernen Aufklärung*, edited by Alexander Altmann, 60–129. Tubingen: J. C. B. Mohr, 1987.

Ashworth-Steen, Robyn. "How Satisfactory Is Maimonides' Solution to the Problem of Evil." *European Judaism: A Journal for the New Europe* 50 (2017) 1: 113–12.

Averroes. *Long Commentary on the "De Anima" of Aristotle*. Translated by Richard C. Taylor with Thérèse-Anne Druart. New Haven: Yale University Press, 2011.

Behnegar, Nasser. "Reading 'What Is Political Philosophy?'" In *Leo Strauss's Defense of the Philosophic Life: Reading "What Is Political Philosophy?"* edited by Rafael Major, 22–42. Chicago: University of Chicago Press, 2013.

Benardete, Seth. *The Argument of the Action: Essays on Greek Poetry and Philosophy*. Chicago: University of Chicago Press, 2000.

____. *Encounters and Reflections: Conversations with Seth Benardete*. Edited by Ronna Burger. Chicago: University of Chicago Press, 2002.

____. *Plato's "Laws": The Discovery of Being*. Chicago: University of Chicago Press, 2000.

____. *Socrates' Second Sailing: On Plato's "Republic."* Chicago: University of Chicago Press, 1989.

Berman, Lawrence V. "The Structure of the Commandments." In *Studies in Jewish Religious and Intellectual History: Presented to Alexander Altmann on the Occasion of his 70th Birthday*, edited by Siegfried Stein and Raphael Loewe, 51–66. Tuscaloosa: University of Alabama Press, 1979.

Blumberg, Harry. "Theories of Evil in Medieval Jewish Philosophy." *Hebrew Union College Annual* 43 (1972): 149–68.

Cerami, Cristina. "A Map of Averroes' Criticism of Avicenna: *Physics, De Caelo, De generatione et corruptione* and *Meteorology*." In *The Arabic, Hebrew and Latin Reception of Avicenna's Natural Philosophy*, edited by A. Bertolacci and D. N. Hasse, 163–240. Boston, Berlin: W. de Gruyter, 2018.

Davidson, Herbert A. "Arguments from the Concept of Particularization in Arabic Philosophy," *Philosophy East and West* 18 (1968) 4: 299–314.

___. "Maimonides on Metaphysical Knowledge." In *Maimonidean Studies*, volume 3, edited by Arthur Hyman, 49–103. New York: Yeshiva University Press, 1992–93.

Alfarabi. *Al-Farabi on the Perfect State.* Translated by Richard Walzer. Oxford: Clarendon, 1985; reprint: Kazi Publications, 1998.

___. "Letter on the Intellect." Translated by Arthur Hyman. In *Philosophy in the Middle* Ages, edited by Arthur Hyman and James J. Walsh, 215–21. Indianapolis: Hackett, 1973. Arabic edition, *Risalat fi'-l-'aql.* Edited by Maurice Bouyges. Beyrouth: Imprimerie Catholique, 1938.

___. *The Political Writings,* volume 1, *"Selected Aphorisms" and Other Texts.* Translated by Charles E. Butteworth. Ithaca: Cornell University Press, 2001.

___. *The Political Writings,* volume 2, *"Political Regime" and "Summary of Plato's Laws."* Translated by Charles E. Butteworth. Ithaca: Cornell University Press, 2015.

Feldman, Seymour. "The Theory of Eternal Creation in Hasdai Crescas and Some of His Predecessors." *Viator* 11 (1980): 289–320.

Al-Ghazālī. *The Niche of Lights.* Translated by David Buchman. Provo: Brigham Young University Press, 1998.

Groff, Peter S. "Cultivating Weeds: The Place of Solitude in the Political Philosophies of Ibn Bājja and Nietzsche." *Philosophy East and West* 70 (2020) 3: 699–739.

Harvey, Steven. "Alfarabi, Averroes, and the Medieval Islamic Understanding of Phrónesis." In *Phronesis – die Tugend der Geisteswissenschaften*, edited by Gyburg Radke-Uhlmann, 177–94. Heidelberg: Universitätsverlag, 2012.

___. "Disgraceful! Maimonides' Use of *Qabīḥ* in the *Guide*." *Oriens* 50 (2022), 280–320.

Harvey, Warren Zev. "Maimonides' Critical Epistemology and *Guide* 2:24." *Aleph: Historical Studies in Science and Judaism* 8 (2008): 213–235.

___. "Maimonides' First Commandment, Physics, and Doubt." In *Ḥazon Naḥum: Studies in Jewish Law, Thought, and History Presented to Dr. Norman Lamm on the Occasion of His Seventieth Birthday*, edited by Yaakov Elman and Jeffrey S. Gurock, 149-162. New York: Yeshiva University Press, 1997.

___. "Maimonides's Avicennianism," *Maimonidean Studies,* volume 5, edited by Arthur Hyman and Alfred Ivry, 107–119. New York: Yeshiva University Press, 2008.

___. "A Third Approach to Maimonides' Cosmogony-Prophetology Puzzle," *Harvard Theological Review* 74 (1981): 287–301. Reprint, in *Maimonides: A Collection of Critical Essays*, edited by Joseph Buijs, 71–88. Notre Dame, IN: University of Notre Dame Press, 1990.

___. "Twersky on Integration of Law and Philosophy in Maimonides." Remarks presented at 25th anniversary of the death of Isadore Twersky. Harvard University, Cambridge, MA January 19, 2023.

Hyman, Arthur. "Demonstrative, Dialectical and Sophistic Arguments in the Philosophy of Moses Maimonides." In *Moses Maimonides and His Time*, edited by Eric L. Ormsby, 35-51. Washington DC: The Catholic University of America Press, 1989.

Ivry, Alfred. "The Logical and Scientific Premises of Maimonides' Thought." In *Perspectives on Jewish Thought and Mysticism*, edited by Alfred Ivry, Elliot R. Wolfson, and Allan Arkush, 63–97. Amsterdam: Harwood Academic Publishers, 1998.

Kalman, Jason. "Job the Patient/Maimonides the Physician: A Case Study in the Unity of Maimonides' Thought." *Association for Jewish Studies Review* 32 (2008) 1: 117–140.

Kaplan, Lawrence. "Maimonides on the Miraculous Element in Prophecy." *Harvard Theological Review* 70 (1977) 3–4: 233–256.

Kellner, Menachem. *Maimonides on Human Perfection. Brown Judaic Studies,* volume 202. Atlanta: Scholars Press, 1990.

Klein-Braslavy, Sara. "The Creation of the World and Maimonides' Interpretation of Gen. i–v." In *Maimonides and Philosophy*, edited by S. Pines and Y. Yovel, 65-78. Dordrecht, Boston: Martinus Nijhoff, 1986.

___. *Maimonides' Interpretation of the Story of Creation* (Hebrew). Jerusalem: Reuben Mass, 1978, 1988.

___. *Maimonides as Biblical Interpreter.* Boston: Academic Studies Press, 2011.

Kochin, Michael S. "Weeds: Cultivating the Imagination in Medieval Arabic Political Philosophy." *Journal of the History of Ideas* 60 (1999) 3: 399–416.

Kogan, Barry. "What Can We Know and When Can We Know It?" In *Moses Maimonides and His Time,* edited by Eric Ormsby, 121-37. Washington, DC: Catholic University of America Press, 1989.

Kraemer, Joel L. "How (Not) to Read The Guide of the Perplexed." *Jerusalem Studies in Arabic and Islam* 32 (2006): 350–409.

___. *Maimonides: The Life and World of One of Civilization's Greatest Minds.* New York: Doubleday, 2008.

Kreisel, Howard. *Judaism as Philosophy: Studies in Maimonides and the Medieval Jewish Philosophers of Provence.* New York: Academic Studies Press, 2015.

Langermann, Y. Tzvi. "Criticism of Authority in the Writings of Moses Maimonides and Fakhr al-Dīn al-Rāzī." *Early Science and Medicine* 7 (2002) 3: 255–75.

___. "Islamic Atomism and the Galenic Tradition." *History of Science* 47 (2009): 277–95.

___. "My Truest Perplexity." *Aleph: Historical Studies in Science and Judaism* 8 (2008): 301–317.

___. "The True Perplexity: *The Guide of the Perplexed,* Part II, Chapter 24." In *Perspectives on Maimonides: Philosophical and Historical Studies,* edited by Joel L. Kraemer, 159–74. Oxford: Oxford University Press, 1991.

Lerner, Ralph. *Maimonides' Empire of Light.* Chicago: University of Chicago Press, 2000.

López-Farjeat, Luiz Xavier. "Avicenna's Influence on Aquinas' Early Doctrine of Creation in 'In II Sent.,' D.1, Q.1. A.2." *Recherches de théologie et philosophie médiévales* 79 (2012) 2: 307–37.

Lorberbaum, Yair. "On Contradictions, Rationality, Dialectics, and Esotericism in Maimonides's *Guide of the Perplexed*" *Review of Metaphysics* 55 (2002) 4: 711–50. Hebrew version, "The Seventh Contradiction: On the Contradictions in the *Guide*—A Reevaluation" *Tarbiz* 69 (2000): 213–37.

Maimonides, Moses. *Ethical Writings of Maimonides.* Translated by Raymond L. Weiss and Charles Butterworth. New York: Dover, 1983.

___. *The Guide of the Perplexed.* Translated by Shlomo Pines. Chicago: University of Chicago Press, 1963; Judeo-Arabic edition, *Dalālat al-ḥā'irin.* In *Le Guide des Égarés.* Edited by S. Munk. 3 Vols. Paris: A. Franck, 1856–66. Revised and reissued by Issachar Joel. Jerusalem: Yunovits, 1931.

Millerman, Michael. "On 'The Literary Character of the *Guide for the Perplexed*': Aporia and Euporia." *Interpretation: A Journal of Political Philosophy* 42 (2015) 1: 51–67.

Neria, Chaim Meir. "Al-Fārābī's Lost Commentary on the Ethics: New Textual Evidence," *Arabic Sciences and Literature* 23 (2013): 69–99.

Ogden, Stephen R. *Averroes on Intellect.* New York: Oxford University Press, 2022.

Ormsby, Eric, ed. *Moses Maimonides and His Time.* Washington, DC: The Catholic University of America Press, 1989

Parens, Joshua. "Alfarabi's Harmonization: Authentic and Exoteric," *ISHRAQ*, Islamic philosophy yearbook, 301–320. Moscow: Institute of Philosophy of the Russian Academy of Sciences and the Iranian Institute of Philosophy, 2022.

___. "Death and Dying, Mortality and Immortality in Moses Maimonides." In *Political Theory on Death and Dying*, edited by Erin A. Dolgoy, Kimberly Hurd Hale, and Bruce Peabody, 161–70. New York and London: Routledge, 2021.

___. *Leo Strauss and the Recovery of Medieval Political Philosophy.* Rochester: University of Rochester Press, 2016.

___. "Maimonidean Ethics Revisited: Development and Asceticism in Maimonides?" *Journal of Jewish Thought and Philosophy* 12 (2003) 3: 33–62.

___. *Maimonides and Spinoza: Their Conflicting Views of Human Nature.* Chicago: University of Chicago Press, 2012.

___. "Maimonides's *Guide of the Perplexed*: Its Genre and Its Three Great Themes." Lecture delivered at St. John's College, Santa Fe, on November 16, 2018.

___. "Prudence, Imagination, and Determination of Law in Alfarabi and Maimonides." In *Enlightening Revolutions: Essays in Honor of Ralph Lerner*, edited by Svetozar Minkov and Stéphane Douard, 31–55. Lanham, MD: Lexington Books.

Parens, Joshua and Joseph Macfarland, eds. *Medieval Political Philosophy: A Sourcebook.* 2nd ed. Ithaca, NY; Cornell University Press, 2011.

Pines, Shlomo. "Limitations of Human Knowledge according to al-Fārābī, Ibn Bājja, and Maimonides." In *Studies in Medieval Jewish History and Literature,* edited by I. Twersky, 82–109. Cambridge, MA: Harvard University Press, 1979. Reprint, *Collected Works of Shlomo Pines.* volume 5, edited by W. Z. Harvey and Moshe Idel, 404–431. Jerusalem: Magnes Press, 1997.

___. "Les Limites de la métaphysique selon al-Fārābi (sic), Ibn Bājja et Maïmonide; sources et antithèses de ces doctrines chez Alexandre d'Aphrodise et chez Themistius." In *Miscellanea Mediaevalia, Akten des VI Internationalen Kongresses für Mittelalterliche Philosophie.* August-September 1977, 211–225. Berlin: De Gruyter, 1981.

___. "Truth and Falsehood Versus Good and Evil. A Study in Jewish and General Philosophy in Connection with the Guide of the Perplexed, I,2." In *Studies in Maimonides*, edited by Isadore Twersky, 95–157. Cambridge, MA: Harvard University Press, 1990.

Raffel, Charles M. "Providence as Consequent upon the Intellect: Maimonides' Theory of Providence," *Association for Jewish Studies Review* 12 (1987) 1: 25–71.

Ravitzky, Aviezer. "Maimonides: Esotericism and Educational Philosophy." In *The Cambridge Companion to Maimonides*, edited by Kenneth Seeskin, 300–323. New York: Cambridge University Press, 2005.

___. "The Secrets of the *Guide of the Perplexed*: Between the Thirteenth and Twentieth Centuries." In *Studies in Maimonides,* volume 7, edited by Isadore Twersky, 159–207. Cambridge, MA: Harvard University Press, 1971.

Ravitzky, Aviram. "The Balanced Path and the Path of Asceticism: The Unity of Maimonides' Ethics." *Tradition* 47 (2014) 1: 28–47.

Reines, Alvin J. "Maimonides' Concepts of Providence and Theodicy." *Hebrew Union College Annual* 43 (1972): 169–206.

Rousseau, Jean-Jacques. *Émile.* Translated by Allan Bloom. New York: Basic Books, 1979.

Samuelson, Norbert. "Maimonides' Doctrine of Creation." *Harvard Theological Review* 84 (1991): 249–71.

Schwarz, Dov. "The Debate over the Maimonidean Theory of Providence in Thirteenth-Century Jewish Philosophy." *Jewish Studies Quarterly* 2 (1995) 2: 185–96.

Seeskin, Kenneth. *Maimonides on the Origin of the World.* Cambridge, UK: Cambridge University Press, 2005.

___. *Searching for a Distant God.* New York: Oxford University Press, 2000.

Shayegan, Yegane. "The Accidentality of Existence in Avicenna and Its Critique in Averroes." *Journal of Persianate Studies* 10 (2017): 218–39.

Stern, Josef. *The Matter and Form of Maimonides' "Guide."* Cambridge, MA: Harvard University Press, 2013.

Strauss, Leo. *The Argument and the Action of Plato's "Laws."* Chicago: University of Chicago Press, 1975.

___. *The City and Man.* Chicago: University of Chicago Press, 1964.

___. "Farabi's *Plato*." In *Louis Ginzberg*, Jubilee volume, edited by Alexander Marx, Saul Lieberman, Shalom Spiegel, and Solomon Zeitlin, 357–93. New York: American Academy for Jewish Research, 1945.

___. *Persecution and the Art of Writing*. Glencoe: The Free Press, 1952. Reprint, Chicago: University of Chicago Press, 1988.

___. *Philosophy and Law.* Translated by Eve Adler. Albany: SUNY Press, 1995. German edition, *Philosophie und Gesetz*. Berlin: Schocken Verlag, 1935.

___. "The Place of the Doctrine of Providence according to Maimonides." Translated by Gabriel Bartlett and Svetozar Minkov. *Review of Metaphysics* 57 (2004): 537–49.

___. *On Tyranny*, revised and expanded edition. Edited by Victor Gourevitch and Michael S. Roth. New York: Free Press, 1963, 1991.

___. *What Is Political Philosophy? and Other Studies.* Glencoe, IL: The Free Press, 1959. Reprint, Chicago: University of Chicago Press, 1988.

Twersky, Isadore. *Introduction to the Code of Maimonides* (Mishneh Torah). New Haven: Yale University Press, 1980.

Wolfson, Harry Austryn. *The Philosophy of the Kalam.* Cambridge, MA: Harvard University Press, 1976.

___. "The Terms *Tasawwur* and *Tasdiq* in Arabic Philosophy and Their Greek, Latin, and Hebrew Equivalents." *The Moslem World* 33 (1943) 2: 114–28.

Yaffe, Martin D. "Providence in Medieval Aristotelianism: Moses Maimonides and Thomas Aquinas on the Book of Job." *Hebrew Studies* 20/21 (1979/1980): 62–74.

# INDEX

Abraham, 17n2, 108, 188–9, 277
Abulafia, Abraham, 180, 272
Account of the Beginning, 6–8, 33–6, 83–4, 239–80
Account of the Chariot, 6, 8, 22n535–6, 83–4, 94, 102–3, 203, 231–3, 250n9, 251–5
admissibility premise (also see Mutakallimun), 45–8, 47–8nn34–5, 54–5, 143, 146–7
Alexander of Aphrodisias, 10, 13, 71–2, 103–111, 117, 126–7, 216–18, 264–5
Altmann, Alexander, 68, 70–75
angels (see intellects, separate)
Aquinas, Thomas, 42, 60nn58–9, 135, 164n31, 184–5n22, 210, 238n57
Aristotle, works of
*De anima*, 85n34, 184–5n22, 248–9n7
*De caelo*, 102, 116–18
*Categoriae*, 58n54
*Ethica Nicomachea* 51n41, 73, 145n10, 154n21, 161, 187n27, 188n29, 212–13n17, 248–9n7
*Metaphysica* 84, 91, 140n3, 204, 21n16, 248n7, 258n20, 261nn25–6, 264, 277–8
*Physica* 10, 41n22, 75, 84, 85, 89, 91–2, 133n41, 140n3, 142, 207, 231, 282–3
*Topica* 117
Ashworth-Steen, Robyn, 165n33, 232n53
astrology (or astral determinism; also see fideism), 19–20, 37–9, 62, 213
Augustine, 151, 210
authority, 11, 13, 105–12, 116–17, 119, 121, 128, 132, 229–31, 246–7n5, 263, 282, 286–7
Averroes (Ibn Rushd), 11n4, 40–41, 51–2, 56–7n51, 72, 184–5n22, 210, 264n30, 273, 279
Avicenna (Ibn Sīnā), 20, 40–42, 51–7, 62, 255–64, 264–5
Benardete, Seth, 167n36, 281–3
Berman, Lawrence V., 160n28
Blumberg, Harry, 165n33
Cerami, Cristina, 41n22
Crescas, Hasdai, 41, 56–7, 172, 180, 264n30, 272, 264n30, 273n37, 255–64, 272
creation and eternity, viii, 7, 10, 14, 26–9, 33–6, 41, 45, 62, 90, 101, 112, 114–26, 131–6, 167–8, 174–81, 239–80, 281–2, 285, 289, 290–92; eternal creation, 42, 44, 55. 56–7n51, 131–3, 171–2, 179–81, 241, 272–4, 273n36, 277–9, 289
Davidson, Herbert A., 14, 53n46, 66, 68–9, 72n12, 73–5, 79–80, 121n25, 170, 174–8, 191n34, 285, 289
defense: of the Law or city or religion (see also *kalām*), 3, 4–8, 12, 65–6, 89–90, 131, 284–6, 290; of philosophy, 3–9, 12, 65–6, 285, 290
demonstration, 9–10, 47, 101

dialectic, 9–10, 13, 88–9
disgrace, 13, 110, 112–31, 286–7; contrasted with shame, 112–13
dogmatist or dogmatic, 1–2, 56, 65, 68–9, 285
doubts, space of, 12–13, 98–9, 101–2, 106, 282, 285–6; weighing of, 9–11, 12–13, 99, 101–2, 110, 131–2n39, 279, 286
Epicurus, 219–20, 268
esotericism, 1, 44–5n29, 80–81, 90
evil, problem of (also see privation and providence, privation of), viii, 210–26, 250, 287–8, 289–90
Alfarabi (al-Fārābī or Fārābī), 4–5, 56–7n51, 184n21, 221, 225, 232n52, 265
Feldman, Seymour, 56–7n51, 132n40, 264n30, 272–3, 279n42
fideism, 19–20, 33, 37–9, 45, 62, 88, 198, 201–2, 206, 213, 245
freedom, 9–11, 19–20, 37–9
Alghazali (al-Ghazālī or Ghazālī), 53–4, 163n30, 239–40, 245, 254, 267, 270–73, 279
God (see also Prime Unmoved Mover and YHVH), omnipotence of, 11, 48n35, 62–3, 115n19, 127, 131–2n39, 135, 216n23, 220–21; omniscience of, 218–19, 220–21, 224
Groff, Peter S., 232n52
Half-and-Half Teaching, 2–3, 12, 17–39, 252, 283
Harvey, Steven, 112n15, 224n36
Harvey, Warren Zev, 14, 41–2n23, 66, 68–9, 80–83, 89n36, 131–2n39, 169–70, 173–4, 179–81, 191nn33–4, 255–6nn15–17, 271–2, 277–8, 285, 289
hindrance (see privation)
Hyman, Arthur, 9–10, 10n10
Ibn Bajja, 69–70
imagination (also see intellect), 34, 48n35, 54–7, 143, 184–7
impediment (see privation)
impossibility, 29, 33, 47–8nn34–5, 55, 121, 125, 127, 172, 176–7, 207, 216, 236; logical vs. natural, 48, 118
intellect, 71–2, 75–6, 78, 82, 84–5, 89n36, 95, 111n14, 125, 153, 158, 163, 183–6, 226, 229, 234, 236, 290–91; acquired intellect, 230n49, 258–9n22, 265n31; and imagination, 48n34–35, 54–7, 126, 143, 183, 215–6, 274; and will, 20–24, 28, 58–63, 136, 207–11, 223–4, 240, 247–51, 265, 277; as ruling faculty, 97n43, 223–4, 229–30, 290–91
intellects, separate (see also Prime Unmoved Mover), 73–6, 80, 183–4, 230n49, 236, 258–60, 264; Active Intellect, 73, 122, 183–4, 241, 264–8; as angels, 76, 86–7, 98, 183, 188n28, 258–9nn21–2, 265
Ivry, Alfred, 18n3, 68, 77–8
Job, 23, 27, 94–8, 129n36, 226–31, 244
Jonathan ben Uziel, 22n5, 240, 250–55
*kalām* (dialectical theology; see also Mutakallimun), 107, 128, 129n36, 135; *kalām,* enlightened or intelligent, 8–9; *kalām,* vulgar or popular or imaginative; Ash'arite, 128–9, 135, 164, 206–9, 220–23, 227, 227–8n43, 270–71; Mu'tazilite, 50, 107,

128–9, 220–23, 225, 226–7, 227–8n43, 235
Kalman, Jason, 218–19n27, 222–3n34
Kant, Immanuel, 1–2, 68n5, 69–70, 126n29, 284
Kaplan, Lawrence, 14, 170, 172–4, 178–9, 190–91, 191nn33 and 35, 194–6, 289
Klein-Braslavy, Sara, 35n14, 120n24
knowledge, limits of, vii, 1–2, 5, 8–9, 11, 12–13, 56–63, 281–6; vagueness of, 2, 5, 8–9, 13, 65–6, 87, 89–90, 98, 101–2, 105, 265, 282, 285–6
Kochin, Michael S., 232n52
Kogan, Barry, 18n3, 72n13
Kraemer, Joel L., 9–10, 66, 81–2, 213n19, 255–6n15, 285
Kreisel, Howard, 41–2n23, 131–2n39, 253n13, 256nn16–17
Langermann, Y. Tzvi, 67, 70–71, 78–81, 105n4, 118n21, 285
López-Farjeat, Luiz Xavier, 41–2n23
Lorberbaum, Yair, 44–5n29
Maimonides, works other than the *Guide:*
*Commentary on the Mishnah*, 246–7n5
*Eight Chapters*, 19–20, 36–9, 47–8, 118n21, 158–9, 163–4, 185n24, 215, 230n49, 231–2nn50–51
*Letter on Astrology*, 97, 171, 197–9, 289–90
*Letter to Joseph*, 185n23
*Mishneh Torah*, 80,84n33, 154
*Treatise on the Art of Logic*, 49
matter (see also privation), viii, 13, 213, 287
metaphysics (or divine science, see also Account of the Chariot), 6–7, 10, 44. 72, 84, 231
miracles, 3n5, 10–11, 18, 28–36, 39, 42–3, 49, 90, 93, 132, 135, 169, 175–9, 183, 191n35, 192–3, 198, 283–4, 289
Moses, 21, 74, 97, 108, 112, 163, 170–71, 185–9, 197, 221–2, 243n1, 283–4
Moses Narboni (or of Narbonne), 172, 179–80, 272
Mutakallimun (dialectical theologians, also see *kalām*), 28, 32, 40–56, 107, 143–52, 164, 193, 287–8
nature of being or existence (*ṭabīʿat al-wujūd*), 32, 42–56, 103–4, 119–21, 129, 135, 193, 215; as opposed to order of existence, 125
necessary existence argument, 21, 40–41, 51–4, 77, 240–41, 255–65
necessity (also see purpose), 3, 27–8, 32, 42, 47–8nn34–5, 54, 57, 88, 109–10, 121, 174–5, 241, 275, 279, 286; and purpose, 254, 271, 273–5
negative theology, 8, 18n2, 20–23, 51, 56–63, 65, 73, 77–8, 95, 284–5
obstacle (see privation)
Ogden, Stephen R., 184–5n22
Onqelos the Proselyte, 22–3, 240, 251–3
overflow (also see prophecy and providence), 14, 35n14, 56n51, 67–8, 95, 98, 162–4, 168, 181, 183–4, 186–7, 202, 223–4, 230, 233–5, 249–51, 264–6, 290–91

Parens, Joshua, 5n12, 38n19, 69n7, 97nn43–4, 113n17, 128n35, 153n18, 158n27, 192n38, 211n14, 212n15, 214nn20–21, 220n30, 222n31, 224n36, 232n52, 273n37
particularization, method of (see also admissibility premise), 46–8, 70, 88–9, 124, 140, 146, 148–9, 151–2, 177, 202–3, 238, 242, 267, 276, 285, 291
philosophy and Law, 3–5, 9, 13, 18, 37, 40, 81, 95, 131–2n39, 140, 180–81, 218–19, 226n39, 232–3, 247, 279, 287, 289–92
physics (see also Aristotle works), 1, 5–7, 33–6, 44, 75, 84–5, 89–92, 114, 142, 207, 231, 282–3, 291; physical or causal explanation vs. mathematical prediction, 79–80, 87–9, 91–2, 267, 276, 285–6, 291
Pines, Shlomo, 1, 65–83, 113, 118nn21–2, 120nn23–4, 123nn26–7, 124n28, 126nn30–31, 141n3, 144n8, 203n2, 207n10, 217nn25–6
Plato, 7, 83–4, 152n16, 172–81, 210–12, 225, 281–3, 289
possibility, 28, 47–8nn34–5, 121, 259–60n23, 261–2, 279
preponderance, method of, 52–4
Prime Unmoved Mover (PUM, see also intellects, separate), 17–8, 17n2, 24–6, 40, 55–63, 77, 148, 258, 260, 265, 284–6
privation, 13, 120, 282–3; as hindrance or obstacle or impediment (*'a'iq* or *māni'*), vii–viii, 11–2, 24–6, 29, 115n20, 134, 136, 141, 164–8, 182–90, 208–10, 264, 291; hindrance of recipient, 122, 168, 181–2, 186, 234–5, 268; and matter, 13, 139–40, 145–52, 156–9, 164, 287–8; as veil (*hijāb*), vii, 11, 162–4, 167n34, 185n24, 233; and will, 239–80
privation, particularized, 13, 51, 139–52; as opposed to absolute privation, 142, 144, 150–51
prophecy, 67–8, 92–4, 97, 167–8, 173–4, 181–99, 281–2, 288–90
providence, viii, 14, 67–8, 92–3, 95n41, 167–8, 281–2; providence, general, 38–9, 97–8, 235–8, 243, 267–8, 276; providence, particular, 7, 30, 93–8, 126–31, 202–38, 289–91; privation of, 202, 239–80, 287–8
purpose (end, final cause; also see will), 33, 88, 239–40, 245, 267, 271, 274–5, 279
Raffel, Charles M., 218n27, 226–31
Ravitzky, Aviezer, 44–5n29, 154n19
reason and revelation (also see philosophy and Law), 205, 219, 239
Reines, Alvin J., 218n27, 225n37, 229
relation (category of), 17–8, 57–60
rhetoric, rhetorical, 4, 18, 67, 109–10, 119–21, 128, 131, 189, 211, 214–18, 258
Sabians (and Sabianism), 21
Samuelson, Norbert, 133n41, 218–19n27
Schwarz, Dov, 218–19n27
skeptic or skeptical, 1–2, 12, 44, 65–9, 76–8, 80–83, 80n29, 87, 99, 102, 214–16, 256–7, 284

Seeskin, Kenneth, 17n2, 57n53, 131–2n39
Shayegan, Yegane, 52n42
solitary, 106–8, 232, 284–5
Spinoza, Baruch, 150, 272
Stern, Josef, 1, 2nn2–3, 17n2, 36n15, 41n21, 43n28, 44–5n29, 56n50, 65n2, 66–9, 70n8, 71n9, 78n25, 102, 131–2n39, 140n2, 152n17, 216n24, 219n28, 255–9, 287
Strauss, Leo, 1, 2n2, 3–8, 44–5n29, 108n8, 201, 235
Strauss, Leo, works of
*The Argument and the Action of Plato's "Laws,"* 281–2
*The City and Man*, 204n4, 281–3
"Farabi's *Plato*," 220n29
Introduction to the *Guide*, Pines ed., "How to Begin to Study *The Guide of the Perplexed*," 6n14, 76n22, 108n8, 142n6, 177n8, 203–4, 237nn54–6, 243n4, 258n21, 293–5
"The Law of Reason in the *Kuzari*," 221n31
"Literary Character of the *Guide of the Perplexed*," 4–5, 47n33, 51n41, 60n59, 72n14, 113n18, 154n20, 155nn22–4, 180n14
*Philosophy and Law*, 2–5
"The Place of Providence according to Maimonides," 6, 141n5, 167n35, 201n1, 203–4nn3–4, 290
"Restatement on Xenophon's *Hiero*," 3–5
"Jerusalem and Athens," 214n21
Themistius, 10, 43n27, 103n1, 264–5
touch, sense of, 51n41, 154–6, 158–9, 185
Twersky, Isadore, 131–2n39, 154n19, 181n17, 256–7
will (also see intellect), 20–26, 32–3, 38, 61–3, 88, 146–7, 239–80, 289–90; and necessity, 27–8, 31–3, 239–41, 254, 267, 271, 272n33, 276–8; and purpose, 240–41, 254, 267–80, 273–4
wisdom (also see intellect), 25–6, 33
Wolfson, Harry Austryn, 43n28, 53–4, 53nn44–5, 54n47, 111–12n14
YHVH (also see will), 17–8, 17n2, 20–25, 40–42, 55–63, 65, 95–6, 148, 190, 242, 276, 283–4